SONG

SONG

A HISTORY IN 12 PARTS

JOHN POTTER

YALE UNIVERSITY PRESS
NEW HAVEN AND LONDON

For information about this and other Yale University Press publications, please contact:
U.S. Office: sales.press@yale.edu   yalebooks.com
Europe Office: sales@yaleup.co.uk   yalebooks.co.uk

Set in Adobe Caslon Pro by IDSUK (DataConnection) Ltd
Printed in Great Britain by TJ Books Limited, Padstow, Cornwall

Library of Congress Control Number: 2023937781

ISBN 978-0-300-26353-4

A catalogue record for this book is available from the British Library.

10 9 8 7 6 5 4 3 2 1

CONTENTS

ILLUSTRATIONS

ACKNOWLEDGEMENTS

Huge thanks to Yale's commissioning editor Julian Loose, whose concept this was, and without whom it would have been an entirely different book or no book at all. Thanks, too, to Rachael Lonsdale, Lucy Buchan and Frazer Martin at Yale for seeing it safely through the production process, to my eagle-eyed copy-editor Richard Mason, and to the anonymous Yale readers for their thoughtful advice and encouragement.

In a long career performing songs of one sort or another I've been privileged to work with some fantastic musicians. I'd particularly like to record my thanks for wonderful music-making (roughly in chronological order of repertoire) to Richard Wistreich and Red Byrd, Rogers Covey-Crump, Christopher O'Gorman and the Conductus Ensemble, harpist Jan Walters, the Hilliard Ensemble, the Dufay Collective, the Dowland Project, the Broadside Band, Alternative History, lutenists Ariel Abramovich, Jacob Heringman and Stephen Stubbs, harpsichordists Jeremy Barlow and David Roblou, and pianists Stephen Banfield, Elisabeth Haddon, Paul Hamburger, Trevor Hold, Christopher Robinson, Nicky Losseff and Joanne Metcalf. Between us we have performed almost all of the music mentioned in this book. I'd also like to thank Stef Conner, Linda Hirst, Gordon Jones, Nicola LeFanu, Laura Moody, Mark Padmore, Ned Potter and Roderick Williams for enormously stimulating discussions on the questions that musicians ask themselves anew with every performance; a particular thank you, too, to Tessa Reid and Lucy Reid, daughter and granddaughter of Peter Pope.

I'd like to dedicate these ramblings to my fellow performers and the community of scholars and composers without whom the book wouldn't exist. And, of course, to my wonderful family, Penny, Ned, Alice, Emily and Grace.

POINTS OF DEPARTURE

The golden discs aboard the two *Voyager* spacecraft, launched in 1977 and currently around 40,000 years away from their next encounter with a planetary system, contain among the messages and pictures from Earth twenty-seven musical examples, about half of which most of us might call song. Inevitably, choosing an album's worth of songs to represent the whole of humanity was a difficult and controversial process, and possibly the only people entirely happy with the selection were the scientists, musicologists and artists who put it together. The problem for Carl Sagan's NASA committee (leaving aside more banal questions such as budget and copyright) was that whereas song appears to be a universal concept, individual songs are culturally determined, can be owned and fought over, and ultimately signify something deep within the individual psyche.

Having recreated a gramophone (the time capsule includes a needle – this was the cutting edge of 1970s pre-digital technology), the intergalactic anthropologist might discover that Earth's songs could take many wonderful forms, but removed from their original context, there would be no way of assigning cultural or musical value to any of them. Despite the earthly compilers trying long and hard to overcome their instinctive and institutional biases, there are notable omissions from the discs. These include the Beatles (for whose record company the earthly copyright period was potentially more rewarding than the several billion years on offer from NASA) and songs from the classical tradition (Mozart's 'Queen of the Night' aria being the closest). There is very little literature and almost no poetry. Our alien listener would never know what it was missing.

Every culture has something that every other culture would probably recognise as song. It's a personal thing: we all have a word for it as an artefact even if we differ over the details. It involves singing, tunes (probably) and words (almost certainly). It also implies a listener, an audience of some sort (though not necessarily). Song may or may not have rhythm, and there seems to be a general consensus that it is a relatively short form which probably rules out most of the epics of Babylon and medieval Europe, though they might give us clues to shorter stories. More recently a song might come in at under a minute (like one of Webern's miniature masterpieces); if being plugged on a radio station, the limit was under three minutes for a pop song before Queen decided to risk a longer one.

Until the appearance of recording at the end of the nineteenth century, song also always had a visual dimension, which it has since rediscovered with video and film. Before the gramophone and radio, the listener would always be in the presence of the singer. It's an intimate medium: the singer is immediately in touch with you, bombarding you with their thoughts and unleashing your imagination which instantly provides interpretations of its own, unique to you (or possibly not). Once the idea of something being communicated is understood, a whole hinterland of possibilities opens up: the song tells you something about the singer, what is being sung about, and about the listener and the circumstances of the performance (if it is a performance).

The story of song begins with the precursors and pre-history of the genre, at a point where an unknowable oral tradition comes into focus with the first musical notation some 5,000 years ago. The evidence is frustratingly fragmentary and it's easy to over-interpret these early signs, but we can speculate on the possible shape and function of what we might call song. Sumerian epics tell heroic stories; courtiers stare out from Egyptian tombs, possibly celebrating their rulers' lives in song. We can make better guesses about ancient Greek music for which elaborate but still-mysterious notation survives, and the epic reappears in the mead halls of early medieval Europe, bereft of its music but with many references to harpists and singers. At about the same time, monks are memorising, reading and chanting, and parallel oral and written traditions develop which will eventually produce the first religious songs that have a life beyond the liturgy. The early church is a key source, and it has a direct effect on the way songs work: it has little time for instruments or women, so with some extraordinary exceptions the first written songs will be male, godly and monophonic.

From the twelfth century onwards we encounter monophonic songs – a single line of music that may or may not have been accompanied by an improvising instrument and may have had a much older existence in people's heads – preserved in songbooks from all over Europe. These could be sacred in the form of conductus, berating sinful man, or secular as created by the troubadours, *trouvères* and *Minnesänger* who sang of courtly love, the natural world and political intrigue. We glimpse the first women makers of song, and later polyphonic song enables a more convivial music-making. Songs are improvised, composed and improved upon; exquisite manuscript survivals suggest the emergence of temporary core repertoires with many local variants: no one ever sang the same thing twice.

In the later Middle Ages music becomes an essential element in courtly display and cultural competition, and patrons vie for the best singers and the best songs, which might now be composed polyphonically rather than just 'found', as the Troubadours put it. The lute emerges as the accompanying instrument of choice and will remain so until the seventeenth-century harpsichord takes its place, only to be replaced itself a generation or two later by the piano which is still with us (just). Almost any vocal music can be turned into song by Renaissance musicians, intabulated in that pragmatic notation only understood by lute players, that tells them where to put their fingers but not what the notes are. In Italy a host of female composers stretched societal norms to become in significant ways the equal of their male counterparts. In England and France, as the sixteenth century merged into the seventeenth, a generation of lutenists created songs we still sing; their early Baroque successors deconstructed old songs and created new ones, exploring mythology and the pains and possibilities of love. Towards the end of the century the song descended from its aristocratic heights and found its way into the first public concerts: melody became public property, and everyone had a tune in their head.

The eighteenth century saw the development of the detachable operatic aria, another step towards democratisation, which would be repurposed as domestic entertainment alongside more spiritual tunes. By the nineteenth century most classical music had become too complicated to make up without considerable creative graft, and the composer himself was invited into bourgeois drawing rooms where delicate sensitivities could be safely explored in song, and women musicians often flourished against the tide of history.

Then, in the 1890s, our silent speculation resolves into sound and we can finally hear what was going on; instead of going out to hear a song, soon the best singers would perform for you in your own parlour at the drop of a needle. The gramophone began to supersede the piano as the main focus of the drawing room, and in the early twentieth century composers pushed the boundaries of harmony close to breaking point in the knowledge that only specialist performers would ever be able to sing their music. Fiercely complex songs were produced, gaining ever more academic and critical acclaim as their potential audience fell away to seek solace in jazz and increasingly sophisticated popular music.

The return of song to a kind of connoisseurship in the second half of the twentieth century coincided with the rediscovery of the Renaissance and Baroque in the form of the early-music movement, bringing songs of the past back into the present, repolished. As art song retreated, popular music achieved an unforeseen legitimisation with the era of the Beatles; musicologists would compare Lennon and McCartney with Schubert. Progressive rock musicians collaborated on songs that stretched the form way beyond its customary three-minute length and into the rich harmonic territory inhabited by Schoenberg before he claimed to have secured the future with only twelve notes, as in serial music. Art song and pop song finally caught up with each other when Sting, his own songs sometimes compared to those of Dowland, recorded Dowland himself.

Reducing a history of song to twelve titles reflects all the problems of the NASA committee as well as many of the interpretative and contextual problems of the alien investigator, who will at least have the advantage of being able to hear them all (an appropriate auditory system permitting). Meanwhile, back on Earth, the writer of musical history before the last decade of the nineteenth century is essentially deaf to what music sounded like in the past, so there can be nothing definitive about this very selective history. Songs can be intensely personal (whether you hear them or sing them) and none of us would choose the same twelve songs as anyone else. My choices are based on decades of performing experience in many different genres, but I hope they will reveal aspects of our common humanity as the story evolves from the Middle Ages to the present; the final chapter will offer some pointers to readers who wish to explore the bits I've left out.

The titles that head each chapter give us a historical dimension and a timeline but are essentially points of departure for explorations of what they may represent, who sung them, to whom and in what circumstances. The story is not evenly spread: history doesn't actually divide into convenient periods; each chapter is designed to be self-contained but within a wider unfolding narrative. The penultimate chapter takes a broader view as classical and popular manifestations of song begin to coalesce towards the end of the twentieth century, and I hazard some guesses at what the cacophonous future might hold.

HILDEGARDIS *a* Virgin *Prophetess,* Abbess *of*
S*t* Rvperts Nunnerye. *She died at* Bingen A*o* Do:
1180. *Aged* 82 *yeares* .

W. *Marshall sculpsit .*

Hildegard von Bingen, still the inspiration for Thomas Fuller's
The Holy State *(1642).*

1

HILDEGARD VON BINGEN
'COLUMBA ASPEXIT'

M ost of this history is silent, which makes it rather speculative. An art historian who had Vasari's *Lives of the Artists* but was unable to see any of the paintings referred to would produce a very different history from one who had the paintings but no Vasari. But like the art historian we're not reliant on just one form of evidence, and although the artefact itself may be absent it leaves traces in art and as literature: we can see pictures of ancient singers, we can read about people singing and we can read the texts of the songs they sang; eventually we can interpret the signs they used to remind themselves of how the songs sounded, and around a thousand years ago medieval scribes devised notation we can read. The connection with words is symbiotic, but literacy makes songs visible: a written song is a lot easier to document than an oral tradition. The 'art' song that is a consequence of all this is no more or less significant than a folk song, but we have more tools at our disposal to analyse or document it. It's not surprising that music histories tend to begin with notation, music you can see: the inaudible invisible can seem unknowable.

The awkward fact remains, though, that until we can identify music that we can actually sing ourselves, we can't be sure that the various words ancient languages use for song and singing are in any way equivalent to our modern terms. Our interpretation of the evidence that reveals itself painfully slowly until around the end of the first millennium may be conceptually very wide of the mark, and is inevitably informed by our own certainty of what we assume song to be. When we see pitches we hear in our heads temperament and tuning, discrete intervals that are always the same; what a medieval scribe heard in his head when he was transcribing a song will never be known. The brave modern singer who has attempted to get to grips with the rhetorical pronouncements of Quintilian or Cicero (for example) can be forgiven for thinking that the differences between ancient singing and speech, poetry and performance, are so unfathomable as to be unrecoverable in any meaningful way.

In the twenty-first century we seem to have harmony embedded in our very existence, with songs providing a background to everything from TV weather forecasts to dentists' drills and shopping malls. This composed richness which integrates the horizontal tune with the verticality of harmony has only been with us for a couple of centuries. Go back beyond that and you find the tunes and bass lines of the early Baroque, the harmony improvised and so lost to history; before that, Renaissance and medieval polyphony essentially consisted of simultaneous melodies, the 'harmony' a by-product of rules designed to reconcile conflicting tunes. Go back further still and you find only tunes, and beyond that only words.

The blur of pre-history comes into focus when an oral tradition seems to appear miraculously in written form. It's not just that people's memories are too full to contain countless numbers of very long songs: the context and function of songs, their performance and transmission, assume an additional dimension. Songs and songbooks can be gifted, moved from place to place, reflected upon, and rather than be in a state of continuous reinvention, begin to assume a more permanent form, less dependent on memory or formulaic recreation. Crucially for the historian, once written down whether performed or not, they can travel into the future sitting safely on library shelves. Written language has a significance all of its own: when sung in the vernacular a song may carry completely different meanings from one sung in a more stylised, high form of the language, or in a different language altogether. The relationship between the oral and written is subtle and complicated; after all, words and letters began as mnemonic devices in just the same way as the seemingly impenetrable squiggles of the first music notation, as aids to memory.

Although it leaves a visible imprint of cultural events, literacy is not quite the evidential El Dorado that it appears to be. In the first millennium the written, scholarly and clerical seem almost to obliterate the oral, secular and popular, the more so because the European writing that existed was itself written in Latin, a language not spoken by anyone outside the court and church. The idea of literate song having a higher cultural value (especially if it was in a language not one's own) was there from very early on, and being essentially monkish any secular agenda was cleverly hidden beneath exhortations to godliness, abstinence and general good behaviour. The mnemonics of notation were not simply a performative convenience: for the early church, which we have to thank for the earliest surviving songs, increasingly sophisticated forms of notation were also a means of standardising the message by regulating the mode of delivery.

The history, or rather pre-history, begins with a number of threads which are already loosely interwoven by the time we can glimpse the sources, and which come into a kind of alignment around the beginning of the second millennium. The vast and ancient Graeco-Roman tradition of recitation was poetic and literary, rhetorical and performative, a branch of oratory and a world away from the silent reading that we might do today. Cicero's famous rules for memorising long speeches were part of a centuries-old tradition of declamation, meaning the difference between singing and speech in the context of poetic song was a very fine one; the resulting hybrid poetics blurs the distinction between the written and the spoken, unlike our modern tendency to understand the two modes as mutually exclusive. Public singing and speaking shared the same ability to persuade, to play upon the emotions of listeners, and speaking could become so heightened and exaggerated that Romans sometimes couldn't tell which was which. Some of the earliest notation signs are found above classical speeches, as exercises in rhetorical delivery; if the original performers had trouble distinguishing between singing and speaking, what chance do we have two millennia later? There was no repeated melody as we would understand it, as the poet's words became identified with the persona of the performer rather like a modern actor.

There was similarly no need for notation as we now know it: the performer embodied the song and could change it at will, aided by occasional rhetorical marks and depending on the listeners' responses. Classical declamation and its rhetorical music only lasted as long as a performance, but a great deal of Roman poetry survived in written form, reappearing up to a thousand years later as medieval song and confirming a fundamental criterion for song: it has to be written down in some form to achieve lasting worth. Orality and literacy are never mutually exclusive, but the timescale from a broadly oral performance culture to a systematically literate one is breathtaking compared with the current exponential evolution of songs. From the Beatles to Beyoncé is less than a generation, from Bach to Britten a matter of a couple of centuries; the first recognisable European songs may have taken almost a millennium to germinate.

A second thread that becomes woven into the performative experience is the church. Christianised after Constantine's conversion in 312, the Roman Empire became the conduit through which a Jewish literate tradition became absorbed into Roman Christianity. The first Christian music was oral and formulaic, but in time the need to formalise and regulate the ritual led to its being written down; as the music itself evolved into something more complex, notation became a record of what might have been sung in the past with a view to reproducing it in similar form in the future. The Judaic inheritance complemented the legacy from pagan Rome, freighted with a secular literature so strongly embedded in the cultural intelligence that its survival was ensured by the church itself: Christianity was the state religion and Latin the language of the Roman Empire, its ecclesiastical and governmental *lingua franca*.

The decline of Rome, though punctuated by historically visible catastrophes such as the sack of the eternal city by Alaric's Visigoths in 410, was a complex process. The slow disintegration of the empire was mitigated by the gradual assumption of elements of *romanitas* by the very tribes that threatened it, such was the awe which the seemingly timeless Roman culture inspired in the aspirational Goths, Franks and Vandals. The Roman obsession with their own language led them at first to dismiss the tribal languages as gibberish – the *blah blah* that gave us the word 'barbarian' – but it was 'barbarian' culture that enabled cultural and musical evolution. In the sixth century we can see the extraordinary intertwining of ancient traditions (not yet a synthesis) in the lives of Boethius and Venantius Fortunatus. The patrician Boethius, born supposedly in Rome *c.* 470–75, had a classical education based on his interests in rhetoric, literature and philosophy. He was in the service of the Ostrogothic king (and *de facto* Roman emperor) Theodoric the Great, who had been raised on the shores of Lake Balaton and brought up as a hostage in Byzantium. Musical settings of poems from Boethius's *De consolatione philosophiae* reappear in manuscripts from the ninth to the eleventh centuries; his *De institutione musica*, an attempt to explain ancient Greek ideas of music to the Romano-Germanic world he was born into, survived to be one of the earliest musical tomes to appear in print in the fifteenth century.

Venantius Fortunatus, born in 540, sixteen years after Theodoric had Boethius executed, had a similar classical education but took to the road as a wandering minstrel after the chaos following Theodoric's death. He was in Metz in 566 in time for the marriage of the Merovingian King Sigebert to Queen Brunhilda, daughter of Athanagild the Visigothic king of Spain. He wrote them a celebratory ode, one of many for various aristocratic patrons, and eventually became bishop of Poitiers. Two of his hymns, 'Pange lingua' and 'Vexilla regis', are still sung today (though it's the words rather than the tunes that we're sure about). He also wrote several *planctus*, laments on the death of a famous figure. The *planctus* would reappear as the troubadour *planh* and later still in the famous laments of Baroque opera. The most bizarre musical afterlife, however, was that of the Romanised Visigoth King Theodoric, not himself a musician, but whose feudal feats (actual and invented) were still entertaining German audiences of the sixteenth century in a parallel universe in which he has morphed into the knight Dietrich of Bern.

Music histories tend to explain song as an evolving thread within the canon of great composers' works. The performing reality has probably never been quite as simple as that, and the accumulation of musical sources extends across both time and geography. Unravelling the genesis of the earliest European songs involves a kind of historical time-shift, jumping forward to the second millennium to discover songs in the oldest surviving collections written many hundreds of years previously. *Beowulf*, the greatest of the Anglo-Saxon (or Old English) epics, survives in a manuscript compiled between 975 and 1025 but probably refers to events (both real and mythical) in sixth-century Scandinavia. *Widsith*, the song of a *scop* or travelling entertainer who claimed to have unlocked his 'word-horde' at courts all over the known world, has similar beginning and end dates, and many of the French chivalrous *chansons de geste*, dating from the twelfth century, refer back to the 'great deeds' of Charlemagne in the eighth.

We know nothing of what happened to these poems between the time of their subject matter (and therefore probable composition) and their appearance in written form hundreds of years later. Was there a thriving oral tradition that survived depredation, war and decay as the Latin world was absorbed by the Germanic, or were they copied and recopied, eventually to lie silently chained up in libraries? We can only guess at what a performance might have been like; the poems themselves sometimes mention harps or fiddles, but how these were wielded is a matter of creative conjecture. *Beowulf*, in the reconstructed performances by Benjamin Bagby, can take many hours; some *chansons de geste* consist of tens of thousands of verses that presumably took several days to get through, perhaps using repeated musical phrases (no music survives). We have no idea why or when they were first written down, and how many manuscript versions existed before the first surviving copies, or whether written versions offered reflective possibilities for subsequent oral performances.

Many songs were presumably not written down at all and after their oral reach withered were then forgotten. Bede, in his *Historia ecclesiastica gentis Anglorum* (Ecclesiastical History of the English People) of 731, described how Caedmon, a monastic servant and cowherd in the monastery of Streanaeshalch (now Whitby Abbey), was taught how to sing and compose in a dream. He was so embarrassed by his inability to sing that when the harp was passed round and everyone expected to contribute a song he would quietly leave the table and go home. On this particular night he had retreated to the cowshed to be with his beasts, having taken fright when the circulating harp came in his direction. A figure appeared beside him and asked him for a song. Caedmon explained his musical and poetic deficiencies, whereupon the man taught him what we now know as Caedmon's Creation Hymn – in the vernacular as Caedmon presumably had no Latin. The story of the apparition reached the abbess, who declared it a visit from God himself and asked Caedmon to compose more songs, eventually admitting him to the order as a brother. Bede tells us that Caedmon went on to write countless other songs for his fellow monks and nuns, who would teach him scriptural themes (which his previous outdoor life had given him little knowledge of) upon which he would create new songs, making him the first composer known to write to commission. We have only Bede's word for it as none of the songs survived; we are dealing with a very thin historical thread here.

It is another 400 years before we come across the first songs in the English language to survive with musical notation. These are attributed to Godric of Finchale, who like Caedmon received them direct from the ether during a dream. His three surviving short songs were realised courtesy of the two Marys, St Nicholas, his dead sister Burgwen and at least two angels. Like Caedmon he had led a secular life, born in East Anglia and becoming a successful merchant (and possibly a pirate), before devoting himself to prayer and penance. He remained a layman, choosing austerity and solitude in a Northumbrian hut rather than the monastic community of nearby Durham. The deprivations of the ascetic life are known to induce hallucinations (Godric also claimed to have dined on the riverbank with St Matthew among others), but that does not explain how an ex-pedlar and sometime sailor produced well-crafted songs. Godric may have been illiterate and claimed to know nothing about music, though in his Fenland childhood he would never have been very far from the chanting of monastic foundations that knew both Latin and the vernacular.

His songs required two sorts of scribe: one who could write or transcribe Old English, and one who understood musical notation. There were more of the former, and more sources survive without notes. Were it not for Godric's legendary and miraculous saintliness, no one would have bothered to record the songs and their peculiar genesis; there must have been unknown numbers of less spiritually fortunate composers whose efforts went unrecorded. Godric died in 1170 and was buried in Durham before his body was returned to Finchale, where over the next few hundred years the priory grew until it was dissolved in 1536. The ruins still stand on a bend in the River Wear, and Godric would probably enjoy the caravan park that sits within its grounds. I once tried to evoke the saint by singing his St Nicholas song in the roofless church, the 'schone hus' that even without its roof was probably a good deal more comfortable than his original hermitage.

That any songs survived at all is due to the scribal labours of generations of monks, who made copies of copies for their own libraries and for those of others. The so-called Cambridge Songs, for example, were copied in St Augustine's Canterbury (now a ruin not far from its more famous cathedral) sometime in the eleventh century, having started life in the Rhineland perhaps soon after the death in 1039 of the German king Conrad II, one of several Frankish monarchs celebrated in the collection. The songs are part of a manuscript known as MS Gg.5.35, bequeathed to the Cambridge University library in the seventeenth century and with a colourful history both before and after it was acquired by the library. Having lost various leaves probably during periodic rebindings, a page containing verses of Boethius was removed by a scholar in 1840 and eventually bequeathed to the Frankfurt University library where its provenance was recognised in the 1980s, leading to its subsequent return to Cambridge.

MS Gg.5.35 is a substantial collection containing Latin poetry (Horace and Virgil as well as post-classical poems by eighth-century scholars such as Bede and Alcuin), prayers transliterated from Greek to Latin, medical texts, riddles and hymns. Bound in with this eclectic material are more than eighty poems in Latin and Old High German, some with an early form of notation. The song leaves include laments for kings and bishops, love songs (some in a woman's voice), complex explications of Greek musical theory, and a number of erotic poems that were later censored by an embarrassed cleric. Karl Breul, in his edition of 1915, maintained that the poems were a songbook, subsequently bound in with a larger collection of material, which represented the repertoire of an eleventh-century Goliard or travelling musician. For musicians of the early-music revival this was an irresistible programming opportunity, though some must have wondered about the appeal of hymns, prayers, songs about German emperors, music theory and erotica to Goliardic programme planners. More recent examination of the foliation suggests the songs were not a separate collection but another facet added by an enthusiastic collector; nevertheless the collection gives us a rare glimpse of a flourishing Latin secular song tradition in Germany and Anglo-Saxon England.

Like later collections such as the German *Carmina Burana* manuscript (in which some of the Cambridge Songs reappear), only a very small number of the Canterbury poems have notation to guide the singer (some can be guessed at from later sources). Does this mean that some were for a reciter rather than a singer? Or could it be that the ones without notation were easier to remember, whereas some needed a more specific kind of reminder? Or perhaps they were simply copied from different kinds of sources and had all the information needed by the singer whose songbook it may have been. Perhaps the songs were just a part of a stockpile of edifying and entertaining material that monks enjoyed in their spare time.

The collision of the oral and the written remains problematic until we can read actual pitches, and we have to wait even longer before we can say anything very certain about rhythm. The earliest attempts at musical notation used neumes, marks or lines which gave the contours of a melody and presumably triggered the pitches that the singer already knew. At some point, someone must have first equated a visual process with an aural one. How we equate hearing 'up' in a scale with seeing it written on the page is something that neuroscientists still debate, but the first neume notator must have associated the angle of a written line with rising or falling pitch. Over a period of two hundred years or so, these signs were refined until they were eventually formalised in the eleventh century by Guido d'Arezzo, whose system of lines and spaces was based on the configuration of a hand, held horizontally. Subsequent scribes experimented with a variety of lines before settling on five by the thirteenth century. A four-line stave is still used for plainchant in many Catholic choirs today.

For a modern singer, notation has to be the shortest possible route to understanding how the music should go: we want accurate information about as many parameters as the composer chooses to give us, and then the rest is up to us. The first sight of a new piece is uniquely exciting, and what we mostly see are notes to which words have been added. In the late twentieth century, when the early-music movement began to revive medieval song and chant, many of the most successful singers came from the English Protestant choral tradition and had very little experience of singing plainchant from a four-line staff with its additional neume-derived superscript signs. In the rush to realise the pitches we missed many of the clues left by the first notators, and where possible we would use later sources that give us the pitch information so we could get on with the job. The problems faced by our medieval predecessors were of a different order: they already knew the notes, they just needed to be able to recall them well enough to perform them or teach them to students; what a medieval scribe saw was text, possibly overlaid with hints about enhancing it with music.

We don't really know what made a Frankish scribe in eighth-century Aachen or Metz feel the need to devise a notation system, so we can only speculate on what it was intended to do. Written language, like musical notation, is in the first instance a representation of sounds, and the earliest notation signs appear at a time of extraordinary linguistic change, a process which divides scholars as much as questions of early notation divide musicologists. For reasons of political geography as well as cultural inheritance the Carolingian church and court had a keen interest in the pronunciation of Latin; they went to great lengths to preserve what they could of an uncorrupted pronunciation (an early example of the pursuit of excellence, perhaps). Medieval scribes could refer to a body of classical literature written in a Latin that was still spoken in church but which at home or in the street may have been well on the way to becoming Romance, the commingling of vulgar Latin dialects that would eventually sediment into the languages we know today.

The language question presented particular challenges and opportunities to singers and composers. The silent written language required attention to the sound of language in performance; as the vernacular Romance languages evolved further away from the Latin source, the rise and fall of the classical language, its appropriate stresses and cadences, could be helped along by notational marks. Beneath the mysterious scribblings that are the earliest neumes we can perhaps detect an excitement among the scribes tasked with recording existing tunes or devising new ones. Where the music was already known, the notation marks need perhaps only to give a reminder of pitch and shape, the poetic metre of the text producing its own phrasing and rhythm, but new music would require new signs that would override the rhetorical autopilot. Eventually, instead of a song being a dramatic quasi-musical recitation looking back to Rome, we find text and music fusing into the single expressive entity that composers still work with today. There is no evidence of written Romance dialects until much later, which suggests that Latin may have remained the high form of both the written and spoken language (though linguists argue about this). With a small number of early exceptions, the vernacular languages had to wait until they achieved a written status a couple of hundred years in the future, when they would enable a cornucopia of secular song.

***

The church was institutionally male and authorship was rarely attributed, so it is something of a shock to discover that one of the first composers whose music survives and whose name is known to us is a woman, Hildegard von Bingen (*c.* 1098–1179). Although women were welcomed into the church and could live a similarly fulfilling cloistered life to men, the higher spiritual and administrative edifice was entirely male, an inheritance from its origins in Judaism. That is not to say that women were absent from the creative processes enabled by the church, but since authorship was mostly anonymous a female presence is hard to determine (it becomes even harder in the later Middle Ages when universities replaced monasteries as centres of intellectual endeavour and tended to marginalise women). Even when we know of a significant woman poet or musician, the fact that history has until recently been written mostly by men has tended to reduce even the most extraordinary women to footnotes in an essentially male narrative.

Although revered in Catholic circles for her religious writings for many subsequent generations, Hildegard is virtually absent from musical history until the late 1970s and the 800th anniversary of her death. She was perhaps fortunate that this event occurred as the early-music movement was becoming enormously successful as an artistic and commercial phenomenon. In the early 1980s the German ensemble Sequentia staged Hildegard's sacred music drama *Ordo virtutum*, in what would be a decades-long exploration of her works; in the UK, Christopher Page's Gothic Voices recorded sequences and hymns which sparked the public imagination, triggering research and performances that continue to this day to illuminate Hildegard's works, especially her vast collection of sacred songs entitled *Symphonia armonie celestium revelationum* (Symphony of the Harmony of Heavenly Revelations).

Hildegard was the tenth child of minor Rhinehessen aristocracy who offered her to the church as a tithe, encouraged by a precocious religiosity which she apparently demonstrated almost as soon as she could talk. At the end of the first millennium the territories of France and Germany as we know them today were contained within the conglomeration of kingdoms, duchies and city states that made up the geo-religious entity known as the Holy Roman Empire, a sometimes fractious duopoly with its hereditary emperor at one end and an elected pope at the other. Although unmistakably Germanic for several centuries, the inhabitants of the Rhineland Palatinate of Hildegard's birth still considered themselves to be part of Roman Gaul. At the age of eight (or possibly fifteen – the sources, including Hildegard herself, aren't entirely clear) she became an anchoress, walled up within the nun's quarters in the monastery of Disibodenberg, together with two other women, Jutta of Sponheim, her spiritual mother and mentor, and a relative of lesser rank who presumably saw to their less godly requirements.

The process of walling up women (and sometimes men) was a ritual entombment, involving what was in effect a burial service, the final bricks or stones laid by a priest or, in Hildegard's case, a bishop. A single aperture would be left, through which food could enter and waste products leave. An anchorite could expect to be incarcerated for the rest of her life, in the expectation of something less austere in the next one. The Hildegard hagiographies describe the ceremonial burial in some detail but are less forthcoming on subsequent life in the cell; medieval saintly biographies never give us the nitty gritty that we really want to hear about. We are told that under Jutta's guidance she read the psalter and played the psaltery, and as the cell was opposite the monastic church the women presumably heard the monks chant their daily ritual. Wealthy unmarried daughters could find a comfortable and safe communal lifestyle within monastic walls, and Hildegard and her fellow brides of Christ were presumably able to mitigate the discomfort of their cell somewhat. They certainly observed proper dress and deportment in their daily lives. While they may have spoken German informally to each other and when negotiating with the outside world, their music-making may have been exclusively formal and in Latin, already the preserve of a literate elite. Hildegard claimed no knowledge of music and may have dictated it to an assistant; we know nothing about how she came to compose her songs. We also have no idea of how much the sources reflect actual performances in an age when memories were long and large and didn't usually require music to be written down.

From our twenty-first-century vantage point it is perhaps not a surprise that in her sometimes harsh and self-inflicted isolation

Hildegard experienced waking visions. In fact, they seem to have started long before her incarceration, which gave her the time and space to reflect on them in between often long bouts of severe illness. Her visions (Hildegard was adamant that they were not dreams but a kind of enhanced consciousness) were first diagnosed retrospectively as migraines by medical historian Charles Singer after consulting the extraordinary illuminations in her major work *Scivias* in 1913. Hildegard researchers have acknowledged the possibility ever since (notably in Oliver Sacks's 1970 study *Migraine*) and many of her episodes do indeed seem to display classic migraine symptoms such as intense pain and sickness, geometrical shapes, lights and stars, and they may have begun at around the age of three, as is often the case with modern sufferers.

But the complexity of both visual and auditory dimensions suggests that she may have suffered from other conditions which confuse or obstruct the neurological signals from the eye to the brain such as temporal lobe epilepsy or scintillating scotoma. Hildegard herself wrote about epilepsy in two medical tomes, especially in *Causae et curae* (Causes and Remedies), and associated the symptoms with a moral dimension, but she was reluctant to discuss her visions until God gave her a suitable sign. This occurred sometime after she was elected to lead the Disibodenberg community on the death of Jutta in 1136. Within ten years her reputation had attracted so many acolytes that God suggested that she leave the relative comfort of a well-endowed establishment to refound a decayed monastery on the Rupertsberg, a day's ride away at Bingen where the rivers Nahe and Rhine meet.

At some point during this period she seems to have begun to create the poems and music that became the *Symphonia*. The collection survives in two manuscripts, one probably compiled under Hildegard's own direction and the other shortly after her death. This implies significant local usage, but the lack of later sources suggests her musical star waned much sooner than that of her scientific and spiritual works, and like all monophonic music they eventually lost out to the (male) creators of the first polyphony. Her medical writings are still held in high esteem by those interested in alternative and natural remedies (Hildegard is the patron saint of the German Green Party) and various popes proposed her canonisation. While her botanic and medical writings may not stand up to scientific scrutiny, the songs have found considerable resonance among modern listeners, performers and scholars. There are almost eighty of them, fully notated and almost all composed for formal use within the Benedictine rite, both texts and music credited to Hildegard herself. This much we know, but how and why she wrote them, and their place in the wider history of plainchant, is still much argued over.

In Hildegard's songs, and those of her anonymous immediate predecessors and successors, we can glimpse something of what it must have been like to be a singer-composer-poet in the first millennium. The key elements of text and tune, heightening the text by turning it into music, are fundamental to the concept of song, but what lifts music finally away from oratory and rhetoric is when the notes leave the text behind (literally) and enter that abstract performative realm that transcends the simple delivery of the words. Words can be interpreted, but the purely musical sections of a song – the voice singing on just one syllable – involve a mutual creativity between composer and performer which the singers of the time had long been aware of. When describing the fifth-century *jubilus*, an extended succession of notes known as a *melisma* that is first found at the climax of an *Alleluia* during Mass, St Augustine talks of the joy created by singing on a vowel (often the last syllable of a word), articulating the inexpressible. In the twentieth century, Meredith Monk would call it a direct line to the emotions.

Such descriptions will be familiar to anyone who has sung the long meandering melismas of plainchant or the later forms of organum or conductus, or even a florid Mozart aria. But singing Hildegard in the present, however transformative it may be for us, will not replicate the medieval experience. Today's singers are likely to be professional soloists or, perhaps, one of the surviving Catholic monastic choirs. Members of the latter will be self-selected singers united in their faith, singing daily from the *Liber usualis*, the chants for the complete liturgical year assembled in the 1890s and finally unifying hundreds of local chant traditions. The monks and nuns of Hildegard's time had a centuries-old tradition behind them, singing their way in unison in a language not their own through every single day of their life in the cloister. Many of them would have been placed in a convent or monastery as children and would over a period of several years memorise a local equivalent of the modern *Liber* (which runs to more than 2,000 pages).

Hildegard may have sung her songs alone as an aid to her own personal devotion, but notating them, an expensive and time-consuming process, suggests she had in mind at least the possibility of future choral performance. A chant would ideally be singable by everyone, beginning on a note that would reassure the singers that it would be within their range and slow enough to enable simultaneous contemplation of the text; singing the same repertoire from memory often over a lifetime would have given medieval monastic choirs an instinctive aural cohesion. They were performers and audience, singing to and for each other, a form of therapy that reinforced social cohesion and mutual respect. The unison choir with no form of accompaniment is almost unknown today except where the tradition still continues in a small number of monastic foundations, and it has never gained traction in the secular world (children's songs and football chants being notable exceptions). The symbiosis of singing and song, born of intuition and lifelong devotion to both God and the community, would have produced a unique kind of song. We can't recapture this, but we can empathise with such depth of feeling in a monastic singer, even if in our secular age we are simply revelling in the sheer joy of singing, shifting beyond the words into an inchoate abstraction of tension and release enabled by a woman who died hundreds of years ago. Put this into a poetic framework heavily influenced, as many of Hildegard's songs are, by the colourful imagery of the Song of Songs, and you begin to see why Hildegard's songs still make such an impact today.

'Columba aspexit' is the song that has probably had most attention from modern scholars and performers. It is a sequence, a repeated pattern of pairs of verses (AA, BB, CC, etc.), traditionally used for the reading or chant that preceded the Gospel recitation in the Mass. It opens with the image of a dove peering in through the leaded lights of a church as Mass is celebrated by St Maximin:

Columba aspexit	The dove peered in
per cancellos fenestre	through the window tracery

The dove is dazzled by an ectoplasm-like balm radiating from the saint:

ubi ante faciem eius	where before its face
sudando sudavit balsamum	a balm emanated
de lucido Maximino	from the light of Maximin

The music of this first strophe then repeats, as Hildegard describes the heat of the sun piercing the darkness:

calor solis exarsit	the heat of the sun flamed
et in tenebras resplenduit	and streamed into the darkness

It strikes the jewel that is Maximin, the creator of the temple and its loving heart:

unde gemma surrexit	from where a jewel sprang
in edificatione templi	in building the temple
purissimi cordis benivoli	of the purest benevolent heart

The music is low and slow, contemplative and understated, beginning so close to pitched speech that there is no danger of the singing overwhelming the music. So rich is the imagery that anything more elaborate might break the spell that Hildegard is beginning to weave. In the next two pairs of verses the saint is likened to a tower made from cedar of Lebanon encrusted with precious stones, to a deer splashing in a fountain running with spices, the builder of the temple who longs to fly like an eagle, surrounded by perfume makers. Hildegard then addresses Maximin himself, a spiritual force beyond nature, rapture and awe, in a final *envoi* subsiding into a vision of the saint interceding for the congregation as they reach in praise towards a mirror of light:

ubi intercedes pro populo	where you intercede for the people
qui tendit ad speculum lucis	who reach to the mirror of light
cui laus est in altis	for which there is praise in the highest

It's heady stuff, the music not so much illuminating the text as burnishing it, allowing the blazing colours of Hildegard's imagery to shine through. It's a gift to a singer or a choir: Hildegard has already done the work for you, and your listeners will complete the picture in their own heads.

Although we don't know if she sung them herself, or if she heard her songs chanted by the monks over the dividing wall, we do know that Hildegard's fame spread beyond the Rupertsberg. Maximin was the fourth-century patron saint of the Benedictine monastery at Trier (a day's walk from Bingen), where his much-moved remains had reached their final resting place in the ninth century. The abbey that Hildegard would have known survived fire and remodelling until it was entirely rebuilt in 1674, finally succumbing to an air raid in the Second World War. If Hildegard had the monks at St Maximin in mind when she wrote 'Columba aspexit', she may have been imagining the dove gazing in from the window above the altar, below which was the crypt containing the body of the saint. The dazzling shafts of sunlight piercing the gloom from the east window and illuminating a vision of the rite, accompanied by the heady perfumes of balm and incense, would have summoned up the spirit of Maximin himself. For the monks and nuns the text, rich and colourful though it is, is merely an earthly construct, localised in the here and now, of a much-revered saint and common biblical experience. Yet merged with Hildegard's music, its phrases perfectly mirroring those of the poem, the song surely became something transcendental for both singers and listeners as the single thread of melody wove its way into the acoustic of the church.

Modern performers can capture something of this, but most will approach the piece from a more secular point of view. Musicians research their repertoires, and those involved with the early-music movement research more than most, so they will have some understanding of the context. But secular musicians are not monks or nuns and tend to keep the religiousness of sacred repertoires at arm's length just as an actor assumes a role rather than becoming it; you have to keep some distance otherwise you risk becoming your own audience. The mystical and spiritual union hoped for by the brides of Christ is replaced for the modern singer by the sensuality of Hildegard's summoning of Maximin. It is irresistibly expressive, and in the context of an unmeasured chant every nuance can be painted and lingered over according to whatever fires the individual singer's imagination. You don't even have to be a 'singer': Hildegard almost certainly sang as she spoke.

The Hildegard discography is huge and has acted to some extent as a counterbalance to the ubiquitous male early-music ensembles, though many of the latter have also embraced the creative opportunities offered by the rich text and soaring melismas of Hildegard's antiphons. The Hilliard Ensemble performed Hildegard in great cathedrals all over Europe, each of us singing our own version simultaneously from different parts of the building while Jan Garbarek's saxophone took flight into the vaulting. For the four of us, having sung in Gothic cathedrals since childhood yet admitting of no religion, it was an ethereal but purely musical experience. For the audience, some of whom would cradle a candle or lie on the hard stone floor, it might have been something more, evoking the spirit of Hildegard herself.

The illuminations accompanying *Scivias* have more recently been used for multimedia presentations of songs from *Symphonia* especially by female ensembles, the colourful and puzzling abstraction of the paintings matching the mystery of the music. Hildegard's place in the history of song is now secure, though we will never know quite what her music meant to her and how the manuscripts were used. We may be completely wide of the mark in thinking in terms of performance at all: the books may have been devotional objects for contemplation which produced music entirely in the head.

For the next few centuries, with the exception of a small number of *trobairitz* and the occasional famous nun, the female voice is almost unheard, but Latin song continued to flourish. The evidence is fragmentary apart from the few grand presentational codices, but it suggests clerics were writing for their own amusement and not just for the liturgy. Working copies don't usually survive: they wear out or become unfashionable and are discarded. A serendipitous exception is the manuscript known as the *Later Cambridge Songs*, a scruffy booklet of eight sheets containing thirty-five non-liturgical songs, probably compiled between about 1180 and 1230 and which happened to be reused to bind a later book. There are no brilliant illuminations and no one has felt the need to gloss anything in the margins, suggesting that it was assembled by monks (possibly at Leicester Abbey) who copied the songs for their own informal use. Some of the songs are not found in any other source but many appear in manuscripts all over Europe: songs that travelled and were remembered.

As well as monophony there are songs for two and three voices, the voices loosely woven together, perhaps an experiment in the as yet less common art of simultaneous singing by more than one voice on different lines. The notators were a little careless and often seem to have been working in a hurry, perhaps recording performances shortly after they happened. A scribe writing the first copy of any song must have been working either from memory or from the singing of a fellow cleric. The *Later Cambridge Songs* may provide a fleeting glimpse of this crucial earliest stage of manuscript transmission, the rough copy that would eventually be discarded or updated and which we normally don't get to see.

Hildegard was not the first woman to write songs and dramas. The tenth-century Hrotswitha of Gandersheim (apparently unknown to Hildegard) was one of a number of women with a similarly distinguished career. In the thirteenth century, visionary prophetesses such as Hadewijch of Brabant and Mechtild of Magdeburg achieved more than local fame. The *lais* of Marie de France survive in a manuscript from Reading Abbey probably dating from the 1260s (which also has 'Sumer is icumen in', long thought to be the oldest song in English). Hildegard's modern reputation depends on so much of her work having survived, unlike that of her more famous near-contemporary

Peter Abelard of whom we have only one readable piece and six laments (half in a woman's voice) in staffless neumes. It also rests on two other factors that probably meant very little to Hildegard herself: that we know her name and that she was a woman, two elements that perhaps say more about us than they do about her.

Bernart de Ventadorn gracing an illuminated capital in a Provençal
chansonnier *(c. 1260).*

2

BERNART DE VENTADORN
'CAN VEI LA LAUZETA MOVER'

The twelfth century saw a proliferation of songs in Latin, now a dynamic medieval language with fading links to its Roman heritage and an increasingly colourful secularity. Alongside it, and finding a different audience, are its offspring, lyrics in a plethora of vernaculars that would evolve into languages of their own. This literary revolution is frustratingly invisible to us at its moment of creation, and by the time we see it a hundred years or so later it has blossomed into a riotous profusion of poetic indulgence. The Latin 'Columba aspexit' began with the Holy Spirit appearing in the form of a dove; Bernart de Ventadorn's song in Occitan, the *langue d'oc*, features the secular rhapsody of the skylark.

For the historian it's a huge refocusing of the cultural microscope as songs that our instinct tells us must have existed emerge from the pages of sumptuous songbooks. In the feudal world, the continent-wide migrations have produced many princedoms in which the knightly class discovered that the joys of love, both real and hoped for, could be just as manly as fighting each other (though routine chivalric skirmishing continued much as before). The cultural competition of medieval courts provided the perfect context for musical and literary experiment. Vernacular song evolved from a restless and relentless focus on valour and violence to a variety of forms encompassing a gentler and more reflective aesthetic. This found its expression in lyric verse, a new song form with strophes, regular rhymes and syllable counts, where the throes of unrequited love replaced the hectic business of permanent warfare.

Musicians were of course still too busy doing music to write much about it, and we are dependent on autobiographical hints in the poems themselves and the occasional literary reference for evidence of what must have begun as a purely oral phenomenon. By the thirteenth century, writing has begun to catch up with the oral world and the first magnificent troubadour and *trouvère chansonniers* can tell us something of what we have been missing. The connoisseurs for whom they were compiled must have been aware of the fragility of oral transmission, but above all they valued an older art form and knew the potential of writing to preserve songs for future use.

It's not just the poetry that mysteriously evolved during this period. Just as difficult to trace is the morphing of spoken Latin into local variants which evolved via the dialects of Romance into the languages we know today. Charters and inscriptions began to appear in dialect as an alternative to Latin, and the newly emerging languages started to acquire a value of their own. The medieval songbook is a cultural artefact – you can hold it and turn its pages, not just listen to it, and most of the surviving sources are artistic collaborations involving separate craftsmen for music, text and decoration. They are far too ostentatious and valuable to have been performing copies but were probably copied from scrolls or booklets, now lost, that singers used to remind themselves of words and music. The *chansonniers* represent a kind of performed literature, an elaborate visual encapsulation of what had been an oral performance; in the absence of a physical performer the songs lived on as a visual memory. Songs in performance die even as they are created, but when written into a songbook they both gain a potential future and are simultaneously embedded in our past. These codices also celebrate an extraordinarily vibrant and secular cultural present, the enabling of a more reflective and elaborate creative process that doesn't need to be held entirely in the head.

The collections which survive in the modern territories of France, Germany, Italy and Spain are presumably only a small fraction of the songs that made it into written form, and an even smaller fraction of the pre-troubadour vernacular songs that didn't. From the south of what eventually became France, and including much of northern Italy and Spain, we have troubadour culture in Occitan, a language close to modern Catalan; in the north a little later troubadour forms were incorporated into a French repertoire devised by *trouvères*. The key word is the Occitan *trobar* (hence *trobador*) from which the modern terms are derived. Its origins are obscure but it may come from the Latin meaning 'to find' (as in modern French *trouver*) or discover; the term reflects a new creative process, adventures in a unique literary and musical genre. The art form spiralled outwards from its Occitanian origins; in German-speaking territories *Minnesänger* – singers of love songs – took the troubadour tradition to their hearts, as did their fellow composer-poets in Italy and the Iberian Peninsula. In many respects it was the dawn of European song as we know it.

Although within the cloister music was increasingly written down, the assumption is that the first vernacular songs were created by their singer-composers in performance. They were then refined, possibly by other singers, and may have gone through several versions before their appearance in manuscript. We still can only guess at how such well-crafted poems can be produced in a completely oral culture, and it is possible that writing played a part in the transmission of the songs before the exemplars used by the *chansonnier* scribes. Perhaps in the heat of the creative moment a troubadour would make notes with a stylus on a writing tablet, or first drafts were committed to manuscripts which were then lost. The missing century was certainly not silent but it is invisible, and the question of origins is likely to remain permanently adrift in the realm of scholarly speculation. Even the brief biographies of the singer-poets (known as *vidas*) that often head the collections of troubadour works were mostly written long after their subjects were dead, and they may well be repeating fanciful details of figures who by then were semi-legendary.

We know the names of more than 450 troubadour poets, though fewer than fifty of them have left us any notated music. They were not all men, but of the surviving songs by the twenty or so known *trobairitz* the only one with music is a *canso* by the mysterious Comtessa de Dia, who may not have been a countess nor from Dia but whose 'A chanter m'es al cor' is perhaps the oldest surviving secular song by a known female composer. There are more than 2,500 surviving troubadour lyrics, about 10 per cent of which have music written into only four of the many sources (one from Provence, one from north Italy and two from northern France which are primarily *trouvère* collections). The apparent absence of so much music has puzzled scholars. Some text manuscripts have lines ruled for music which was never copied, but there are almost no musical sources without words. The fusing of rhetorical performance skills with an obsessive exploration of rhyme, assonance and syllable counts may mean that the difference between spoken and sung poetry was sometimes too close to call, and the term *canso* was used for both. Could it be that the sheer sonic richness of a poem was music enough, allowing the performer to exploit the sonorities of the text anew each time? Dante, historian of language and disciple of Cicero, defined poetry as a combination of music and rhetoric, and if the troubadours knew their classical rhetoricians they would know how to manipulate pitch, tone and pacing however a performance was realised.

There is no original well-spring to be found: many songs exist in multiple versions, perhaps reflecting scribal intervention or a certain haphazardness as well as the idiosyncratic singing styles of the original performers. The poems tend to be more consistent from version to version than the surviving notes, and the structural integrity of the poems clearly outweighed the relative simplicity of the music. Singers could adjust their performance to fit their own interpretation of the poem, especially as the songs entered the repertoires of other singers, so there were probably many different versions of any given song. It was also possible to put new words to old tunes, a process known as contrafacture. The creation of a song was a fluid process quite unlike modern classical composition, and perhaps more akin to that of a singer-songwriter whose songs once drafted may remain works in progress for others to complete. Those of us who have recorded songs and then listened to them many live performances later are sometimes surprised at the differences that have crept in over the performing life of a song, the core remaining the same. There is no definitive beginning or completion of a song but a potentially infinite number of possible versions, one of which happens to start the process of realising some of them.

In the nineteenth century, when troubadour song became the subject of serious research, many scholars considered the earliest extant copies, most of which had no musical notation, to be the beginning of a great European literary tradition. More recently, research has focused on how (and why) such fully formed poetry appeared apparently out of nowhere. The genre sedimented into several forms that reflected many of the domestic and political topics found in Latin song, but it is the *canso* (from which we get the modern French *chanson*) which has left the biggest impact on the history of song. A *canso* is a love song, a personal and quasi-erotic poem celebrating or bemoaning the poet's passion for a woman who is potentially seducible but probably unobtainable. The troubadours called it *fin'amor*, but we tend to use the term courtly love, following Gaston Paris's coining of the term *amour courtois* in 1881. *Fin'amor* implies an adulterous relationship, which caused all sorts of intellectual wriggling for nineteenth-century Christian scholars and which still resonates with contemporary scholarship from feminism to literary theory.

Although the various forms of troubadour song were refined and sophisticated, the creators came from all walks of life (though the female *trobairitz* were almost always aristocrats). Poetic skill and a certain charisma were essential, but in an oral culture the poet-composer didn't need to be literate in its modern sense. They were all possessed of a creative spark and the means to keep it alive in their heads. We know a little about the circumstances of twelfth-century performance, but the performances themselves are very much a matter of speculation. There are many references to *joglars, jongleurs* and minstrels, something like modern buskers or street entertainers, and some troubadour songs undoubtedly found their way into the streets. But the typical performance venue must have been in the courts to which the successful performer would hope to be attached. Aristocratic courts everywhere compete for cultural prestige, and by a quirk of history (helped along by a legal requirement to divide inherited territory equally between offspring) the landscape of Provence has more castles per hectare than almost anywhere in Europe, providing an abundance of opportunity for troubadour art to flourish. It was a highly militarised society and therefore quintessentially male, but in troubadour song the knightly class was able to show a new respect for women, and although they were few in number many *trobairitz* were able to achieve a similar status to their male counterparts.

Guilhem IX of Aquitaine (also VII, Count of Poitou; 1071–1127) is considered to be the first person to create songs in the literary language of Occitan (there must have been oral predecessors, but Guilhem makes a convenient starting point). He is largely ignored by musicologists as only a fragment of one of his songs survives with music. Literary studies, however, have had a field day with all eleven of his surviving poems, at least three of which (depending on how you read them) would be considered obscene by today's concertgoers. He may have been the first poet to compare a woman to a filly and the c-word in his poems is definitely beyond courtly, though he does establish the principle of a vassal hopelessly in love with a lady who is not (yet) available. The poems are clever, well crafted, and surely amused his aristocratic listeners who would, like Guilhem himself, have been familiar with similar performances in the same genre, all of which are now lost. His education would have equipped Guilhem with a knowledge of rhetoric and oratory, and with the constant interaction between church and local aristocratic circles he would almost certainly have been familiar with Latin lyrics from the monastery of St Martial in Limoges (the source of some of the earliest writings in Occitan). Guilhem spent some years fighting in Spain and crusading fruitlessly in the Holy Land so he may have heard all manner of verses beyond southern France, all or none of which could have influenced his poetry.

This is speculation, of course, and scholars are still divided on how Guilhem managed to be so at home in a medium of which we have no prior knowledge. I suspect he would be surprised at his modern reputation as the first troubadour, despite his boasts of sexual indulgence. At the time he was famous for his recklessness on the battlefield and his occasional difficulties with the church, though he eased his conscience perhaps by endowing the Abbey of Fontevraud, where his granddaughter Eleanor of Aquitaine lies to this day (as do the remains of her son, troubadour and king, Richard *Coeur de Lion*). Eleanor, sometime wife of the English king Henry II, would become a famous patron of both *trouvères* and the later generation of troubadours, notably Bernart de Ventadorn with whom she had a particularly close relationship.

***

The first generation of troubadours included Jaufre Rudel, also an aristocrat and of whom four songs survive with melodies, and Marcabru, an itinerant composer-poet who survived on his talent rather than his position in society; forty-four of his poems survive, four of them also set to music. One of Marcabru's poems is a Crusade song, though he doesn't seem to have gone to the Holy Land (unlike Rudel who died there). Bernart de Ventadorn (*c.* 1152–*c.* 1195) was one of a second generation of troubadours who flourished in the second half of the twelfth century. Nineteen of Bernart's forty-five songs survive, set to music. 'Can vei la lauzeta mover' (When I see the skylark) appears in some twenty-eight sources, more than any other troubadour lyric.

There are two short *vidas* of Bernart, one of which is a slightly more colourful version of the other and neither of which can be independently verified. Both agree that he was brought up in the castle of Ventadorn in Limousin and that his mother was a baker in the service of Viscount Eble II. Eble, a musician and poet himself and a patron of performers, recognised the talent of the charismatic young Bernart, who must have seen and heard many a troubadour at Eble's court, if only from behind the arras. In proper troubadour form Bernart fell in love with the viscountess and when Eble found out, Bernart was obliged to leave. He found a position at the court of

Eleanor of Aquitaine and he duly fell in love with her too. He may have accompanied her to England when she married Henry II (there is no evidence beyond the *vida*), but if he did he returned to the mainland when this affair was also discovered. He may then have secured a position at the court of Raimon of Toulouse, after whose death he retired to a monastery in the Dordogne and vanished from the pages of history. The broad shape of this biography may be true, and he does seem to confirm the affairs in his songs, but we can't be sure about the details.

Bernart sings about himself and his predicament, the frustrations of being so physically close to the object of his desire and yet socially so impossibly far away. He sometimes addresses her directly, but more often bewails her ignorance of his condition or even of his existence. His love mirrors the seasons, depressing him in winter but finding a fleeting optimism in spring and summer. In many of his songs he emerges from a wood or strikes up in a garden and he is frequently consoled by that fellow singer, the nightingale. He gives his loves fictional names and isn't afraid to rebuke them for slighting him. He discusses his emotional state and castigates himself for his stupidity (he is like a fish who has foolishly taken the bait). He sometimes outlines how he wants the song to go, flags up his topic, and may even ask the listeners' advice about it. He will talk to the song itself, embodied as a messenger to his love. He will end a song with a conspiratorial *envoi* (*tornada* in Occitan) referencing people and events that would have been familiar to his audience but mean nothing to us (a tricky thing for modern singers to bring off). Some of his songs are *tensos*, dialogues between himself and another named poet. His is the shy quasi-eroticism of courtly love rather than the vaunting near-obscenity of Guilhem. Bernart never gets his lady, but her charms and beauty suffuse the landscape and on a good day make the sun shine on him. He likes a good song and he knows when he's written one but he doesn't boast, apart from briefly noting the fact that it's no wonder he's a better singer than anyone else as he's more sincere than anybody when it comes to love. This is how *fin'amor* works.

As the tradition evolved, the troubadours turned their attention to all sorts of topics, ranging from corruption in the church to the attributes (good and bad) of chivalry. The love-poetry-music matrix is something we can identify with today, and Bernart's *canso* 'Can vei la lauzeta' is a first and wonderfully complete expression, an exemplar not just for his fellow troubadours but also for songwriters of generations to come. Rewritten versions of the poem appear in Old French and Catalan (quotations from it still appearing in the mid-fifteenth century) and the tune surfaces with new texts (*contrafacta*) in the repertoires of *trouvères* and *Minnesänger* decades later. The song has a *razo*, something like a modern programme note, based perhaps on a spoken introduction first performed by a *jongleur* explaining how Bernart witnessed the events in the story.

'Can vei' has been the subject of more literary and musical analysis than any secular song before the Lieder of Schubert. It teases out the key attributes of *fin'amor* – the singer's total obsession with his lady, her indifference, his despair and pleas for mercy, his leaving the scene for pastures new, finally telling his friend Tristan that he's going to give up singing altogether. These outpourings come in various permutations according to which verses were sung to the different scribes who presumably notated (or improved) actual performances. Musically, the song has something of the shape of plainsong (Hildegard would have recognised it), and having a range of an octave and rarely using more than a fifth of that it is within reach of any singer. Today's performer, like Bernart's contemporaries, can choose which verses to sing, and no one can fail to be moved by the opening lines: the poet looks up to see the joyful beating of wings as the skylark slips and swoops against the rays of the sun:

Can vei la lauzeta mover   When I see the lark beating its wings
De joi sas alas contral rai   For joy against the sun's rays

The sheer joy of flight, with all its risks and possibilities, is the perfect image for his condition, and the music reflects this in an extraordinarily subtle way which the listener may not even be aware of. The transcription starts on D (it's in the Dorian mode, the equivalent of a scale of D using only the white notes on a keyboard), but apart from a couple of brief ornamental swoops it only returns to a D for the very last note. It's a gravity-defying musical tour de force, and although the image only applies to the first verse it constantly unsettles the subsequent strophes, as Bernart makes his complaint. All troubadour songs are sophisticated literary constructions, but before Bernart few had an emotional range that was matched in the music. It is one of the first songs that not only puts us in touch with the distant past but also has a timelessness which, like the greatest songs, will always mean something in the present.

Geoffroi de Vinsauf urges troubadours to perform with their voice, their countenance and gestures, to be at one with the subject, and make properly spoken introductions. The troubadour would perhaps be called upon after dinner, an informal act within a highly structured social scene. There would have been little help from the acoustics, the walls hung with textiles, the listeners richly and sweatily dressed and unlikely to be as silent as their modern counterparts. The ability to interact with the courtiers, to hold the room, would be a major factor in a troubadour's success: something of the chutzpah of today's stand-up comedian or the authority of an actor giving a one-man/woman show. A successful performance might mean a gift of clothing, fuel or food or even a horse, but perhaps more importantly confirm the troubadour's place in the chivalric order of things. Their reputations would have preceded them, and their audience, much like a modern one, would be predisposed to enjoy themselves; after all, they were about to witness a version of a song that would be created for them and never heard again in quite the same way.

The topics would be familiar, local and often a little risqué. The performers still had their classical rhetorical skills but now employed them to deliver a love song in the language spoken by their listeners, who would be untroubled by a dodgy dative or a misplaced pronoun in more rarefied Latin verse. A notationless music must have started with the singing of the poem. We can imagine an improvised beginning of a piece using a small number of pitches, but the simultaneous improvising of a number of strophes with regular syllable counts and rhyme schemes is a much taller order. This perhaps explains why songs which survive in multiple versions are so different: they continued to be works in progress, constantly refined and reinvented until captured by a scribe. The latter's task would have included guessing what the composer-singer meant to say, rather than literally transcribing what he saw or heard. By the time the poems were written down rhetoric had become poetry.

None of this is easy for a modern performer to get across, and without a landmark recording to compare with Gothic Voices's interpretation of Hildegard there are few models to stimulate the imagination (not helped by the lack of authoritative modern editions). The classical recital format immediately places physical, psychological and artistic barriers between singer and listener. The black-and-white formality of the stage has to stand in for a grand and multicoloured medieval domesticity, and a modern audience will have little understanding of either the language or the poetic tradition. The challenge for today's listeners is that, ultimately, the genre is essentially a literary one, and the experience of listening without understanding must surely be a meagre one compared with those who first heard these songs. Guesses at performance practice have come and gone, and historical musicologists now tend to be cautious about who sang what with whom. The rich compositional palette that evolved during the nineteenth century has left us addicted to harmony. (The twenty-first-century troubadour Pharrell Williams's song 'Happy' has only one essential note: it is the harmonic sequence beneath it that made it a global hit.) Our addiction inevitably conditions the nature of the debate about accompaniment in ancient music. Neither harmony nor accompaniment would have meant anything to a troubadour, and although there is iconographical evidence of instruments (fiddles, harps or lutes) in the same room as singers, ideas about their role change with the musicological wind. It is hard enough to figure out what a performer sang when there was no notation, but at least a singer was only responsible for one note at a time; what a multi-stringed fiddle or lute might have played in an age of monophony is anyone's guess. The late twentieth century's enthusiastically over-arranged ensemble performances attempted to evoke some medieval colour, and the unfamiliar sounds of reconstructed instruments undoubtedly held the audience's attention, perhaps distracting from the fact that this is monophonic music without the support of the functional harmony we always expect in a song.

Ironically, the more minimal accompaniment (or none at all) favoured by current scholarship may have put successful performances further out of reach, and today's singers can be forgiven a certain reluctance to record versions that may not survive future scrutiny. Absent performers are rarely able to impress their personality on the listener at home (podcasts and live radio may have lessons for us here) and we have to temper our predilection for the reverberant acoustics appropriate for sacred music; a big acoustic simply obscures the more intimate clarity necessary for small-scale secular songs. Reverberation, both natural and electronic, has been a hallmark of many early music recordings, but in order not to sound unconvincingly ecclesiastical we have to do without acoustic distance as a metaphor for the distant past.

These problems arise after the performer has worked out how to pronounce Occitan and made a decision about rhythm. The musical sources show only pitches, leaving the modern performer to work out how the poetic metre relates to the music. Today's performers are generally relaxed about rhythm, and will happily read from scores with bar lines (which they are free to ignore) or unstemmed noteheads which give them a choice. It has taken a long time for scholars to sanction a loosening of the bonds of the bar line. In the twentieth century many musicologists, most from a modernist background in which all music is rhythmically organised, found it hard to imagine that singers could perform without metred rhythm and sought refuge in the theory of rhythmic modes. The theory didn't get off to a good start in 1909 with the young Jean-Baptiste Beck accusing his older fellow scholar Pierre Aubry of stealing his theory of modal rhythm, resulting in both scholars wrecking their careers and possibly causing Aubry's death practising for a duel with his accuser the following year. The musicological pendulum swung back and forth over the century, many scholars insisting on bar lines while most performers ignored the music altogether.

Very few early scholars appear to have been singers; they knew the poetry and tunes inside out but from looking at them, not living them. Had the first scholars to investigate the manuscripts been rock or jazz singers they would surely have approached the problem from an entirely different viewpoint. Popular music is an oral music, and transcribing it has always been, to say the least, approximate. A modern pop song will almost always start with a performative act, helped by scribblings of text or perhaps chord symbols and snatches of melodic shapes. Even a recorded version, the equivalent to writing down a troubadour song, is still only a record of one iteration of the song, which then has a performing life of its own (evidence of which may survive in bootlegs, the modern equivalent of medieval secondary sources). Nobody reading from a transcription of a song by Paul McCartney or Ella Fitzgerald would expect to reproduce the note values on the page; this is the prerogative of the performer whose task is to get across the text in the most effective way, and this cannot be reflected in any notation that would be simple enough to understand. A troubadour or *trouvère* would surely be mystified by the idea that anyone would want to transcribe his or her rhythm beyond appreciating the cleverness of their syllable counts.

There is also the question of *musica ficta*, the process whereby a performer would be expected to add sharps or flats to conform to a modal logic assumed by the composer and so not notated in the score. Many modern troubadours will have come to monophonic song via later polyphonic music where competing lines of music need a consistent application of the rules. This is a crucial area where the oral and written don't quite mesh, and we don't know how far the rules apply to solo song or who applied them. Perhaps the best we can do is to accept the limits imposed on us by the past and think of the lack of evidence as a creative opportunity. This is quite a challenge for classical performers brought up on a more disciplined diet of later music with its pedagogical certainties. In my own work with music of the period I've tried to make a distinction between performances that are the result of musicological research and therefore have some sort of connection with the past, and those which use the material as inspiration in the present. The Dowland Project's version of 'Can vei' rests on a lute drone, taking a musical idea for which there is very little historical evidence but which appeals to our sense of musical logic and has been rooted in medieval performance practice since the 1980s. Between verses there are solos from saxophone or viola, giving the audience a chance to reflect on the poem. The only thing remotely historical about this kind of arrangement is that it is located firmly in the performers' present, just as it would have been a thousand years ago.

If we were to focus solely on troubadour poetry we might conclude that the songs were created at a time when enlightened knights serenaded superior women in peaceful if draughty domesticity while monks calmly chanted the office in the cloister. Whereas Hildegard's songs undoubtedly reflect significant aspects of her theocratic society, the love songs of the troubadours seem more like a form of cultural escapism in the context of the heavily militarised courts in which they flourished. The relationship between church and court was complicated by the secular resources of the pope, who could call on feudal allegiances to defend the faith against heresy. The Crusades, called by various popes in often disastrous attempts to recover Jerusalem from 'the Moors' (as historians tend to refer to the Muslim incumbents), were violent and chaotic campaigns which had a certain chivalric attraction for several troubadours and *trouvères*. There are some three dozen Crusade songs in Occitan (and a slightly smaller number in Old French), but the music the creators may have heard on their travels seems to have made little impact. The Fifth Crusade of the second and third decades of the thirteenth century, variously described by modern historians as a civil war or a genocide, was nearer to home and had terrible consequences for Occitan culture.

The story of the so-called Albigensian Crusade, in which the northern French nobles accepted the pope's challenge to eliminate Catharism from Occitan society, is told in the *Canso de la crozada*. The first 2,800 verses were written by Guilhem de Tudela from the Crusaders' point of view (the poem contains the earliest known use of the word 'crusade') and it is continued for almost 10,000 more by an anonymous poet who was horrified by the atrocities visited upon the Occitanians. Of the many heresies that threatened Catholic orthodoxy, Catharism, a rogue belief system originally from Bulgaria, gained the most traction among all levels of Occitanian society. Its creed focused on the Gospels rather than Catholic exegesis but acknowledging a dual concept of God. It promised (among less tangible and more bizarre consequences) freedom from the secular corruption of the institutionalised church. It was brutally suppressed by vassals of successive French kings who offered participants plunder aplenty, and Pope Innocent III who guaranteed remission of sins. The pope followed up the suppression of Catharism by establishing the Inquisition, which would attempt the ultimate elimination of all future heresy by means of cruel and unusual punishments for those who dared to challenge religious orthodoxy.

Troubadours had generally supported crusading in Palestine, but many were disgusted by the unleashing of the church's military aggression against fellow Christians. Corruption in the church was a recurrent trope in Latin verse, but the vernacular anti-clerical songs of Peire Cardenal and Guillem Figueira stand out as early examples of principled protest songs. Many courtly patrons of the troubadours were destroyed along with their castles, and those who survived sacrificed their Occitanian identity to the stirrings of what would in time become the French state. The last troubadours melted away into the southern reaches of old Occitania in Castile, Aragon, northern Italy and the Kingdom of Sicily, where some took to satire or replaced the object of their amorous entreaties with a newly discovered devotion to the Catholic Virgin, and local vernaculars eventually replaced literary Occitan.

It is around this time that the troubadour and *trouvère chansonniers* were compiled. One of the most sumptuous has been known since the eighteenth century as the *chansonnier du roi*. As is the case with most medieval sources we can't be sure of the provenance, and we don't know whether the king in question was a seventeenth- or eighteenth-century owner or one of its earlier guardians. It may have started life as two or more different collections, and it was subsequently added to during the fourteenth and fifteenth centuries before having some of its exquisite miniatures and several pages excised. It was bought by Cardinal Mazarin in 1640 and acquired by the French Royal Library in 1668. It contains more than four hundred *trouvère* melodies and some fifty notated songs in Occitan (including Bernart's 'Can vei' and 'A chantar m'es al cor' by the *trobairitz* Comptessa de Dia), as well as one of the earliest collections of polyphonic motets and a rare collection of instrumental music. This glorious codex illuminates not just a song collection, but a cross-section of aristocratic taste at a turning point in musical history.

One school of thought is that it was commissioned by or for Guillaume de Villehardouin (?–1278), Crusader, *trouvère*, and ruler of the post-Byzantine Frankish territory of Morea in southern Greece. Guillaume, fluent in Greek and French, contributed two songs to the great book and was in some ways the perfect *trouvère*, a prince of exemplary religious faith, extraordinary military prowess, and a generous patron of music and literature. Attached to the collection is a supplementary *libellus* containing sixty songs by Thibaut de Champagne (1201–53), King of Navarre, great-grandson of Eleanor of Aquitaine, and considered by many (including Dante) to be one of the greatest of the *trouvères*. His poetry reveals a strange chivalric delicacy and an occasional religious zeal (though he spares us the details of his enthusiastic mass burnings of heretics).

Such is the importance of the manuscript for scholars that it has a different siglum depending on who is studying it: M for *trouvère* scholars (Mt for the Thibaut gatherings), W for troubadour specialists, and R if you're looking at the motets. If the manuscript was commissioned by Guillaume, and then passed with a transfer of fealty to his successor Charles I of Anjou as seems probable, then it means that the reach of troubadour and *trouvère* song extended from Flanders to French Greece. It is also significant that the proportion of French to Occitan roughly matches the ratio for all surviving sources, confirming that by the time the songs were written down, French had become the dominant language. Thibaut was one of the most prolific of *trouvères* and may even have supervised his own collected works. But the motets are a sign of changing times, as polyphony begins to compete with solo song for the eyes and ears of aristocratic patrons.

Some of the earliest copies of troubadour song were made by Occitan-speaking scribes in Venice and Treviso, and some have rudimentary Occitan grammars, perhaps suggesting an attempt to keep alive a doomed literary language alongside that of Dante. Dante himself considered writing in Occitan and discussed the language of Provence in his essay on vernaculars, *De vulgari eloquentia*, eventually concluding that a poet should write in his own dialect. The stylistic imprint of Arnaut Daniel, one of eight troubadours who feature in *De vulgari* (and the only Occitan speaker in the *Divine Comedy*), also hovers in the background of Petrarch's *canzoniere*, but by the time of Petrarch's death in 1374, Occitan was an antiquarian interest, preserved in codices but overtaken by new songs in Italian vernaculars. There are hints at a continuing tradition of improvised poetry performances by *cantari*, poets who sang their verse, but the greatest musical achievement of the Italian *trecento* was the creation of a vast song repertoire for two or sometimes three voices.

The less exalted but more democratic form of the *lauda* has enjoyed something of a modern revival, both in colourful but speculative reconstructions of songs from the Cortona and Florence manuscripts and at the hand of the British composer Gavin Bryars, whose sets of *Laude cortonese* extrapolate on each of the songs from the eponymous ms. The original songs, devotional hymns of praise with repeated refrains, were sung in Tuscan or Umbrian dialect by *laudesi*, para-liturgical fraternities of tradesmen who wanted a more inclusive ritual less distanced by church Latin (which many of them may not have understood). By the fifteenth century the drift to polyphony overtook the *lauda* too, and the part-time cobblers, weavers and carpenters who had enjoyed communal music-making resorted to hiring professionals to sing them the more rigorously notated music. It was an urban and often *al fresco* street music, sometimes rivalling secular courts in its elaborate processions and theatrical displays. There was a peculiarly masochistic sub-set of *laudesi* in whose self-flagellating processions the songs could include extra verses urging greater physical rigour.

Occitan had flourished in the northern Iberian courts, but the pull of territorial vernaculars was too much to sustain it much beyond the end of the fourteenth century. Alfonso X ('the Wise') of Castile and León, whose exuberant and multicultural court had sustained the careers of many troubadours, chose to commission the *Cantigas de Santa Maria* in Galician-Portuguese. The *Cantigas* also implicitly acknowledge the primacy of Catholicism with regard to both the reconquest of Muslim Spain and the secularity of the troubadour tradition. Alfonso's liege lady was in effect the Virgin Mary, and each of the *Cantigas* tells the story of a miracle effected by her. The four manuscript copies are sumptuous, with each miracle illustrated by a series of miniatures. These songs, some written by Alfonso himself but most by musicians, poets and artists in his entourage, are books to be read and admired as works of art.

Echoes of the troubadour tradition can be heard in the monasteries and courts of German-speaking territories; the very word *Minnesinger* – singer of love songs – hints at a German version of *fin'amor*. *Minnesänger* had nightingales, dawn assignments and impossible loves just like their French and Provençal predecessors and contemporaries, and like them demonstrate a sparseness of notation and a written existence much later then their first performances. For the first generation of *Minnesänger* there are no notes at all, and the music of many of the most famous German poets of the second generation survives only in fragments. 'German' in this context includes those dukedoms and kingdoms north of the Alps stretching into Hungary and Bohemia, in which the language flourished as a vernacular. One of the earliest and certainly the largest collections of *Minnesang* was assembled in a monastery somewhere in the Alps in the early twelfth century, from where it made its way to the Bavarian monastery of Benediktbeuern perhaps a century later. There it remained, consulted often enough to need rebinding and rearranging before being left on a shelf until it was rediscovered by a secular librarian when the monastery was dissolved in 1803.

The so-called *Carmina Burana* (Songs of Benediktbeuern) consist of more than two hundred songs on almost every conceivable subject, forty-eight of them in German, many dating back hundreds of years and collected from southern and central Europe. We know nothing about the compilers of this vast hoard of songs, but their taste was towards the Goliard tradition of anti-establishment satirical poetry despite showing all the signs of having been compiled for a wealthy patron. There are love songs that owe something to the troubadour and *trouvère* tradition, some frankly obscene (the publisher of the 1847 edition printed the offending material in tiny type at the back, recommending sensitive readers to take a pair of scissors to it). There is a separate section of drinking songs (student efforts perhaps) and many colourful pronouncements about gambling, gluttony, lust and the failings of the church. Only a handful of the Latin poems have notation, undecipherable neumes a few dozen of which are currently guessable from concordant sources.

The poems are mostly anonymous but also include some of the earliest examples of songs by *Minnesänger* such as Walther von der Vogelweide (cited in Richard Wagner's *Tannhäuser* and *Die Meistersinger*), and French poets including Walter of Châtillon and Philip the Chancellor as well as poems based on classical authors.

Walther von der Vogelweide (1170–1230), the first poet to call his songs *Minnesang*, is acknowledged as one of the greatest of all German poets, but his surviving music is represented by just a couple of notated songs and a handful of fragments. Walther may not have revolutionised the music of song (in his 'Under der Linden' the nightingale witnesses a secret tryst under the trees with only four notes borrowed from a *trouvère* melody, an achingly sweet and simple tune that doesn't give musicologists much to work on), but his poetry certainly did. Since the nineteenth century, German scholarship has emphasised the importance of *Minnesänger* in the literary canon but Anglophone musicology has mostly ignored them; *Minnesang* is much less visible in the modern early-music scene. This is a shame, because Middle High German gives the songs that have come down to us a unique colour and shape. The apparent lack of music (despite the fact that the poems are invariably referred to as songs) has discouraged musicologists, but more recent studies of the larger collections have begun to reveal clues to performance, which inhabited that world between the oral and written and which is so opaque to us today. Later composers, further into an increasingly written culture, are more musically accessible. The one-eyed and multilingual Tyrolean knight errant Oswald von Wolkenstein, an early-fifteenth-century aristocrat and diplomat, supervised collections of his songs, many of which are autobiographical, obscene and extremely colourful.

The *Carmina Burana*'s twentieth-century fame was largely due to Carl Orff's 1937 cantata which set twenty-four of the poems. The music is Orff's own but its vivid orchestration reflected the energetic brilliance of the poetry, and the work undoubtedly drew curious musicians to the original manuscript. Since the 1970s early-music specialists have been unable to resist colourful but highly speculative attempts to recreate or reinvent the songs, often working backwards from later versions. Modern scholarship takes a more interdisciplinary and codicological approach which is beginning to yield remarkable insights into how this and the many other collections that are missing notation might have functioned.

The *Carmina Burana* looks back at a repertoire that must have been well known to its scribes. In an oral soundscape there would only have been a need to write the poems down if they were in danger of being forgotten. The tunes were still in people's heads: it was the words that were at risk. In the absence of notation musicologists have tended to assume that the songs were monophonic, and that we should look for concordant sources to unlock the melodies. There aren't many concordances but some of them are polyphonic, and closer examination of the layout of some of the texts on the page suggests that the scribes intended to give readers enough information for them to be able to create a polyphonic performance if they wanted to. Much work remains to be done, but we are perhaps beginning to learn how to read the sources more like a medieval musician might have done.

Polyphony would determine the shape and nature of song for the next century or two, as musicians and their listeners experimented with a more sociable kind of music. This didn't mean an end to the pure melody of unaccompanied song, but it becomes less and less visible, kept in the head to allow more space on the page for the complexities of polyphony. In the German-speaking lands the successors to *Minnesänger* flourished as *Meistersänger* in guilds of tradesmen who competed in song according to strict rules. Hans

Sachs, the famous cobbler, poet and singer from sixteenth-century Nuremberg (as featured in Wagner's *Die Meistersinger*), was also a Lutheran. The decadence of Oswald von Wolkenstein was replaced by the decorum of rule-based fellowship. It was the survival of an oral tradition, reinvigorated by a realignment of music and class.

In the Francophone world the romance of the troubadour survived at the upper end of the social scale. In 1364, Philip the Bold became Duke of Burgundy, a collection of territories in the Low Countries and northern France so extensive and dispersed that its capital was wherever its itinerant ruler laid his head. On St Valentine's Day 1401, Philip, by then the most spectacular and munificent of rulers, declared a new social and artistic enterprise at his residence in Paris, the *cour d'Amour*. Harking back to the semi-mythical *cour amoureuse* of Eleanor of Aquitaine, the annual event required members to compete in poetry and song celebrating women (or, more particularly, the love of men for women). It was an entirely male society, but it did attempt to elevate the position of women by tapping into the ideals of courtly love first expressed by Bernart. The courtiers were mostly aristocratic amateurs, but some composer-poets are to be found in the lists of members, all of whom were expected to create fashionable *chansons*, *virelais* and *ballades* for the occasion. It all happened in the moment, and once performed they were gone. As with so much medieval song, we know the names of many of the performers, but we will never know what they actually sang.

Woodcut of Josquin Desprez from Petrus Opmeer's Opus chronographicum *(1611).*

3

JOSQUIN DESPREZ
'LA DÉPLORATION SUR LA MORT D'OCKEGHEM'

It's not very fashionable but it is convenient for performers to use the terms medieval, Renaissance and Baroque. We know what we mean: we know that there is nothing middling about the Middle Ages and that there was no rebirth of classical music in the Renaissance (though one can argue the case for an attempt at the latter in the early Baroque period). But as history becomes more visible and less anonymous (and there's more and more of it) we can begin to see how various dots join up, often over many generations. We would all agree that from the thirteenth century onwards we are in an age of polyphony, but that's not to say that there was no polyphony before that, nor that our understanding of the term is anything like what it meant then. This period is also an age of improvisation – of music that we can't see let alone hear but whose most dynamic practitioners were as famous as today's improvisers. It's a time when the written and the unwritten, the improvised and the artfully constructed, mesh together to produce songs that were enjoyed not just in castles and monasteries, but in the more modest drawing rooms of merchants, craftsmen and intellectuals. Solo songs continue to be composed but the attention of history is on the newer and more sociable forms of song where musicians gather to sing together. The church, as a significant employer of musicians, inevitably influences the various musical strands that appear, but the sacred and the secular are sometimes hard to tell apart, with music for the church often appropriated for domestic entertainment and secular songs incorporated into the movements of the Mass.

For the last hundred years or so we have made a broad distinction between popular songs and 'classical' songs. It's not entirely binary, but we know what we mean when we use the terms and one thing most might agree on is that 'popular' means appreciation by the many and 'art' implies creation and reception by an informed minority. History is never going to be truthful about popular music – we can't hear any of it before the very end of the nineteenth century and its pre-audible story is inevitably written by the literate middle class. Were troubadour and *trouvère* songs 'popular'? We don't know the societal reach of the songs but there are hints of a wider circulation, especially in the expanding towns of central and northern France. It was certainly a genre created by poet-musicians and enjoyed by an elite, but it has many of the characteristics of modern popular song. The concept of *trobar*, in which poet-composers perform their own songs, would not resurface until the singer-songwriters of the late twentieth century and recording captured their songs for posterity, just as the *chansonniers* did 700 years ago. The highest form of song, in the meantime, took a different course with a diversion into polyphony which altered the link between creation and performance, and *trobar* gave way to what we would call composition.

Music history has focused almost exclusively on polyphony, the visible written manifestation rather than the opaque orality of performance. But the first polyphonists were brought up in an environment which placed equal value on solo song and on improvisation. The solo songs of the early medieval period seem to vanish after Guillaume de Machaut (1300–77), displaced by the great Franco-Flemish polyphonists that have been such a rich feature of the early-music movement. The mostly anonymous compilers of the great European songbooks of the thirteenth and fourteenth centuries were in effect saving the songs for posterity, dignifying them with a written existence alongside the newly evolving written polyphony. In Machaut and Adam de la Halle (*c.* 1245–*c.* 1288) we also see musicians with an eye on their place in history, assembling and editing collections of their own songs and motets. The impact of written polyphony proved very resilient: 700 years later the discographies of Adam and Machaut would feature their polyphonic works almost exclusively, with their solo songs now only of academic interest and mostly unrecorded. Their anonymous contemporaries have been even less fortunate.

Adam de la Halle was one of the last of the *trouvères*, his songs of *amour courtois* expressing similar sentiments to those of the first French or Occitan poet-composers, notated in the free rhythm of the *ars antiqua*. His first attempts at polyphony were created by fusing together a new tune with an existing one; not so much polyphony as simultaneous monody, and for this he opted for a metrical notation (which made it more likely that all voices would finish at the same time). Many songs of the period exist in both forms, and a manuscript copy is not a sure guide to the number of singers or what they actually sang. Sometimes alternative parts were supplied or lines could be omitted if there wasn't a quorum. For many generations there would have been no hard and fast distinction between monophony and polyphony. This linear and melodic conception of multi-voiced composition persisted until late Renaissance composers began to think vertically in terms of harmony as we know it, in chords rather than tunes.

This, though, is only half the story: the boundaries between solo song and polyphony may have been blurred but there was a more obvious distinction between written and unwritten music. Historians, naturally enough, focus on the written: it can be seen and analysed. Orally created music was never visible and is only dimly perceivable at all via occasional references to performers, notable performances and the occasional instruction manual. Until very recently, polyphony was assumed to start with the Parisian composers Léonin and Pérotin, whose organa (chants with added voices) seemed to be strikingly different from what had gone before. Here were two musicians we could put a name to and call composers; Pérotin even wrote in four parts and used rhythms and repetition just like Steve Reich. How extraordinary must it have seemed when two or three soloists sang together in a world where a single chant line was the daily musical diet.

But was polyphony really so rare? And was plainsong actually plain? We are beginning to understand more about memory and improvisation, unrecorded elements that have left us nothing to analyse, no names or dates to focus on, and yet have become a kind of early-music elephant in the room. We are so saturated with literacy that it's almost impossible to conceive of a musical society where complex operations which we need to work out on paper or laptop can actually take place in the head. Even the tiny few who were literate depended on memory for basic storage and the managing of information, whether arithmetical calculation or the learning of Latin. These are skills that we have under-used for centuries, and modern scholarship is only gradually coming to terms with this aspect of epistemological history. There is an increasing awareness that there are no surviving medieval composers' sketches because there may not have been any such sketches: both oral and written music began life in the minds of their creators.

We first learn of polyphony in *Musica enchiriadis* and its companion commentary *Scolica enchiriadis*, dating from the second half of the ninth century. These anonymous treatises tell us, among much else, the rules for constructing organa, adding a second line over an existing plainsong to be sung in church. There are no 'scores', simply rules for directly creating sounds (the earliest surviving actual pieces are found in the Winchester Tropers around a hundred years later). The rules themselves presumably existed long before they were written down, and during the following centuries more elaborate instructions were devised enabling up to four voices to create harmony in their heads by applying previously memorised formulae. The Parisian organa of Léonin and Pérotin are the spectacular results of this process. They were not, after all, 'the first great dead white male composers', as Anna Maria Busse Berger memorably described them. The Parisian organa were probably created towards the end of the twelfth century, but there is no record of them until the manuscripts of around half a century later. They bear a close relationship to the instruction books of the period; if you have a lot of patience and a high boredom threshold you can create your own pseudo-Léonin by following the obsessively detailed instructions in the so-called Vatican Organum Treatise which pre-dates the Parisian manuscripts.

The earliest written manifestations of these two 'composers' represent the maturing of an oral process rather than the beginning of a written one, an evolving series of semi-improvised oral iterations that were eventually captured by a scribe. That may not have been the end of the process either, just a glimpse of an artistic development still in train until overtaken by a change of musical fashion centuries later. It is the continual refinement of this interchange between the oral and the written that is the key to understanding how secular song developed over the ensuing centuries.

Singers were trained from childhood to improvise, adding parallel voices according to learned formulae which enabled them to be creative and to start and finish without crashing dissonances. A written treatise enabled pedagogical paradigms to travel unaccompanied by a singing teacher. When whole pieces appeared in manuscript particular versions could be preserved or used as reminders or to inspire new versions. And rules were surely written down to discourage singers from breaking them. The breaking of rules is fundamental to creativity and artistic growth, and in a culture where little is visible and fixed it is likely that creative boundaries were porous. Writing the rules (again and again) was an attempt to restore some discipline, as would be the case with many future treatises. It was perhaps creative rule-breaking that gave rise to the more sophisticated polyphonic improvising techniques of descant and counterpoint which enabled anyone to create song (sacred or secular) with fellow singers or instrumentalists. It's also a reminder that a treatise is likely to represent what the writer would like to happen rather than what musicians actually played or sang.

Descant replaced the parallel movement of traditional organum technique with contrary motion, freeing performers from the known melody and enabling the creation of independent parts. Skill in *cantare super librum* – singing upon the book – was an essential requirement for church and court musicians, swift-witted composer-performers who could create new music on the hoof. Eventually the writing of music, *Resfacta* as the theorist and composer Tinctoris called it, even if conceived initially in the head, began to yield advantages of scale and structure; without instant performance you could pay more attention to the rules. Musicians increasingly took the Machaut/Adam route, realising that you could perform the same piece more than once and to some extent own the results, at least until someone else got their hands on it.

The rhythmic notation of the French *ars nova* was developed to exploit the creative possibilities unleashed by fitting several voices together simultaneously, but as the new notation evolved it was also applied to some solo songs (such as the *lais* of Machaut, at least two of which are in fact canons so need to be coordinated). The old and the new existed side by side, and in the case of solo song it's hard to know how rigorously the new forms were applied. The nineteenth-century term *formes fixes* given to the three French verse-and-refrain forms *ballade*, *rondeau* and *virelai* implies more rigid structures than may actually have been the case. There has been much musicological speculation (often of the angels-on-pinheads variety) on exactly what the difference is between the three forms. It depends where the refrain comes (which may not be clear from the layout of the poem), and a source will often call itself a collection of all three but not say which is which (a performer's decision, presumably).

Many of Machaut's monophonic *virelais* seem to be for dancing, which would need more attention to rhythm than the amorous ramblings of the *trouvères*, hence a metrical notation. One copy of his *Louange des dames* has a miniature of a poet at work in a garden. Is it Machaut himself, composing a first draft onto a scroll, surrounded by rejected drafts? The process of researching and then editing texts and music of the late-thirteenth- and early-fourteenth-century codices has partly obscured the wider view of what they represent. We want to be able to read the music and perform it in an appropriate manner (maybe), but the great *chansonniers* are not performing editions: if singers needed to read from notation they would have used single sheets more like those shown in the picture of the scribbling poet, perhaps gathered into the small folders or booklets known as *libelli*, of which a tiny number survive.

Machaut is another composer with a claim to be the last of the *trouvères* and like Adam wrote magnificent solo songs even as he was experimenting with polyphony. He was also one of the greatest poets of his age and as secretary to King John of Bohemia he saw chivalry close up both on and off the battlefield. The death of John in 1346, some years after Machaut had left his post, was one of the many heroic tragedies of the Battle of Crécy reported by Froissart, who was in turn influenced by the poetry of Machaut. The blind king, his horses tied to those of his fellow knights, charged into the fray knowing it was his final act, and he and his slain companions were discovered the next day, still roped together with their dead steeds. Despite his huge legacy of solo songs, very few singers (nor most scholars) would now consider Machaut a *trouvère*. For music historians he is the greatest polyphonic composer of his time, but that's partly because so much of his music survives and because he represents the newly invigorated *ars nova*. Philip de Vitry (1291–1361), a fellow radical composer and probable begetter of the new style, was too busy playing politics to ensure the survival of more than a handful of his pieces. Our perspective on his solo songs is rather compromised by our modern tendency to see history in terms of polyphony and compositional cleverness, but Machaut himself (and his contemporaries) certainly considered his grand solo *lais* to be among his finest works.

The equal importance given to solo song and polyphony (and the sometimes vague borderline between the two) is visible in *Le Roman de Fauvel*, an iconic manuscript that is one of the great codicological, literary and musical conundrums of the early fourteenth century. The *Roman* started life as an allegorical poem satirising corruption in the French court and the church. Its hero is a fantastic horse, whose name and colour are a metaphor for the condition of society; he is *fauve*, the dun colour of deception, and his name, a veil of falseness, is comprised of an acrostic: *Flaterie, Avarice, Vilanie, Variété, Envie, Lâcheté* (flattery, greed, villainy, fickleness, envy, cowardice).

There are two versions of the original poem, completed in 1310 and 1314 respectively, but sometime before 1318 the otherwise unknown and strangely spelled Chaillou de Pesstain was responsible for the creation of a sumptuous, illustrated conflation of both, complete with a silent soundtrack of 169 songs, motets, chant and poetry readings. Stories illustrated by images and music were not unknown (both Adam de la Halle and Machaut produced something similar) and Reynard the Fox had previously appeared as an animal satire, but the scale of the Bibliothèque Nationale manuscript Fr 146 in which the *Roman* is found is astonishing. This mute cacophony embodies a hundred years' worth of polyphonic development from the *ars antiqua* style of the Pérotin era to multi-texted motets possibly composed by the architect of *musica nova* Philip de Vitry. Until a facsimile was published in 1990 most attention was focused on these thirty-four polyphonic pieces, which were the only musical representation of the *Roman* in a modern edition. The facsimile revolutionised study of the manuscript, opening it up to interdisciplinary codicological study as well as an understanding of the monophonic music. The latter comprised the vast majority of the pieces, and included the only source of the *ballades* of Jehannot de Lescurel, whose *trouvère*-like songs sit somewhere between those of Machaut and Adam.

The plot follows the adventures of the love-sick horse, whom the entire world flatters and grooms (we get 'currying favour' from currying Fauvel). He leaves the stable for a grand palace where Fortune has made him master of the royal household, and where he rules church and state as a pompous and corrupt prince. Book Two describes the nefarious goings on in grisly detail as Fauvel attempts to marry Fortune, who offers him Vainglory instead. Happy with this, the horse has a fabulous wedding followed the next day by jousting in which, to his dismay, the Vices (Carnality, Adultery, Pride and so on) are eventually trounced by the forces of Virtue (Virginity, Hope and the like). Fauvel and Vainglory return home and go on to people France with lots of mini-Fauvels, at which point the author gives a Gallic shrug and invites everyone to join him in a drink.

What does it all mean, and what does *Fauvel* tell us about the history of song? The poem is a political satire and must have had aristocratic patronage, but the subject of the allegory and the targets aimed at are still a matter for debate. We don't know what the function of the *Roman* was, who might have read it or performed it. In a sense, the book is itself an ideal performance interpreted in their own heads by those who turned its pages untroubled by physical performers. There is a sense of immediacy in the layout; unusually, it doesn't seem to be a fair copy of another source, and additions were being made right up to the last minute. A representative performance of the whole book is impossible (it would take days, and how would you perform the pictures?). I once produced a student performance in the form of a giant pop-up book which tried to capture its bookness, but even with a small army of student scaffolders and set painters we could only hint at the richness of the original, and we used only a fraction of the musical and poetic resources. *Fauvel* isn't a prescription for a performance of any sort, but a socio-cultural project realised as a *book*. The reader performs the contents by witnessing them; for all its extravagance the book has the intimacy of a one-to-one relationship with the person who opens its covers. A digital multimedia production using all the resources of twenty-first-century technology might be the one way to realise the book while remaining true to itself, and viewing it on a small screen might give a similar illusion of intimacy.

As a snapshot of song history, *Fauvel* is an ironic still point in the noisy narrative of song which enables us to look both backwards and forwards. It's one of the most comprehensive sources of fourteenth-century polyphony and yet some four-fifths of it is monophonic (some pieces could go either way). The polyphony makes no judgement about style: old and new sit side by side and sometimes one could be interpreted as the other (which among other things could convert triple time into duple and vice versa). Metrical rhythm is used extensively, alongside pieces in older and freer notation, as composers grappled with how to express more complex rhythmic divisions. Were they trying to give the songs the regularity of dance or were they grasping at a more precise way of trying to notate speech rhythms? There are poems (*dits*) that might be declaimed or read silently perhaps; songs might be *ballades*, *rondeaux* or *virelais*, according to taste. Whoever opened the book had plenty of choices to make: the main lesson we can learn from this remarkable document is that every potential boundary is blurred; if there are rules, nobody much bothered about them.

The performance of the earliest polyphonic *chansons* might have sounded to the first listeners as a kind of organised chaos, with each of the voices singing a different text. The *Fauvel* motets (if they were performed at all) might have at least two texted parts plus *incipits* for a chant text and melody that the singer was expected to know already. The composer was no longer a poet-composer but a musician for whom the text was subordinate to musical form and construction; the rhetorical basis of the poetry was replaced by text as sonority.

The singers may have seen and heard things differently. The new music was as much an urban phenomenon as a courtly one, and performances probably took place in smaller rooms to audiences of self-made connoisseurs who may have enjoyed trying to puzzle out how the songs fitted magically together. The singers' rhetorical instincts and training would have ensured a coherent delivery of the text as far as the music allowed, but the overall effect was likely to have been a purely musical one. This was awkward for singers of the early-music revival who came to medieval music from the Renaissance or Baroque where they were expected to make the text and its meanings as clear as possible. The other problem was the physical geography of the *formes fixes* of *ballade*, *virelai* and *rondeau* on the page. The music is binary, but the texts repeat in different patterns for each form, making navigation potentially hazardous (a *ballade* is a relatively straightforward AAB; a *rondeau* has eight verses, ABAABBAB, but repeats the words for the first, fourth and last A's). It may also have been a fourteenth-century problem too: we know that singers didn't always keep to the intended form (perhaps through having got lost too many times) and manuscripts tend to bunch pieces of the same form together, perhaps because if you were going to perform more than one, everyone could agree on the route through the material.

After years of performing multi-texted motets and *chansons*, you begin to accept all this as normal. It's another condition that puts you directly in touch with the ghosts of your fourteenth-century predecessors. You cannot privilege your text over those of your fellow singers, and making the differentiated lines balance requires a particular skill: you sing for each other. This is far from the ego-driven performance of troubadour song, and it marks the beginning of a different relationship between composer, singer and audience. Most obviously, the composer may have had a certain authority as the author of a song, but he (the first composers of polyphony seem to have been exclusively male) is dependent on his performers to execute it; the performers negotiate with each other, using the composer's notes as an adjustable template (hence the different versions which survive). A troubadour or *trouvère* would do everything possible to get across the meaning of their song; after all, that was part of what writing in the vernacular was all about, and a successful performance would involve most of the audience getting the same message. But listeners to the multi-texted motets and *chansons* could not possibly all take away the same meanings, and were free to use their own imagination. In deriving multiple meanings (or none beyond an immediate acoustic pleasure) from a plurality of texts, audiences for the medieval secular motet were perhaps not unlike modern classical audiences and their instinct to give performers the benefit of any musical or poetic doubt.

Once musicians had evolved a system for organising rhythm, the question of number became the most important single structural criterion. Despite the efforts of various popes to discourage composers' obsession with number rather than text, the motet (both sacred and secular) became an arcane art that only a tiny number of people could understand or perform, a true art song. At its most reductive the system of rhythmic proportions known as *isorhythm* was so intricate that text and simultaneous melodies had to be subordinated to the numerical proportions of the whole piece (elements of which would get faster and faster as the same rhythmic cell was repeated in smaller note values).

The tendency to notate the voices in individual lines (rather than underneath each other in score) created more opportunities for visual game playing that could have no bearing on performance (beyond increasing the likelihood of it all falling apart). Notation often became an end in itself, challenging performers, intriguing those who commissioned manuscripts, but completely bypassing most listeners. Machaut's 'Ma fin est mon commencement' (My end is my beginning) is an early example of a Webern-like cleverness of construction, where the triplum line is the cantus sung backwards and the tenor line is a palindrome, reversing halfway through. The scribes didn't even need to write out all the parts: giving clues as to how to construct them was all part of the fun. The isorhythmic scheme of Guillaume Dufay's (*c.* 1397–1474) 'Nuper rosarum flores', sung at the dedication of Brunelleschi's dome of the cathedral in Florence, was once thought, not entirely fancifully, to have been constructed on similar proportions to those of the dome.

The early-music movement relished the first modern encounters with fourteenth- and fifteenth-century Franco-Flemish polyphony. The revolution began in earnest in the 1970s with David Munrow's Early Music Consort whose Netherlands polyphony was sung by Anglican ex-choral scholars for whom the meandering weirdness was quite unlike anything we had sung before. The English choral tradition, so influential throughout the Western world, didn't go back much beyond Thomas Tallis and William Byrd, whose serial embracing of both sides of the religious divide has left us with a substantial repertoire in both Latin and English; they seemed to use harmony that had proper chords with logical progressions. Their music and that of their contemporaries formed (and mostly still forms) the bedrock of English cathedral and college chapel music. Latin pre-Reformation masses and motets have only ever found a very limited place in the Protestant liturgy and as most of us came to the secular via the sacred we knew very little about the fifteenth-century *chanson*. The late medieval and early Renaissance repertoires were as new as the avant-garde which many of us had also been experimenting with (and few of us understood the compositional principles of either old or new).

We still argue over how the songs of Gilles Binchois and Dufay were performed. In the early days of the early-music revival no opportunity was lost to use the newly rediscovered instruments to create what now seem improbable orchestrations. While this attracted a new audience (and provided work for lots of players), there was little evidence for instrumental participation; the few comments in contemporary sources were ambiguous at best. After a musicological course correction which decided the mostly three-part songs should be performed only with voices even if two of the parts had no words, a more relaxed approach now generally accepts that we will never know for certain, and that a plurality of practice was much more likely. You can now hear the *chansons* of Binchois, Dufay and their contemporaries performed as pristine *a cappella* or as solo songs arranged for one or more instruments, safe in the knowledge that somewhere your choice will have some musicological respectability.

The advocacy of David Munrow and his contemporary trailblazers benefited some countries and periods more than others. French music from the twelfth and thirteenth centuries and Franco-Flemish music of the two following centuries were the main beneficiaries; Italy too in the latter period, though mainly as the place where northerners such as Josquin and Heinrich Isaac (1470–1517) found employment. There was a flourishing song culture in *trecento* Italy which had an *ars nova* all of its own but which has never quite sparked the modern imagination. The earliest surviving signs of it, dating from a decade or two after *Le Roman de Fauvel*, are found in the Rossi Codex, a manuscript probably compiled by musicians at the Veronese or Paduan court of Alberto della Scala (whose father had been Dante's patron). The distinctive two-voice texture with both parts newly composed hints at a lost connection with the conductus repertoire and there are some stylistic quirks from troubadour poetry, but these madrigals (which bear no relation to the sixteenth-century term) are distinctively Italian songs owing little to French or Occitan antecedents. The manuscript also contains monophonic *ballatas*, confirming that both forms of song were current at the court.

The Rossi pieces have been largely overlooked by modern performers, as have most of the works in the slightly later and more magnificent Squarcialupi Codex, compiled in Florence at the beginning of the fifteenth century. This is an altogether grander affair, with more than 350 madrigals, *ballatas* and *caccie* (canonic songs in up to three parts, many very elaborate and huge fun to sing). It has almost the entire known output of Francesco Landini, the blind organist, lutenist and singer whose performances of his music were famous throughout the land, as well as the music of Jacopo da Bologna, Niccolò da Perugia and many other more obscure contemporaries. Each composer's section of the manuscript was supposed to contain a miniature portrait, but the collection seems not to have been completed. Paolo da Firenze has a portrait and space for his music but the composer seems not to have made it in time. The Squarcialupi Codex might also have been the biggest source of music by Giovanni Mazzuoli, but instead we have many blank pages, decorated ready for a composer whose works don't exist anymore. It's a reminder that the great codices probably represent only small windows on the music of the time.

English musicians feature in many manuscripts and account books across Europe in the first decades of the fifteenth century. Robert Morton and John Bedyngham, two English singer-composers about whom we know almost nothing, are among the most popular European composers of songs. Walter Frye's 'Ave Regina' is found in secular songbooks and was famous enough to feature in several paintings; Yolande de Laval even had it painted onto the ceiling of her oratory in the château of Montreuil-Bellay (where it floats miraculously to this day). Scholars have argued the case for a significant English influence on mainland compositional style, encouraged by references in Tinctoris and in Martin le Franc's *Le Champion des dames*, a poem dating from the early 1440s in praise of women.

Among its more than 24,000 lines are six strophes that mention music and which include reference to a 'Contenance Angloise', suggesting Dufay and Binchois were influenced by John Dunstable. This evidential gold dust has puzzled Anglophone scholars, who have dissected every nuance of the text but been unable to agree what Martin le Franc really meant. It's not helped by the fact that the survivals of each composer are not evenly spread by genre, making comparisons difficult; only two secular pieces of Dunstable survive (and they may not be by him), Binchois was a supreme secular melodist, and Dufay excelled at everything.

It's a puzzle to many performers too, who would consider each composer a completely distinct musical entity with little stylistic overlap between them. The alleged English 'sweetness' (lots of thirds and sixths) is actually more audible in the works of Walter Frye, Pyamour and John Plummer (all of whom can be found in European sources) rather than Dunstable. In the same poem Le Franc tells of Binchois and Dufay being astonished at the playing of a couple of blind fiddlers improvising at the Burgundian court. The rather endearing picture in one of the copies of *Le Champion des dames* has Dufay standing by a portative organ chatting to Binchois who is holding his harp; there is not a note of music to be seen. How we'd love to know what they are talking about; perhaps they were discussing how the English musicians performed rather than what they wrote.

The intimacy that characterises the Dufay–Binchois miniature sometimes appears in the music itself. As early as the fourteenth century we find motets which celebrate the art and science of music and the musicians who make it, naming much respected fellow singers and composers, noting their individual skills and personalities. Ironically, many musicians' names are known only from the texts of these motets, composed by someone whose name we don't know.

The motet, literally a song with words, eventually came to mean a polyphonic piece with a religious text, but when the term first appears it applies to songs performed in private spaces too, where the words need not be sacred.

There is a manuscript in the library of Durham Cathedral which Frank Harrison suggested was compiled for the court of Jean II of France while he was a prisoner in England awaiting ransom between 1357 and 1360. Jean had been captured while leading the French armies to defeat at the Battle of Poitiers (1356) and was accorded all the privileges due to his regal status, including a substantial retinue of servants and musicians. The triplum (upper voice) of 'Musicorum collegio' names seven singers in the French court, at least one of whom was English, briefly sketching a vignette of each one and celebrating their shared enjoyment of singing together. Beneath the rapid biographical patter is a slower more serious text riffing on the number seven, in which the poet links the singers of the triplum to the seven-branched candelabra of the Book of Revelation, the whole built upon a slowly evolving untexted line of chant. In 'Musicalis sciencia', a French motet of similar date, the poet greets the stars of the musical firmament of the day, including Philip de Vitry and Machaut, over a clever complaint in which Rhetoric tells Music that singers often get it wrong.

Companionable composition continued into the next generation: in 1423, Guillaume Dufay drinks a toast to nine singers, presumably his co-workers at the court of Malatesta di Pandolfo. The early-music revival has also extended the process across the centuries: trying to understand how medieval song was performed brings us much closer to our musical forebears than simply reaching for, say, a volume of Schubert which we perform more or less as we've been taught. We come into the closest contact with our medieval equivalents in the great *tombeaux* in which composers commemorate their own predecessors. There are many reasons why a living composer might want to be associated with a famous dead one and there is a certain formality to some of them, but tributes to Johannes Ockeghem (*c.* 1410–97) – who himself composed a tribute to his teacher Gilles Binchois – are exceptionally moving.

Ockeghem was the most revered composer of his time, having served three French kings over the course of his long life. Like many composers famous during his lifetime (and Josquin, especially) he has had a fluid worklist, with some compositions later reassigned to other composers. He was, like all his contemporary composers, a singer, and his dozen or so masses combine a singerly expressiveness with almost obsessive mathematical game playing. These would always have been a challenge to sing, and he must have had supreme confidence in his singers. His twenty surviving *chansons* are simpler, sociable songs mostly for three voices.

Many composers honoured Ockeghem during his lifetime by incorporating references to his music into their Mass setting, and he appears as one of thirteen composer-singers celebrated in Loyset Compère's 'Omnium bonorum plena'. Ockeghem's death was the occasion for many outpourings of musical and literary grief. There were formal tributes: the poet Guillaume Crétin wrote a substantial rhetorical lament in French, complaining that the great poets of the past were not there to assist him, and calling on all living poets, especially his younger contemporary Jean Molinet, to write *déplorations* of their own. Molinet duly stepped up and contributed 'Nymphes des bois', and some years later Erasmus of Rotterdam was inspired to create a Latin dirge which was in turn set to music by the mysterious Ioannes Lupi many years later still. Antoine Busnois's flamboyant and joyful 'In hydraulis' compares Ockeghem to Orpheus and the greatest of ancient musicians, the whole energetic enterprise carried along over a three-note untexted tenor to which one can sing the word 'vale' (farewell) or, better still, the dead composer's name.

***

The most moving of all the tributes is by Ockeghem's most famous successor, Josquin Desprez (*c.* 1450–1521), who also had a keen interest in combining canons with the expressive phrasing loved by singers, and who would after his own death go on to become one of the most celebrated composers in Europe. His 'Déploration sur la mort d'Ockeghem' fuses together a setting of the requiem chant and Molinet's poem 'Nymphes des bois'. Molinet, with an affectionate series of puns, exhorts wood nymphs, goddesses of fountains and expert singers everywhere to raise their voices in mourning for the passing of the great composer. Towards the end the poet introduces Josquin himself, together with his fellow musicians Brumel, Compère, Caron and Pierre de la Rue, weeping for their dead 'bon père'. In summoning up the names of these musicians for us to sing, knowing that all of them would eventually join Ockeghem to be celebrated in turn by later generations, Josquin speaks directly to us in the most sublime way. You never want your performance to slip from rhetoric to reality, and singing the names of the composers, themselves dead for 500 years, is a severe test; we too are the 'chantres experts de toutes nations' called upon by Josquin and Molinet. It's only when the last chord has melted into the acoustic that you can afford to reflect on the centuries-long connection you have just made.

'Nymphes des bois' appears in the luxurious Medici Codex presented to Lorenzo di Piero de' Medici, the Duke of Urbino, and Madeleine de La Tour d'Auvergne on their return to Florence after their French wedding in 1518. It is written entirely in black ink (an innovation for mourning music) and has no clefs or mensuration signs, meaning that only a very select few would understand how to perform it. Molinet's poem was later used as the basis of a tribute to Antoine Brumel in 1520, shorn of its companionable composers, and the Josquin motet appears in a final version copied in Germany sometime after 1560 with a text commemorating the death of Josquin himself (presumably written soon after his death in 1521). We then lose sight of the 'Déploration' until Charles Burney reconstructed a version for his *General History of Music* in 1789.

Almost all written music before the sixteenth century began life as vocal music, and yet if the illustrations in the more luxurious manuscripts are anything to go by, the medieval secular environment was actually peopled with instrumentalists, groups of lute players, fiddlers of various sorts, often with singers, drifting lazily through bucolic landscapes or entertaining at home. They mostly play without music, so we assume that they were improvising or playing by heart, and that perhaps many of them may not have been able to read music at all. As secular written polyphony became fashionable those instrumentalists familiar with notation began to play written vocal music, and from the late fourteenth century it is clear that virtuoso instrumentalists were appropriating the latest polyphonic *virelais* and *rondeaux*. The evidence for this is found in a number of codices that have very decorated versions of vocal pieces, often with no texts and with alphabetical or intabulation signs (known to lutenists as 'tab') as well as neumes.

There is much debate over what instruments were used and how they related to the singers for whom the music was originally written, but the wider engagement of musicians with polyphony must have been led by singers, who would be perfectly capable of singing versions of even the most florid of the supposedly instrumental manuscripts. A lack of text would be no barrier in a culture where memory was every musician's main information processor, and the large number of variant versions of individual songs suggests that anyone with an interest probably had their own two versions inside their head. The most significant conclusion we can draw from all this is that polyphonic songs as they appear in manuscripts do not represent even a first performance, and are essentially source material for any musician to develop for themselves. The polyphonic originals, both then and now, attracted an audience that at least aspired to understanding their complexities, and part of its appeal must have been its exclusivity; an anonymous *trouvère* melody might conceivably have been heard in the street, but a *chanson* by Ockeghem probably not.

Singers had sung from a form of staff notation for as long as notation itself: once you understood the system your brain could easily read a poem at the same time. Accompanying instrumentalists, even performing from the same scores, only needed to focus on their fingers. Some early attempts to transcribe vocal music for instruments simplified the process yet further by using letter names for notes (if a keyboard was the intended instrument) or something more like modern guitar notation for lutes. Tinctoris, in his *De inventione et usu musice* written sometime in the 1480s, drew attention to a change of lute-playing technique when some players began to abandon the goose-quill plectrum in favour of using their fingers. There is always a time lag covering such changes and the new technique may well have first appeared much earlier in the century. Tinctoris says Pietrobono Burzelli, twenty years younger than Dufay, is the greatest virtuoso with the plectrum, but he doesn't comment on the playing of his *tenorista*, an accompanying musician who may have used his fingers to play two parts to Pietrobono's tune, enabling them to perform three-voice polyphony.

The new technique meant that the lute became a truly polyphonic instrument for the first time, which also signified that a polyphonic song in up to four or five parts could be performed by one person singing one part and playing the rest. The preferred notation was tab, symbols that told players where to put their fingers, and it is the intabulated scores that enable us to track the course of accompanied song from the fifteenth to the seventeenth centuries. We will never know when this practice started: there are no Dufay tabs (they may yet surface – we know his peers owned lutes), but tabs of Josquin's music outnumber the staff-notated originals. Once tab became common, the practice of making anything into a song gained a new impetus, and the lute became the accompanying instrument of choice.

The late-twentieth-century focus on composers' *Urtext* (and their presumed intentions) blinded many musicologists to the more likely reality of performance practice implied by the later, so-called secondary sources. A more relaxed approach by both scholars and performers today is enabling a richer array of performance possibilities. The 'Déploration' certainly started life as a motet and probably received its first performance by a small choir or vocal ensemble, but nobody would have considered it in any way authoritative. No tabs of the piece have yet come to light, but it is likely that many of the friends of both Ockeghem and Josquin made their own versions of this very personal tribute, turning it into song. We are now much more likely to see a late medieval or Renaissance vocal manuscript as a blueprint, the first stage in the creation of an edifice that may use whatever materials are available to construct it. This may turn out to be the lasting gift of the early-music movement to the history of song, returning the music to its performers.

The unique form of 'Nymphes des bois' lends itself to any number of creative interpretations in addition to the *a cappella* versions that loom so large in the Josquin discography. I sang the piece many times with the Hilliard Ensemble and others in its pristine 'original' format, but my more recent performances have been with lutes, using Josquin's notes as the blueprint that his contemporaries and successors would have understood them to be. On the *Secret History* album, an experiment in performing *a cappella* polyphony as song, soprano Anna Maria Friman sings the top line, accompanied by the duetting vihuelas of Ariel Abramovich and Lee Santana. The requiem chant is not sung at all, but absorbed like a ghost into the spontaneous ornamental weaving of the instruments. For the second part, after the requiem has finished, we are joined by viol player Hille Perl (who happened to be visiting the church as a guest) and I join Anna for the heart-rending final section where we sing the names of the composer's fellow mourners. The vihuelas cover the other parts, enabling us to create our own song from Josquin's materials. In a recent performance with countertenor David James (Jacob Heringman playing all the other lines on lute) we were able to call up the German ensemble Amarcord from the audience to sing the requiem tenor. Just as it was for our historical forebears, the music is available for anyone to do with it whatever moves them.

Cipriano de Rore imagined by Heinrich Eduard Winter as part of his Portraite der berühmtesten Compositeurs der Tonkunst *(1817).*

4

CIPRIANO DE RORE
'ANCOR CHE COL PARTIRE'

In chronological terms Cipriano de Rore (1515/16–65) is several hundred years away from Bernart de Ventadorn (died 1194), but what links them is a set of creative processes, the nature of performance, and in particular the mysterious and delicate relationship between the oral and the written. The nature of songs from the nineteenth century onwards was in no small way defined by the piano as an accompanying instrument. For singers it's a comfort to see the score, familiar and ergonomically laid out, the same for everyone and both performers sure of what they have to do. In our exploration of the pre-history of the genre the concept of accompaniment hasn't yet materialised in quite the same way; singers worked with whatever or whoever was to hand. Composers, usually singers themselves, had a very fluid concept of the music they created. With the reimagining of the lute as a polyphonic instrument, plucked with the fingers rather than a plectrum, we see the first seeds of an idea of the lute as a sole accompanying instrument for song, which centuries later would become the art song as we understand it. The first examples had to compete with the traditional gatherings for polyphonic song and with the improvised song to which we don't have access (and which may have been the most popular of all).

The life of professional musicians in the early Renaissance was often a peripatetic one, with increases of reputation and status hopefully following in their wake. By tracking the whereabouts of singers and players from the evidence of payrolls, letters and court records we can get some idea of the role and importance of *improvvisatori*, the performers who left behind no written music. There were street performers who entertained in Italian piazzas, *canterini* or *cantastorie* who accompanied themselves on some sort of viol or lute and whose names and repertoire we mostly don't know. Some were extremely successful: Pietrobono Burzelli, the singing lutenist also known as 'Pietrobono del chitarino', travelled extensively throughout Italy while employed by the d'Este court at Ferrara and even spent a year in the service of Queen Beatrice of Hungary. He was born in 1417, which places him midway between the two great polyphonists Dufay (born *c.* 1397) and Josquin (born *c.* 1450). Pietrobono's fame was such that a medal was struck in his honour and contemporary poets praised his efforts in ecstatic terms, describing spell-binding performances of narrative verse. Did he sing, read, recite? We know only that he held his listeners in thrall and that he sometimes accompanied himself: not a note of his music has survived and yet his contemporaries seem to have considered him the foremost musician of his age. This was the ultimate live music: after Pietrobono's performance was done all that remained was a memory; nobody wrote any of it down.

There are clues that we can tease out from references to his teaching, and from the fact that he often performed with a *tenorista*, who may have sung or played a fiddle of some sort or possibly another lute, holding a tune over which Pietrobono would improvise. The custom of creating new songs by adding to an existing melody was deeply rooted in the culture (we have seen it in organa and *cantus firmus* which had for centuries been written versions of this practice). He was sometimes hired to teach a specific number of songs and was paid by the song, which suggests that this was probably done by rote and with no attempt to teach notation. As a court musician Pietrobono would have lived alongside musicians whose stock in trade included written polyphony, and there are tantalising references to his teaching versions of 'Scaramella' (a folk tune that was set by many composers including Josquin and Compère) and Tromboncino's 'L'ocelo da le rame d'oro'. We may not know what he performed but his importance to this delicate historical thread is that he knew existing tunes, and that he could improvise while accompanying himself; he worked at the nexus of the oral and the written. He may even have used notation, but if he did, his working copies are likely to have been scruffy single sheets, a world away from the grand *chansonniers*.

There were many performers in the oral world whose art combined poetry and music in ways that we can only guess at. The elusive Leonardo Giustiniani, who might have ended up as Doge of Venice had he not died in 1446, was a writer of *poesia per musica* who gave his name to a genre. Although fellow poet Pietro Bembo thought *giustiniani* were rather better in the delivery than the content, Leonardo's collected *canzonette* were reprinted many times in the years after his death. Serafino dell'Aquila (born 1466) was a poet who declaimed his own verses and those of Petrarch, accompanying himself on the lute. His speech-song was impossible to notate, but his verses were sometimes copied on scraps of paper or manuscript and began to appear in printed volumes after his death in 1500. He favoured the Petrarchan sonnet and the *strambotto* (from the Occitan *estrabot* meaning a sentimental love song), a six- or eight-line single stanza with a rhyme scheme that varied according to region. Benedetto Cariteo, born in Barcelona in about 1450 but adopted by Naples, was similarly famous for his improvised declamation; like Serafino he too created *poesia per musica*, poems designed for musical declamation.

Orally transmitted music was available to everyone within audible reach, and the *improvvisatori*, singing in an Italian vernacular, appealed to a much wider audience than the elite singers of the written French *chanson* employed by Italian courts. Once the formulaic *strambotto* and its related song types became widely imitated, musicians began to notate the new, more popular forms. By the end of the century the newly legitimised popular song had reached the ears of the Venetian printer Ottaviano Petrucci, whose publications tell us what he thought musicians liked to sing and play, even if they don't tell us how they did it. His first secular publication had been more in the nature of a retrospective and is a landmark in the history of song. The *Harmonice Musices Odhecaton* of 1501 is a volume of *chansons* comparable to the great manuscript anthologies of the medieval period and one of the first to use moveable type for musical notation. The curious title is a conflation of Latin and Greek, meaning something like 'Harmonic Music: One Hundred Songs' (a rounding up as there are only ninety-six). By 1504 this had become a three-volume set of *chansons*, most of which had been composed and performed in Italy by Franco-Flemish musicians over many generations.

A matter of weeks after releasing his third volume Petrucci turned his attention to the *frottola*, producing eleven volumes over the ensuing ten years. The term, like madrigal, is of uncertain origin and may have come from the Italian *frocta* meaning a collection of frivolous things, perhaps a kind of false modesty as the poems were often by aristocrats who had no qualms about writing in language close to dialect. By the time we see the first ones it means a charming, clever but untaxing love song, sufficiently opaque to need a multitude of sub-genres, mostly strophic and defined by their rhyme schemes and the position of any refrain. The old French *formes fixes* catered for in Petrucci's earlier volumes were now competing with more fashionable and straightforward songs in the vernacular (and sometimes Latin). The fourth of Petrucci's *frottola* volumes is subtitled *Strambotti, ode, frottole, sonetti, et modo de cantar versi latini e capituli*, which covers just about everything from peasant verse to Petrarch; it includes 'Scaramella' in Loyset Compère's arrangement, an echo of that performed by Pietrobono perhaps. In Book Six we find most of the above and the first evidence of *giustiniani*, and although Petrucci wasn't very good at identifying which was which, it's clear that the sub-genres of the *frottola* are a musical chemistry that conceals elements of oral practice among the prints. There are even musical templates over which you can declaim or sing the poem of your choice.

The *frottola* is often overlooked in music histories, dismissed as a rather unfocused and relatively trivial episode squeezed between the sophisticated Franco-Flemish polyphonists and the emotional extravagance of the madrigal. It simply wasn't considered arty enough, and many *frottole* are indeed sufficiently straightforward for anyone to have a go at in our own time. But beneath this rather undernourished account is a more intriguing story of a different kind of courtly patronage in which we can see the emergence of a secular song based on chords rather than counterpoint. For Petrucci and his customers the original meaning of the term *frottola* was probably long forgotten even as it became fashionable: it was now a catch-all term for a native Italian song with its roots in oral culture rather than the elaborate density of the northern *chanson*.

The first composers associated with the new genre are Bartolomeo Tromboncino and Marco Cara, who were employed at the Mantuan court of Francesco Gonzaga and his *marchesa*, Isabella d'Este. The outward face of the grand Italian courts was a masculine one, and in Mantua it was Francesco who looked after the ceremonial and chapel music by which his fellow princes would judge his establishment. A typical Renaissance prince, his entire life had been devoted to the masculine pursuits of hunting and soldiery and the necessary musical and artistic adjuncts that confirmed his status. The wives and daughters of Renaissance royalty had an entirely different upbringing, focused on the running of their own household rather than preparing to fight someone else's, and with time to indulge in the arts if they weren't keen on hunting.

Isabella d'Este had been brought up at the court of her father Ercole d'Este, Duke of Ferrara, soldier and a magnificent patron of the arts, and her mother the formidable Duchess Eleonora d'Aragona (dedicatee of Bartolomeo Goggio's *De laudibus mulierum* – In Praise of Women). Isabella grew up surrounded by some of the finest poets, artists, intellectuals and musicians of her time, and became the embodiment of the cultivated Renaissance woman. Her marriage to Francesco gave her free rein to indulge her artistic and musical passions, culminating in the creation of a dedicated *studiolo* in which to display her paintings and listen to music. She was given comprehensive instruction in music theory and singing (and is one of the few singers known to have consulted a singing manual, especially between teachers). A skilled performer on bowed and plucked instruments, she was particularly noted for the purity of her singing and the dexterity with which she accompanied herself on the lute or vihuela. With Francesco's chapel and its singers off limits, her entire attention was focused on secular music, and she became the channel through which poets and musicians were matched to each other; she provided the creative energy for the composition of hundreds of new *frottole*.

If a particular poem appealed to her, Isabella would pass it on to Cara or Tromboncino to be 'frottolised', and it was her request to the poet Niccolò da Correggio for a Petrarch sonnet to be set by one of her singing lutenists that may have steered Tromboncino and his fellow composers beyond the repeated quatrain towards the weightier forms of the sonnet and *canzone*. Tromboncino must have been an extraordinarily charismatic man and musical talent as Isabella continually had to forgive his sometimes scandalous behaviour. He has the distinction of being the only known lute-playing trombonist-composer to have murdered his wife. He was pardoned for this but still left Mantua under something of a cloud, moving on to the rival court of Lucrezia Borgia in Ferrara after the turn of the century. The gentle Cara, on the other hand, gets approval from Castiglione (a favourite of the *marchesa*) in *Il cortegiano*, where both his songs and his singing are highly commended.

Isabella probably performed her commissions herself from manuscripts in the composer's hand. These would have been working scores that got plenty of use and, needless to say, none of them have survived. But in 1509, Petrucci published the first of two volumes by Franciscus Bossinensis, whose *frottola* arrangements include ornamented versions of songs by Tromboncino among many others. We know nothing about Franciscus other than the clue in his name, which suggests he came from Bosnia, and the dedication of the collection to a prominent Venetian. These publications are collections of *frottole* (126 of them) by the most famous composers of the period arranged for voice and lute, and they give us the clearest picture of how the songs were performed. Bossinensis intabulates just the tenor and bass lines; the alto line from the original *frottola* is omitted and the top line, printed in staff notation, would be sung by the player. The simplified parts make it easier for the performer to give equal attention to playing and singing, and additions to either part can be made at will. The appearance of the lute-song volumes raises the question of what the polyphonic presentation of the other *frottola* volumes really means. Perhaps they are laying bare the entire compositional process as a palette from which performers could create their own orchestrations (as had been the case with polyphonic music for generations), rather than scores in the sense of a plan for performance.

The *frottola* has not fared well in terms of historically appropriate performance. This is partly because in their printed Petrucci form the songs seem relatively simple compared to the French *chanson*, and they have confusing sub-genres with no clear rules about how they should be performed. Tromboncino and Cara do sometimes make it into music-history books, but mostly as 'precursors' of the madrigal. *Frottole* also have a slightly compromising connection with popular music (tricky for modern programme planning), unlike the later madrigal which was considered generally more sophisticated, a reputation that it speedily regained when madrigal singing was rediscovered in the nineteenth century. In the hands of Claudio Monteverdi and his seventeenth-century contemporaries the madrigal would become one of the most creative vocal art forms, consigning the *frottola* to the sidelines of musical history. But the vertical thinking of the *frottola*, chords rather than simultaneous tunes, would be a key element in the post-madrigal continuo song, and beyond that, the early *Lied*.

The relationship between *chanson*, *frottola* and madrigal has been much discussed by musicologists seeking to explain stylistic developments (both musically and geographically). One thing they all had in common was that whatever they looked like when published, all of these genres were mined for performance as solo song. Musicians could either do this for themselves, reading from a print and selecting which lines to play and sing, or they could consult one of the increasing numbers of instructional manuals. In Philippe Verdelot's *Primo libro di madrigali* of 1533 we have the first printed evidence showing that the polyphonic madrigal could be reimagined in much the same way as the *frottola*, and it confirms that for musicians of the time the concept of genre was very flexible. The madrigal that re-appears in the 1520s was a recycling of the fourteenth-century term but with a greatly expanded artistic base; it dispensed with generic formal structures, enabling a much more subtle connection with the poetry. This usually took the form of a single through-composed strophe that had more textural colour than the *frottola*, achieved by mixing homophonic and contrapuntal elements according to the demands of the text, leading eventually to what we would call word painting.

We don't know much about Verdelot; he was probably born in France but migrated southwards, ending up in Florence in the 1520s. There he collaborated with Niccolò Machiavelli on his play *La mandragola*, in which the first madrigals appear. Verdelot's first *libro* was reprinted twice and followed by second and third volumes; these were amalgamated in 1540 into a single publication which itself was reprinted ten times between 1541 and 1566. We can get an idea of Verdelot's status (and that of the madrigal) from the fact that in 1536 Ottaviano Scotto published *Involatura de li madrigali di Verdelotto da cantare et sonare nel lauto intavolati per Messer Adriano*. The Adriano who had intabulated twenty-two madrigals from Verdelot's *Primo libro* was no other than Adrian Willaert, *maestro di cappella* at St Mark's, Venice.

Unlike the Bossinensis *frottole* the Willaert tabs are of all three lower lines (with the voice in the usual staff notation). Why would the earliest madrigals be printed in both staff notation and lute tab? The answer may be to do with the increasing competence of players and intabulators. Andrea Antico (another Venetian printer) had published a volume of Tromboncino and Cara tabs in the 1520s, so there was clearly a market for the solo-song format. Willaert's tabs are of a different order from those of his predecessor, being precise transcriptions of all the parts with nothing added apart from a few small editorial emendations. Perhaps Willaert, the foremost teacher and composer of his age, was trying to show potential performers that the more serious madrigal was open to the same sort of treatment as the *frottola*, and this was how you did it.

***

Both Willaert and Verdelot were northerners, as was the most successful of the early madrigalists, Jacques Arcadelt, whose *Primo libro di madrigali* was reprinted some forty-five times. The madrigal was the means by which the polyphonists were able to blend the contrapuntal elements of the *chanson* with the more homophonic style of the *frottola*. It was another northerner, Cipriano de Rore, who finally established the madrigal as the most dynamic vocal form of the later sixteenth century. Cipriano was born in the Netherlands in 1515/16 and like many of his Franco-Flemish contemporaries moved south to find work with a succession of Italian patrons; he died in Parma in 1565. Little is known about his early life but he undoubtedly benefited from the newly successful Venetian printers Antonio Gardano and Girolamo Scotto. Printing was by now creating music on a significantly commercial scale, which among other things quickly established composers' reputations, potentially generating fame that would outlive them.

Cipriano's madrigals went on being performed for more than half a century, as both ensemble pieces and solo songs. Had he lived to a ripe old age he could have met Monteverdi, whose brother cited Cipriano as the forerunner of the *seconda prattica*, the new more soloistic music of the early Baroque. His madrigal 'Ancor che col partire' first appears in an anthology of 1547 and the tune became one of the century's greatest hits, alongside Lassus's 'Susanne un jour' and Palestrina's 'Vestiva i colli'.

'Ancor' is a love song that can be read on many levels. At its simplest it is the complaint of two lovers about to part but whose subsequent reunions are so exciting that they would happily repeat the process a thousand times a day. Given the metaphorical equivalence of death and orgasm (much enjoyed by madrigalists everywhere), it can also refer to a specifically erotic scenario. The multiple excitements happen in the last three lines of an eight-line strophe, and to ram home the point Cipriano repeats these. It's fun to sing, well within reach of the sixteenth-century *dilettante*, and one can easily imagine a convivial evening of nudging and winking with singers entertaining themselves over prints of Cipriano's four-voice original madrigal. The part-writing is exquisite, beginning with pairs of voices coyly chasing each other and coming together at key moments. These are common enough devices and many madrigals worked in exactly the same way, so it's hard to find textual reasons why 'Ancor' exists in so many versions, which leaves us with purely musical or performance reasons for its popularity.

It took a decade or two for print copies to circulate, and for musicians to make their own personal versions. The song appears in Cosimo Bottegari's lute book in 1574, a working copy with signs of regular use by its singing lutenist/composer/compiler. There were versions for keyboard by Andrea Gabrieli and others, and many of the leading lute composer-singers intabulated their own arrangements. For solo singers there are several extremely virtuosic versions of the top line, published as examples of how to ornament a madrigal and perform it on your own, including three by Giovanni Bassano (published in 1591, one of them based on the bass part), two by Giovanni Battista Bovicelli (1594) and one each by Girolamo Dalla

Casa (1584) and Richardo Rognono (1591). One of Bovicelli's has a sacred text, 'Angelus ad pastores', that would certainly have woken up anyone dozing off during Mass. There are also untexted versions designed for instruments or singers who already knew the words, including a 1624 version by Giovanni Battista Spadi.

They are extremely florid – to the extent that a modern singer who didn't know the original might not know that it was there – giving structure to the cascades of quick notes. The original tune has some 125 notes (depending on how you count them); typically, a 'division' version will have four or five times that (hence the name). None of the subtlety of the part-writing survives when you have only a tune and an improvised accompaniment, so the expressive force of the song is entirely dependent on the performer's ability to turn florid ornamentation into emotive rhetoric. The earliest ornamentation manuals date from the 1530s; aimed at singing students who may not have had access to a *maestro*, they give us a vivid picture of how the unwritten impinges upon the written. The songs that resulted were intimate affairs: it's not possible to project them into a large space as too many laryngeal muscles are involved with simply getting round the notes. That they had considerable currency can be judged from the scathing criticism that 'excessive' ornamentation often came in for: everybody was at it, and good taste was constantly at risk.

The versions that have come down to us are not those that would have been performed by professional singers (who would have devised their own), but they give us an impression of the kinds of performances these singers would have given and to which courtly amateurs might aspire. Each of the printed instructional manuals contains pages of exercises so that the student can develop the techniques to create their own unique version of any tune. The sample pieces are merely examples of the kind of thing you might end up with once you have absorbed all the lessons. A glance at all of the exemplars will reveal that they are all very different from each other, which suggests that it was no problem for any competent professional to create a fresh version every time they sang it. The audience who heard the great soprano Tarquinia Molza perform 'Ancor che col partire' would not expect to hear her sing the same version more than once.

The solo performance of polyphony seems to have reached its apogee in the 1580s, with many musicians putting pen to paper to celebrate the extraordinary music-making to be had by reimagining the text and texture of the madrigal as fiercely virtuosic solo song. For some, the singing that these performances required presented no problem: if you had the *dispositione*, basically a natural facility to get around fistfuls of notes at great speed, you could find a tune that everyone knew and take it somewhere else. The parallels with jazz are not lost on those who have attempted this repertoire, and like jazz it has sometimes been criticised (both now and in the Renaissance) as being technical cleverness at the expense of emotional engagement.

Very few early-music singers have taken on this very challenging music (instrumentalists have often impressed but they don't have to consider text and meaning). Those that can do it have understandably tended to privilege speed over content and reproduce the printed examples rather than devise their own. Once again the early-music movement's high regard for what can be seen but not heard prevents us from imagining how performers who didn't need the examples – those who regularly performed these songs – actually sang them. Sixteenth- and seventeenth-century performers could do whatever they wanted with a song, taking it off the page and creating something that would never be repeated. We will always be both inspired and inhibited by the printed examples left behind, but simply reproducing them won't enable us to enhance the text or unleash the creative potential enjoyed by our sixteenth-century predecessors.

I have to confess to a lack of courage in this area myself. I sang Cipriano's polyphonic version of 'Ancor' many times with the Hilliard Ensemble and others, and as the early-music movement developed towards the end of the twentieth century, early-music singers, many of us by then in retreat from the prescriptive complexities of the avant-garde, were increasingly conscious of the creative possibilities of improvised ornamentation. We were aware of Girolamo Dalla Casa's 1594 arrangement of Cipriano's 1550 madrigal 'A dolc'ombra' with embellishments in all four voices, and our madrigal singing became more personalised; more risks were taken. Discovering the 'division school' solo versions of madrigals and *chansons* was revelatory, but when I had an opportunity to record my own version of Rognono's extrapolation on 'Ancor che col partire' I was so dazzled by the sheer virtuosity of the writing that I reproduced it note for note (which was hard enough). Now, in live performances of this repertoire, I attempt to invent my own (though with key phrases I sometimes find that a seventeenth-century predecessor has beaten me to it).

The clue to making it work is to follow the rhetoric, and that's what the sixteenth-century versions do, each in its own way. We need to be much more inventive with our own versions, transcending both time and early music, if we are to access the personal emotional rhetoric that the original singers must have brought to their own creations as they explored the poem. As a step on the way, in her version of 'Ancor che col partire' which sticks to Rognono's notes (ironically, as she is a jazz singer), Maria Pia de Vito wrings an emotional impact from the song by manipulating the tempo in her recording with John Taylor. Supporting her, the chromatically inflected piano matches her rubato, enriching Cipriano's harmonies with a wonderfully empathetic accompaniment. Of course, had Maria Pia de Vito made her own version rather than following Rognono's, it would have been jazz; rarely have the two genres come so close.

John Taylor's inspired piano playing is a reminder that the accompaniment was also improvised. None of the virtuosic model versions of solo madrigals comes with music for an accompanying instrument. This could mean that they were sung without (Spadi says that's one way of doing it), or that since everyone knew the tunes and how to accompany them it would have been a waste of the printer's time and space. There are so many references to singing lute players that some support from a lute (or possibly a viol) is far more likely, fleshing out some of the original part-writing.

Once more, the point at which the oral and the written coincide inevitably favours the latter: a score survives (incomplete in the case of solo madrigals); its performance is forgotten. As secondary sources some way up the stem of transmission, virtuoso solo madrigals still tend to be considered by today's musicologists and historians as decadent shadows of the composer's original. This mindset – privileging the *Urtext* over its actual use – also hovered over the definition of music for medieval and Renaissance musicians, though as pragmatic singer-composer-poets they mostly chose to ignore it. Practical music-making (that one could actually make and hear) was considered to be intellectually inferior to the medieval interpretation of the Boethian science of music which theoretically underpinned most Renaissance composition (and was largely a matter of numbers). To decipher it, the historian has to make the best of a very small literature written by men who were by and large not successful composers or performers but had points to prove. The late Renaissance correspondence between composers and theorists is littered with abstruse arguments about tonal relationships, intervals and tuning systems, none of which are of remote interest to a singer who is simply trying to get round the notes and express the text. To paraphrase the fifteenth-century scholar Ugolino da Orvieto, theorists write about proportions and so on; performers are practical and acquire the information on a need-to-know basis.

The sixteenth-century focus on virtuosity enabled the singer to bypass (often literally) the rule-bound compositional process that generated the original song, which the composer had to stick to in order to be taken seriously. This still colours our view when looking back at Renaissance music: we think of key composers and their works, and their place in a chronological narrative. The performance history of solo songs has to be sifted out of this compositional timeline as it cuts across stylistic developments and subverts the great-composer narrative; each song was unique, only completed at the moment of performance when the singer added his or her own contribution to a work that may already have been the product of many musical minds. For a brief period everything was up for grabs: Tarquinia Molza improvised a performance of 'Ancor' to her own improvised accompaniment; she gave Cipriano the credit but her audience came to hear her, not him, and her improvisation dissolved into air even as she sang it. The interaction of the oral and the written achieved a synthesis that would not resurface until jazz took a similar course 400 years later.

The beginning of the seventeenth century would see the introduction of bigger lutes and musicians playing from bass lines rather than tab. But for some two centuries lute players had been creating solo songs and leaving us clues in manuscripts copied for their personal use. Most of the surviving medieval and Renaissance *chansonniers* show little sign of use and owe their survival to their value as artefacts, treasured by their owners as cultural capital rather than performing editions. Manuscripts in everyday use inevitably succumbed to first wear and tear and then changes in musical taste, but sometimes the collecting habit led to the preservation of individual collections. At around the same time as the Italian virtuosi were turning madrigals into song, English musicians were recycling the polyphony of previous generations in the form of intabulated lute songs. The wealthy English Catholic gentleman Edward Paston is a rare example of an enthusiast whose obsessive collecting habit was directed towards the acquisition of music he wanted to hear and play rather than simply look at.

There was no equivalent in England to the courts of the Italian city states, but the lesser aristocracy owned often quite substantial country houses with their own musical establishments. These might run to a resident house musician, usually a lutenist-singer-composer-scribe, or a domestic staff that might double as supporting musicians to provide entertainment for the family and visitors. In these households a manuscript culture continued to flourish throughout the sixteenth and early seventeenth centuries alongside the increasing availability of commercial prints. Musicians with access to polyphony, in either manuscript or printed form, copied their own versions to suit the staff available to perform it, based on the tastes of their employer. Paston was a recusant, one of many prominent Catholics barred from court because of their religious beliefs but able to maintain a sufficiently musical household to celebrate Mass at home (in secret, if necessary) in Norfolk. This would be managed with whatever musical forces were available, using manuscript reductions of polyphony arranged for voices and lute.

The need to provide musicians for the Mass engendered a wider musical culture, and combined with a love of collecting for its own sake this enabled Edward Paston to acquire a vast library of music including Italian madrigals, French *chansons* and masses and motets from all over Europe. His manuscripts, dating from the beginning of the seventeenth century, contain some 600 sacred and secular vocal works in up to eight parts intabulated for lute and one or two voices (who presumably sang from separate partbooks which are now lost). Paston was a lutenist himself; his repertoire is old-fashioned and eclectic, ranging from Josquin to Byrd (whom Paston must have known) but stopping at Marenzio and Philippe de Monte with no sign of the *seconda prattica*. He may have owned more recent prints which have disappeared, and he is thought to have had a copy of Nicholas Yonge's *Musica transalpina*, the volume published by Thomas East in 1588 which first brought the madrigal to public attention in England and stimulated the creation of the English genre. Paston supported up to four scribes who intabulated polyphony for him, and uniquely among known English lute players he could read the different national tab styles of France, Italy and Spain.

The survival of Paston's manuscripts, now dispersed in the UK and USA, is very much a matter of luck. His anthologies were exceptionally large but other households maintained musical staff and presumably had collections of their own which have succumbed to over-use or careless curating. The madrigalist John Wilbye spent his entire career in the service of the Kitson family (also recusants) at Hengrave Hall in Suffolk, where he combined estate work with teaching the family and directing its music. An inventory of 1603 mentions substantial collections of music (including Italian madrigals) together with lutes and viols that would have enabled song performance in multiple formats. The Kitsons also had a house in London and Wilbye was a friend of both John Dowland and Thomas East. The second of Wilbye's two books of madrigals 'apt both for voyals and voyces', published in 1609, contains many of his most famous pieces including the five-voice 'Weepe, weepe myne eyes'.

The evidence of ownership and employment doesn't give us enough detail about how this music was performed, and polyphonic song would also be competing with the new lute songs of Dowland

and his contemporaries. The fashion for all things Italian eventually caught up with the radically different Italian songs circulating in London towards the end of the first decade of the new century. *A Musical Banquet* composed in 1610 by Robert Dowland (John's son) and Angelo Notari's *Prime musiche nuove* three years later were both continuo songs (which we shall encounter in Chapter 6). In these pieces, performers were expected to devise their own harmony above a printed bass line which may or may not include the occasional figure to help them out. But the printing history is only part of the story. At some point before about 1620 the owner or scribe of the manuscript known as Egerton 2971 copied 'Weepe, weepe' and made a version for voice and continuo.

Egerton 2971 perfectly reflects the changing times with a mixture of English and Italian songs intabulated or written on two staves as voice and bass line. It contains a version of Giulio Caccini's 'Amarilli', far more florid than either Caccini's original print or Robert Dowland's version in *A Musicall Banquet*. The scribe's version of Wilbye's 'Weepe, weepe' is not unlike an Italian solo madrigal realisation, albeit in a rather restrained English way. Whoever put together Egerton 2971 was familiar with English lute song (there are songs by Robert Jones and Nathaniel Giles), English madrigals (the Wilbye) and Italian continuo song (two Caccini pieces). Judging from the elaborate extrapolations on the latest of these, the scribe knew not just the Caccini originals but something of the virtuosity found in the division school manuals of Rognono and others. He could accompany himself reading tab or sketch in his own harmony over a bass line written in staff notation. The Egerton manuscript gives us a fascinating window on English performance practice and repertoire in the early seventeenth century. The owner was embracing the new and reusing the old, perhaps making little distinction between the two: they were all simply songs.

Portrait of a singing lutenist by Dirck van Baburen (1622).

5

JOHN DOWLAND
'FLOW MY TEARS'

One of the last instructional manuals to include 'Ancor che col partire' was Giovanni Battista Bovicelli's *Regole, passaggi di musica, madrigali e motteti passeggiati* published in Venice in 1594. Two years later, in England, William Barley published his *New Booke of Tabliture* which contains a very different set of rules. If Bovicelli's intention was to liberate performers in a manner that will strike many as not unlike jazz, Barley's was 'to guide and dispose thy hand to play on sundry instruments, as the lute, orpharion and bandora' by telling players where to put their fingers. Although tabs such as those used by Edward Paston had been circulating in manuscript for some time in England, Barley's was the first to make it into print. Among his 141 transcriptions is a piece credited at the end as 'Lacrime by I.D', a pavan for solo lute, the first of many incarnations of what became 'Flow my tears' in Dowland's *Second Book of Songs or Ayres* in 1600. The tune was further arranged by a host of composers for virtually every available instrumental combination of the period over the next several decades. Although it didn't fare quite as well as some of Dowland's songs beyond the end of the seventeenth century, it finally came into its own again when the early-music revival rediscovered the lute in the twentieth. 'Flow my tears' is now considered one of Dowland's greatest achievements.

The very different approaches of Barley and Bovicelli are a reminder that the history of performance has its own multifaceted path that can't be adequately charted via the linear way in which composers and their works are presented in conventional textbooks. Between these two styles – the prescribed accompaniment of Barley and the improvised accompaniment of Bovicelli – was a host of other compositional styles that could be used in many combinations of voices and instruments. France, Germany, Spain and England all had songs that existed in multiple formats, a flexibility that seems strangely democratic in societies that were highly stratified. There were national differences – the Spanish *villancico* is often in only three parts, the early Tudor court in England also favoured 'three men's songs', and the German *Tenorlied* generally has four voices but with the tune in the tenor. In France the polyphonic *chanson* appeared intabulated as lute song, and the *air de cour* seems to have begun as a dedicated lute song which developed as more of a polyphonic genre later in the century. All of these threads have traditionally been studied as separate entities, focusing on the written text rather than a likely performance: they could all end up as a form of song to the lute.

John Dowland (1562/3–1626) had published his first book of lute songs in 1597, heralding a remarkable quarter-century of songs with fully composed accompaniments and poetic texts, just as Schubert would compose centuries later. They were described as being of 'fowre partes with Tableture for the lute' with the option of 'Orpharion or Viol de gambo' – maximising potential sales by being as flexible as possible. There are twenty-one of them, plus a bonus instrumental duet for two players on one lute. This is a novel idea that may have been a selling point; it can't be done without considerable contortion unless one of the players is a child or is sitting on the lap of the other, and it's certainly fun trying. Apart from one or two either side, twenty-one would become the standard number for all composers' subsequent collections, perhaps for technical reasons to do with the printing process. The first book has endorsements from Thomas Campion and Luca Marenzio; Dowland also name-checks Giovanni Croce, *maestro di cappella* at St Mark's, Venice, and mentions his travels in France, Germany and Italy. Most of the poems in lute-song collections are anonymous (Dowland might have written at least some of his own) and some stand comparison with the best Elizabethan and Jacobean poets (notably those of the polymath Campion, who published separate collections of his own verse).

Our knowledge of Dowland comes almost entirely from the prefaces to his publications, a few letters and court records of payments and movements, and a long letter to Queen Elizabeth's secretary of state, Robert Cecil. Courtiers occasionally refer to an actual performance and Dowland's Europe-wide reputation generated plenty of extravagant compliments, but there is no contemporary biography; much of the Dowland literature speculates on the considerable *lacunae*.

The first time we encounter him with any certainty is in 1580 when he leaves England to enter service with Sir Henry Cobham, ambassador to the King of France. Working backwards from Dowland's hints about his age, we can guess he was born in 1563, so he would have been about seventeen. We know nothing of his family or education. In the early twentieth century there was a flurry of speculation suggesting he was of Irish descent (he even makes a cameo appearance in Joyce's *Ulysses*), but it's more likely that he was born to Londoners (though there's no evidence for this either). His childhood must have been a musical one, and we can assume that he was very familiar with lute players and their music. He was presumably a gifted child and born into a reasonably prosperous and well-connected family to have been taken on by her majesty's ambassador. His French trip would have been a life-changing experience, the perfect opportunity to meet some of the great French lutenists, and in court circles he would have heard the most fashionable music of the day.

He would have been born into a thriving musical culture. In 1575, Tallis and Byrd were granted the twenty-one-year monopoly to print polyphonic music, and this may have introduced the young Dowland to the bizarre religious intricacies of Protestant England, the first publication of the two being Latin motets, 'songs which some would call sacred', but clearly of potential use in the Catholic rite. Apart from a contribution to a collection of metrical psalms in 1592, Dowland would steer well clear of church music (though he did tackle biblical subjects in his final book of songs, perhaps as an insurance policy). As a counterbalance to the insularity of Tallis and Byrd, Dowland would certainly have been aware of the Italian musicians employed at court since the reign of Henry VIII. Alfonso Ferrabosco and the Bassano family all regularly revisited Italy and there was a constant influx of *frottole* and madrigals.

Dowland would have come across a similar tradition in France. Henry Cobham had been in post only a year before taking on the young Dowland. He was a much travelled diplomat who had been posted at least twice to Philip II's Spain, where he would have been familiar with the *villancico*, the polyphonic song form also found as lute song. The most significant influences from Dowland's French trip must surely have been the polyphonic *chanson* and the *air de cour*. No fewer than six volumes of Lassus's *chansons* were published by

Adrian Le Roy during the period of Dowland's likely stay in France. Lassus, the supreme craftsman who had experimented with chromaticism in his *Prophetiae Sibyllarum* decades before, composed the most austere religious and ceremonial music, and like so many musicians of the time found his texts changed according to the religious wind. He made up for his religious seriousness in the secularity of his *chansons*, the texts of which ranged from the elegant and lyrical to drinking songs and celebrations of dodgy sex. Most fashionable were the composers of *airs de cour*, which had first appeared in Le Roy's *Livres d'airs de cour miz sur le luth* of 1571, material from which subsequently appeared in England three years later as *A briefe and plaine Instruction to set all musicke of divers Tunes in Tableture for the Lute*, when Dowland was a child.

Dowland may have been in France for four years and on his return he more or less disappears from the radar until 1592, when there is a record of him playing for the queen at Sudeley Castle; at some point he acquired degrees from both Oxford and Cambridge. He must by then have had quite a reputation as a player and in 1594, on the death of the incumbent, he applied for a position as one of the royal lutenists. He failed to get the job; we don't know why, but he felt that it may have been to do with the fact that he had converted to Catholicism while in France. He then left the country for Germany, apparently intending eventually to study with Luca Marenzio in Rome. The German leg of his trip was more successful than his Italian adventure. He was favoured by Moritz, Landgrave of Hesse-Kassel, and in Wolfenbüttel he is supposed to have met the young Michael Praetorius, recently installed as Kapellmeister at the court of the Duke of Brunswick (hard-line Protestant and scourge of Jews and witches). The onward trip didn't work out quite as Dowland had hoped, as we learn from a letter written to Robert Cecil on his way home in 1595.

Cecil, the queen's First Secretary, was one of the most powerful men in the land. He was born with scoliosis, a condition which resulted in a curvature of the spine, and as a short hunch-backed figure he suffered all the indignities that a disabled person could expect in a courtly society obsessed with physical beauty. His father William Cecil, Lord Burghley, had been secretary of state before him and was able to train him in the Machiavellian statecraft and its necessary social skills that would enable Robert to navigate the perilous waters of the court. Unable to present the clichéd charisma expected of courtiers, always aware of the insincerity of flattery and never a threat to Queen Elizabeth herself, he was one of the few courtiers she could depend upon to tell her the truth when necessary. He was also a cultured man and conscious from childhood of man's inhumanity to man, wary of the extreme cruelty meted out to Catholics in the sometimes fragile Protestant era. His position at court made it easy (if sometimes potentially dangerous) to intercede on behalf of those at risk from the religious weather. These included musicians, and the fact that no musicians appear to have suffered the ultimate penalty during Elizabeth's reign may well be due to Cecil's discreet and benign oversight.

Thomas Morley, Robert Jones and William Byrd were among many musicians who dedicated publications to Robert Cecil. In 1609, Dowland dedicated *Micrologus*, a translation of Andreas Ornithoparcus's thesis on singing and composition, to him, commending Cecil's 'protection of the whole state' and the 'speciall favors and graces' granted him by 'the chiefe author of all our good'. This is not a volume of songs and there is no mention of hospitality or the specific niceties that often feature in these salutations. Bearing in mind Dowland's contact with overseas courts, perhaps the patron–client relationship between the two may have been of a more subtle nature than that between Dowland's fellow composers and the Secretary.

Cecil also collaborated with the queen's favourite singer, Robert Hales, when the two were summoned to perform before the queen after an incident at court involving a 'dainty tablet' worn round the neck of Lady Derby. The locket fell onto the floor and the queen insisted on seeing what it contained, which was revealed to be a picture of Robert Cecil. The queen flounced off in a display of mock jealousy, pinning the picture at first to her shoe and then to her dress. It was all a bit of a lark – Cecil was Lady Derby's uncle and the queen was sixty-nine – and Cecil celebrated the occasion by writing an *apologia* to the queen which he asked Hales to set to music to be performed before her majesty.

Hales is known to have performed Dowland's songs on a number of occasions, at least one of them accompanied by the composer himself. This raises the question of whether or not Dowland was a singer. There are no verifiable records of Dowland singing his songs or anyone else's, which is very unusual. There is a similar silence about the lute playing of Robert Hales (it's not beyond the bounds of possibility that Cecil played the lute himself to accompany Hales singing his verses before the queen). Hales may have been a rare example of a singer who wasn't much of a lutenist, and Dowland an even rarer example of a composer who couldn't sing. Almost all musicians were multi-talented, multi tasking composer-performers and it was the norm for them to improvise on existing music or poetry. Almost all music up to the early Renaissance was conceived in the first instance as vocal music and those musicians we call composers were mostly referred to as singers. If Dowland had an interest in song but couldn't sing, one of the options open to him would have been to compose songs, as opposed to busking an accompaniment to a tune which he may not have felt able to sing himself. It may be stretching it a bit (and somewhat ironic) but it could be the case that Dowland's art was expressed as the fully composed accompanied song because he didn't like to accompany himself using existing material – not because he didn't like the music but because he was reluctant to sing it.

Dowland's letter to Cecil is a curious document. He begins with expressions of regret at having converted to Catholicism as a young and naïve student away from home. He then recalls his failed attempt to get a position at court and his subsequent visits to the Duke of Brunswick and the Landgrave of Hesse. The remaining three-quarters of the letter is a detailed account of his accidental involvement in potential Jesuit plotting against the crown while he was in Florence. Much of this Cecil must already have known since Dowland's movements required the Secretary's permission and his office had a Europe-wide network of informants. The letter, written from Nuremberg, has been interpreted as a sign of last-minute panic when the composer realised he might be in deep trouble as soon as he arrived home. Its fulsomeness might be part insurance policy in case the letter fell into the wrong hands. It's also possible that it could suggest Dowland was already serving as Cecil's eyes and ears abroad or was making a case for such a relationship in the future.

Dowland would have heard the full gamut of Italian vocal music on his journey south, but in his political panic (if that's what it was) he had to abandon the idea of studying with Marenzio (if that had really been his intention). As well as the mention of the composer in the letter to Cecil we also have the letter from Marenzio printed in the preface to the first book, but neither of these explains why Dowland wanted to study with the famous and prolific madrigalist. Marenzio published eighteen books of madrigals between 1580 and 1599 and had a high reputation in England. His madrigals had been heavily featured in Thomas East's *Musica transalpina* in 1588 and in *Italian Madrigals Englished* with translations by Thomas Watson two years later. There is no evidence that Dowland ever considered writing a madrigal, and although his lute songs were published with optional parts for alto, tenor and bass, the vocal ensemble versions are not remotely madrigal-like. If Dowland was seriously intending to study with Marenzio, what was it that he expected to learn?

Perhaps we have been misled by thinking of Marenzio solely as a madrigal composer, or by assuming that the default performance of a madrigal (as opposed to its publication) was by unaccompanied voices. In 1589, Marenzio had been a major contributor as both performer and composer to the *intermedii* for *La pellegrina*, part of the festivities celebrating the Florentine wedding of Ferdinando de' Medici and Christine of Lorraine. In this extravagant production, one of the most spectacular ever seen, Marenzio worked alongside the younger generation of composers, Peri, Caccini and Cavalieri, whose songs were as likely to be monodies as ensemble pieces. If Marenzio wrote any monodies they have not survived, but his madrigals would certainly have been performed as solo songs with instrumental accompaniment, quasi monodies; there is no evidence that listeners to the *intermedii* were aware that some of the music was by composers exploring a major stylistic shift and some by a senior traditional composer. Dowland's understanding of Marenzio may have imagined him as on the cusp of a change in style. He may have heard Marenzio performed as lute song, like Willaert's lute-song transcriptions of Verdelot's madrigals (or the tabs of madrigals in the library of Edward Paston which also contains Marenzio madrigals). He may also have appreciated the deep seriousness of the Italian composer, some of whose most exquisite pieces are set to the poetry of Petrarch.

Marenzio might well have been on his way north to take up a position in the Polish court as Dowland was travelling southwards, so the two may never have met anyway, and whatever Dowland's hopes there is no obvious influence of Marenzio in his music.

Dowland did make it safely back to England, where once again his life story continues to elude us. Aware that some of his songs were circulating in unauthorised versions, he set about publishing his own collection. His first attempt went to five editions over the following seventeen years (more than any other songbook). In 1598, by now with a high international reputation, he was appointed lutenist at the court of the Danish king Christian IV, whose sister Anna had married the Scottish king James VI. James's accession to the English throne in 1603 would mean that Dowland's courting of the court would have to start all over again.

Dowland held his Danish post for the next eight years, returning to England from time to time to order instruments or negotiate visits of English musicians to the Danish court. He also supervised publication of a third book of songs in 1603 and his great instrumental exploration of the *Lachrimae* in 1604. While in Denmark he may have travelled to the various German courts favoured by the Danish king, including those of Landgrave Moritz of Hesse and the Duke of Brunswick who had favoured him on his earlier travels, but there is surprisingly little evidence of his playing or composing. All of his publications are intended for an English audience and he doesn't seem to have dedicated any music to the Danish king apart from a single galliard.

Dowland left the Danish court in 1605 and was certainly in England for the notorious state visit of Christian IV a year later. Christian, not yet thirty, was a prodigious drinker, as were most of his retinue. At a banquet at Theobalds, the residence belonging to Cecil and later acquired by King James, the performance of a masque of Solomon and the Queen of Sheba descended into chaos when the performers got so drunk they couldn't stand upright. The Queen of Sheba eventually deposited a tray of 'wine, cream, jelly, beverage, cakes, spices, and other good matters' in the lap of Christian, who then fell himself when attempting to dance with her, 'not a little defiled', as Sir John Harrington reported.

Dowland had prepared the manuscript of his second book while he was in Denmark and sent it to England so that his wife could instigate the publishing process. It was bought by one George Eastland, who arranged for Thomas East to print it (with the permission of Thomas Morley, who then held the printing monopoly and would himself go on to arrange 'Flow my tears'). East and Eastland fell out over costs and settled their various disputes at the Court of Requests. Among the witnesses were the composers John Wilbye and Edward Johnson (who had proofread the volume) and Philip Rosseter, whose elegant songs still find a place in today's repertoires; it was a small musical world even then. A thousand copies seem to have been printed, together with a number of bootlegs made by East's apprentices. Around a dozen examples of the original print run are still extant.

The shenanigans over the publishing rights hint at the money that could, potentially at least, be made from music printing. Dowland's songs were printed as a commercial venture and were presented as part songs in order to maximise sales. The format of all the printed lute-song folios was a trade-off between profitability and practicality. On opening the book the reader was presented with both tablature for lute and staff notation for other instruments or singers. This doesn't make them madrigals – the staff notation is simply a transcription of the tablature; madrigals were published in sets of partbooks, but the lute-song volumes are ergonomically laid out so that a single copy could be used by as many musicians as could fit round the table on which it was placed. These would be very intimate occasions with everyone facing each other – singers, players or a mixture of both. Musicians still sit round tables to rehearse or explore new repertoire, a process that began with Renaissance musicians reaching for their songbooks for an evening of music-making that may have been much more like a recurring rehearsal than a performance. Being able to join in was probably more important than the music itself; Thomas Campion noted in the introduction to his *First Book of Ayres* that anyone overhearing a solo rendering was quite likely to improvise their own harmony, so anyone too far from the table to see the notes might have sung along anyway.

The fact that Dowland's volumes were printed – hundreds of copies available simultaneously instead of one laboriously copied manuscript – was one of the reasons the songs made such an impact. The three decades of the lute song coincided with a boom and then slow decline in the music printing industry after Byrd and Tallis were granted the monopoly in 1575. This early example of musicians monetising their art was always precarious, with a delicate balance between the high cost of labour, rights and ownership, and the challenge of new technologies. There were simply not enough musically literate potential buyers to sustain production at a reasonable price, so all the lute-song volumes have elaborate dedications in return for which the dedicatee would normally make a financial contribution to get the project started. We know almost nothing about who bought the volumes, most of which had a print run of around a thousand copies. Ironically, the number that survive today is tiny compared with manuscript copies of individual songs. It cost nothing to make your own copy tailored to your own performance practice and this bootlegging became the norm when the intabulating of accompaniments was abandoned in favour of improvising from a bass line.

Singers are taught from childhood about the importance of words, and for a modern singer, classical or otherwise, negotiating the relationship between music and text is an essential element of our craft. You know when it works, whether it involves the sophistication of Britten setting John Donne or the seeming banality of a formulaic pop song which can still touch your soul. It's hard to tell (as the oldest evidence is without notation), but for the first troubadours and *trouvères* the words may have come first. Yet as soon as tunes became memorable they could have a life of their own and new words could be put to old tunes. In the shadow world of improvised song that flourished in the fifteenth and sixteenth centuries the words presumably continued to generate the music.

Today's songwriters often begin with the music, playing with a chord sequence or a melodic cell which might have temporary words attached to articulate it. Paul McCartney's 'Yesterday', the germ of which was the opening three notes to the words 'scrambled eggs', is a classic example; Ira Gershwin dummied with 'An order of bacon and eggs' for 'It ain't necessarily so' (perhaps both writers did their best work soon after breakfast). We don't know who wrote the text to 'Flow my tears' but we think the music pre-dated the words. Was Dowland inspired by the dedicatory poem at the end of William Barley's book, which includes the line 'Flow forth abundant teares, bedew this doleful face', or did he perhaps have a scrambled eggs moment? 'Yesterday' is one of the most covered tunes in history (3,000 and counting), and Dowland's became one of the most enduring of the seventeenth century.

What is it that makes 'Flow my tears' a masterpiece? If analysis could tell us the answer we would be able to replicate it in the same way that songwriting *ateliers* provide instant hits for boy and girl bands (and perhaps AI will write lute songs in the future). It's the second piece in the book, and continues the melancholic feel of the first song, 'I saw my lady weep'. In case you think that's enough misery the third song is 'Sorrow, stay' and the gloom is unrelieved until the twelfth song, 'Fine knacks for ladies'. Dowland's singers are unlikely to have sung the whole book through in order, so probably would not have experienced the sudden change in the emotional weather encountered by modern CD listeners when the cheerful pedlar of 'Fine knacks' starts shouting his wares.

For a modern listener 'Flow my tears' has the essential ingredients that mean we can compare it with the best songs in the later classical canon. The Elizabethan cult of melancholy was the channel by which the poet could access the deepest emotions in contrast to the quotidian cheerfulness that society so often required. Dowland called one of his longest pavans 'Semper Dowland semper dolens' – 'Always Dowland, always doleful' – indicating that even a dance form could have an underlying seriousness that edged it towards art and beyond simple entertainment. The song isn't quite through-composed – the form is AABBC with the option of a repeated C – but the effect is of a substantial whole with no let-up in the prospective descent into the abyss. The descending first phrase repeats itself a third higher; tears don't just fall, they keep coming, and music perfectly matches the text (with the odd exception of 'of all joys have deprived') until the bitter end where even those in hell are better off than the poet. It's absurdly over the top, a highly stylised emotional outpouring, written in the third person but about the poet himself: the grief expressed is never tied to a particular event so could apply to anyone, hence its resonance in the present.

'Flow my tears' was not Dowland's most miserable song, though it comes close. That place is taken by 'In darkness let me dwell', a through-composed mini-tragedy in which the poet experiences a living death. Once again we don't know what's causing Dowland's grief, so it's easy to transfer the sentiments to today's performers and audiences. It's the last Dowland song in his son Robert's *Musicall Banquet* published in 1610; in a symbolic foretaste of things to come the song ends with the voice suspended alone after the lute has run its course. Robert's songbook celebrates the cosmopolitan repertoires available to the discerning English amateur at the end of the first decade of the seventeenth century. There are ten English songs including three by Dowland (and one by Robert Hales) and ten by composers from France, Spain and Italy. Among the last are two by Giulio Caccini, whose *Le nuove musiche* of 1602 was one of the first collections in the new declamatory style which left the harmony to the discretion of the player. The collection is performable from tab, but it can also be realised from the bass; it looks to both the immediate past and the rapidly evolving future.

Dowland's fourth and last songbook was *A Pilgrim's Solace*, which appeared in 1612. It was dedicated to his then patron, Lord de Walden at Audley End. The composer became progressively disgruntled as his younger colleagues embraced the simpler but more expressive style of the early Baroque. He eventually did join Robert Hales and his friends as a member of James I's court ensemble, still bewailing his own irrelevance with the passing of time. He was among the musicians who played at James's funeral in 1625, and he died himself less than a year later.

The curious juxtaposition of songs with fully composed accompaniments in England and those published in Italy with accompaniment devised spontaneously by the player lasted for around three decades. The English lute-song school turned out not to be the future of song, as the lyric introversion of Dowland and his fellow lutenist composers was overtaken by the novel Italian declamatory style in which the very concepts of tune and harmony were completely different. Fully composed accompaniments would not reappear for almost two hundred years, when the figuring required by fully developed tonality became so complicated that it was easier to write the actual notes; composers regained control of the score, a situation that had briefly prevailed in the repertoire of the lute-song composers.

The tabs that enabled anyone unfamiliar with staff notation to play the lute had a downside in that unless you were a lute player the notation was unreadable. Tab became obsolete when players started to improvise harmony from bass lines from the sixteenth century onwards, and once Dowland's works fell out of fashion his reputation depended on those who still owned the prints or who copied the top and bottom lines from which they created their own versions to sing with larger lutes or harpsichord. The songs from the original books were still turning up in the 1690s, and the manuscript copies also suggest that Dowland's reputation survived the century. But by the time we get to Burney's dictionary of 1776 the twin effects of time and tab have worked against him. Burney was mystified by Dowland's popularity during his lifetime, but his comments suggest that he may not have been able to read tab. If he saw a print, only the tune would have been readable, and a manuscript copy with only tune and bass line would have seemed very thin indeed to a musician in the age of Mozart. Burney may be the first musicologist whose view of musical history was compromised by not being able to read tablature, a tendency that continued in some branches of musicology until late in the twentieth century.

The prints tell only part of the story. Manuscript copies are found all over Europe, each one copied by or tailored to a particular individual. Needless to say, they are all different and are a priceless resource for the study of performance practice, especially with regard to ornamentation. The later seventeenth-century sources are just the top and bottom lines, and without tab to tell singing lutenists where to put their fingers more attention could be given to personalising the vocal line. In time manuscripts too succumbed to decay or changing fashion and eventually Dowland became little more than a name in a history book.

When the Victorian and Edwardian enthusiasm for part songs embraced the Renaissance madrigal, the lute song was completely ignored. It was not until the 1920s when Edmund Fellowes and

Philip Heseltine produced new editions of the songs transcribed for piano accompaniment that they resurfaced. Heseltine (the composer Peter Warlock) compared Dowland favourably with Schubert, and had he not died in 1930 at the age of thirty-six he would surely have gone on to produce many more editions of lute songs. That task fell to the indefatigable Edmund Fellowes, who edited all the lute songs, transcribing the accompaniments for piano. They could then take their place in the early-twentieth-century recital repertoire while awaiting the revival of the lute and the return to tab in the 1960s.

'Flow my tears' inspired twentieth-century composers from Hindemith to Britten. Henri Pousseur wrote *Tales and Songs from the Bible of Hell* for the four voices of Electric Phoenix and live electronics, using his own four-part realisation of the lute song and deconstructing its elements before recombining them. The lute and its songs had been reawakened by the countertenor Alfred Deller and the lutenist Desmond Dupré. The two met in 1947 and by 1950 they were working on Dowland, at first with Dupré on guitar. The voice of Deller was incredibly persuasive, and the countertenor became increasingly (and mistakenly) identified as one of the fundamental ingredients of early music.

The other great duo of modern times was that of Peter Pears and the guitarist and lutenist Julian Bream whose twenty-year partnership began in 1954 with a performance of Dowland and Philip Rosseter at Wigmore Hall in London. In 2006 the rock singer Sting and lutenist Edin Karamazov released *Songs from the Labyrinth*, an album devoted to Dowland which brought the composer's songs to a global audience, blurring the difference between 'classical' and 'popular'.

'Flow my tears' may not have made it onto the *Voyager* spacecraft but it did find its way into science fiction. The long trail of tears reaches into *Flow My Tears, the Policeman Said*, a 1974 sci-fi novel by the American writer Philip K. Dick, and beyond that into a television series based on Dick's stories called *Electric Dreams*. I received a mysterious phone call one day in 2017 from someone asking if I was an expert on John Dowland. Before I could confirm one way or the other, the caller explained that there was to be a television programme which involved two actors singing Dowland – would I coach them? The film was based not on *Flow My Tears, the Policeman Said* but on another Philip Dick story called 'Sales Pitch'. The Dowland song appeared over the credits, but its main feature was as a key to a voice-activated lock which one of the actors had to teach the other to use. I did coach them briefly, but as they were Steve Buscemi and Sidse Babett Knudsen they needed very little input from me: they sang in their speaking voices, just as Dowland would have done.

The 'Lachrymae Pavan' was probably first enjoyed by a roomful of over-dressed Elizabethan courtiers, dancing the evening away to the accompaniment of lute or viols. A more recent incarnation appears on 'Flow My Dreams, the Android Wept', a dance track by Toby Marks (aka Banco de Gaia) on his 2006 album *Farewell to Ferengistan*. There is a satisfying symmetry in the thought that in the twenty-first century dancers are still sweating their way through Dowland's tune from centuries ago.

Female musician, probably Barbara Strozzi, with a viola da gamba, *painted by Bernardo Strozzi (c. 1630s).*

6

BARBARA STROZZI

'LAGRIME MIE'

The elegant Englishness of Dowland and the flamboyant virtuosity of the madrigal improvisers are almost polar opposites in the rich history of song, but they each contained the seeds of quiet revolutions in composition and performance that occurred in the late sixteenth century. The narrative is complicated (side-tracked, perhaps) by a group of Florentine intellectuals loudly claiming to reinvent the music of the ancients, a kind of conceptual realignment where music finally caught up with the Renaissance but which music historians soon decided to call the Baroque. Anything could still be turned into a song, but the decades either side of 1600 saw a change from cannibalising complex polyphony such as the madrigal and *frottola* to songs that were conceived as songs in the first place rather than being derived from another source.

This new simplicity decluttered harmony (previously a by-product of simultaneous tunes) by allowing performers to improvise their own accompaniment, just the tune and bass line being supplied by the composer. Theoretically, it meant that the delivery of text would be uncompromised by virtuosity, but nothing composers wrote was set in stone and every song performance would continue to be enhanced by improvised additions, tasteful or otherwise. The songs of Barbara Strozzi (1619–77) mark a high point in this process, briefly establishing the song form as complete in itself before the genre had to compete with opera arias as the castrati recalibrated what singing actually was.

Strozzi's life also confirms a significant change in the fortunes of female musicians who since the mid-sixteenth century had been establishing themselves as brilliant and sophisticated contributors to the artistic capital of Italian courtly culture. Most were multi-talented singers who could accompany themselves and each other, as well as compose and improvise. As is always the way, much of their achievement has left no trace beyond their reputations but two composers left a remarkable imprint on the mainstream musical discourse, though their surnames until recently were known to history as those of their fathers. In 1625, Francesca Caccini's *La liberazione di Ruggiero dall'isola d'Alcina* was performed in Florence; it was the first opera composed and published by a female composer and may have been one of the first operas performed outside Italy. In 1618 she had published her first (and apparently only) book of songs. Caccini died in the early 1640s, her reputation having briefly eclipsed that of her father Giulio, whose *Le nuove musiche* of 1602 ensured that it was the elder Caccini whose name we remember today. In 1644 the Venetian singer and composer Barbara Strozzi, adopted daughter of Giulio Strozzi (known to history as the librettist for Monteverdi and Cavalli among others), published the first of the eight books of songs she would produce over the next twenty years; her printed output was greater than any other composer during her lifetime.

The easy explanation for this change of female fortunes is the gradual absorption of humanist values by the intellectual and societal elite from the fourteenth century onwards. While that may be broadly true, it doesn't provide us with physical evidence of women contributing to the late medieval song repertoire which, though mostly about women (and even sometimes written from a woman's point of view), is invariably written by men. Women left no musical manuscripts but they certainly had a musical presence under the male gaze. Dante and Petrarch show us musical women who are a lot more independent than the formulaic subjects of the troubadours' courtly love.

The ladies in Boccaccio's *Decameron*, urban fourteenth-century Florentines escaping to the countryside to beat the Black Death, dance, sing and play morning and night, each day ending with a *ballata*. No music has been found for these and it is likely that none was written down. Giovanni Sercambi later used a similar system in his *Il noveliere* (The Storyteller) based on Boccaccio's frame structure with the women fleeing plague in Lucca with many more songs, none of which have music. The poems of the *Decameron ballate* lack the formal discipline of those set by Gherardello da Firenze and other contemporary composers, possibly because the ladies' music was improvised and they weren't counting syllables quite so conscientiously. They also throw light on how songs were received: after each performance there is generally a discussion, principally of the poetry, dissecting what it might all mean. This is more than an early (and democratic) example of music criticism: as would also be the case until the arrival of public concerts, performers and audience share the same space and the attention is focused on their mutual enjoyment and understanding.

Boccaccio is not a fully paid-up humanist: his women admit to being the weaker sex and at least pay lip service to a need for the reassuring custodianship of men (although in the *Decameron* they get to choose which men), but in scholarship, art and music their achievements can equal those of men – they just have to work twice as hard. But Boccaccio had no time for either pagan or Christian superstition, which at best marginalised women. A decade or so after the *Decameron* he wrote *De claris mulieribus* (On Famous Women), the first collection of women's biographies (104 of them). For the first time women are formally acknowledged in literature as a secular force to be reckoned with and not merely the lower species the church would relegate them to. They don't compose written music, still a male prerogative, but they do have song repertoires. In a culture that was as much oral as literary, women can make songs spontaneously just as well as the men.

Although we know that European courts supported many successful women musicians in the late Renaissance, few of them shone quite so brightly as those of the northern Italian city states. By the beginning of the sixteenth century we can see a remarkable transformation in progress, and a number of women musicians emerge from the shadows to become brilliant stars in the Renaissance's artistic firmament, as humanist poets and intellectuals reach for a different vision of how society might work. To read Ariosto or Castiglione one might imagine that a rebalancing of gender relations was only just over the horizon. As Anthony Newcomb pointed out, there are passages in Ariosto's *Orlando furioso* that could be from a charter of women's social and artistic rights. Castiglione's *Il cortegiano*, completed in 1516 and published in 1528, paints a vivid picture of court life in which women, potentially at least, are in many respects equal to men. *Il cortegiano* is a comprehensive guide to becoming an ideal member of courtly society, expounded as a series of debates among the elite of Urbino over a four-day period (the cultural long weekend was something of a Renaissance fixture).

The references to music have been much pored over by musicologists and performers, but the most progressive conversations happen on the third day, when gender equality comes in for serious discussion.

The increasing assertiveness and accomplishment of powerful aristocratic women was driven by spectacular secularism and despite the opposition of the church. Although the Renaissance church's attitude to women was never in doubt, its attitude to music was always ambivalent. Women's music-making, including composition, flourished in some convents despite successive popes regularly firing off edicts forbidding women to have anything to do with the frivolousness of music or to consort with men who indulged in such decadence. Some convents banned both improvised and composed polyphony whereas others promoted concerts on feast days. The church offered no employment to women to match the creative and profitable career paths open to men, who might, like women, begin as singers but could progress to positions of power and influence as choir directors, teachers or instrumentalists. The papal loathing of women also had bizarre physical consequences for some men: rather than peopling the Sistine Chapel choir with women or boys to sing the upper lines of polyphony, the church opted for the cruellest of compromises, from the 1560s sourcing castrated men who had retained their soprano voices. It was the perfect papal solution: castrati sounded even better than women, had fewer compromising rude bits but still retained the benefits of most of a man's body including substantial lungs to power their child-sized larynxes.

Outside the church there was an increase in private instruction in everything from music (even to prepare for life in a convent) to how to run substantial domestic establishments. It was normal for a well-connected woman to demonstrate musical talent as one of her social graces, and in time these talents became part of the artistic capital that powered competitive city states. At the top of the social ladder stood the princely court, with a musical establishment based in the first instance around the requirements of the chapel, a crucial emblem of courtly patronage and prestige. This body of musicians would provide whatever the prince needed for secular entertainment, anything from a few songs to an entire ballet. The payroll was normally 100 per cent male but there was a subtle relationship between the professional men and the aristocratic ladies of the court, many of whom were serious musicians.

By the sixteenth century the most magnificent of the northern courts was that of Alfonso II d'Este, who became Duke of Ferrara, Modena and Reggio on the death of his father Ercole II in 1559. Alfonso was an archetypal Renaissance prince, a soldier with a love of the arts and a keen interest in dynastic marriage, of which he had three. His first wife, Lucrezia de' Medici (Robert Browning's 'last duchess'), was thirteen when they married and died of pulmonary thrombosis three years later. In 1565, Alfonso married Barbara, Archduchess of Austria, but she died of tuberculosis in 1572. His final marriage was to Margherita Gonzaga in 1579. She was fifteen by the time the marriage contract was completed (dynastic marriages were not about sex) and equipped with all the musical and artistic skills expected of a Renaissance princess. She would outlive her husband by more than two decades, becoming a patron of poets, musicians and artists in her own right, a process which began when Alfonso introduced her to his *musica secreta*.

Evenings at court were for social display; visiting dignitaries and favourite courtiers were treated to music, dancing, poetry reading, card games and the occasional exotic item such as dancing dwarves. When the duke tired of the daily round he would retire to his private apartment accompanied only by the most illustrious guests who might then witness the talents of his extraordinarily musical ladies-in-waiting. This was the private music of the duke, his *musica secreta*, in which ladies of the court would sing and dance under the direction of Luzzasco Luzzaschi, Alfonso's chief composer and harpsichordist since the 1560s. The duke's favourite female musicians in the 1570s included the Bendidio sisters Lucrezia and Isabella, Laura di Scandiano and her stepmother Barbara Sanseverino, all wives and daughters of Ferrarese nobility who would perform separately or in various combinations, sometimes with the legendary bass Giulio Cesare Brancaccio. Margherita's arrival seems to have triggered a paradigm shift in court music-making: Alfonso decided to augment his aristocratic amateurs with professional female singers whose social status, though still impressive, would not normally have been sufficient to admit them to court. The result was the *concerto delle donne*, a flexible ensemble consisting of the finest female musicians Alfonso could find.

The first tranche of new singers included Laura Peverara, Tarquinia Molza and Anna Guarini, all of whom were rewarded handsomely with clothing, accommodation and gifts, and were treated at court (much to the consternation of some older courtiers) in exactly the same way as their noble colleagues. The potential awkwardness was highlighted by the fate of Brancaccio. He was one of the most famous singers in Italy, having devised a new repertoire based on his virtuosic mastery of both tenor and bass ranges within the same song. He also had a reputation as a courtier and warrior of some renown (at least in his own eyes) and it was as a courtly 'amateur' that he assumed he was invited to sing for Alfonso, not as a paid professional. When Alfonso expected him to sing with his professional ladies, he declined, whereupon Alfonso, perhaps tired of Brancaccio's endless stories of his valour in the field, fired him. With the blurring of the distinction between courtly amateurs and paid performers a new distinction arose, that between performers and audience. The change didn't happen overnight, but the pseudo-informality of performance as social grace (à la *musica secreta*) began to go by the board once the miraculous vocalism of the *concerto* in effect embarrassed potential amateur imitators into awe-struck silence.

The accounts of the performances of the *musica secreta* and the *concerto delle donne* give us fascinating but frustrating glimpses into the lives of musicians at the top of society. Very few courtiers were admitted to the inner sanctum and only a few of those wrote down recollections of what they had heard; what impressed them was the beauty, poise and elegance of the women, but most of all their singing. We hear very little about the songs they sang, but the duke acquired a substantial collection of madrigal prints from the arrival of Margherita onwards. Creating a solo song out of a madrigal required exceptional skill in first understanding the structure and then making a unique decorated version while filling in at least some of the harmony, usually on a lute, harp or viol.

The original madrigals were all composed by men; the women may have composed on paper but if they did none of their pieces has survived. Written composition was considered an analytical and manly task as opposed to the instant communicative charm expected of female improvisers. This was not entirely a question of gender: although aristocrats would happily turn their hand to a modestly crafted motet or madrigal, it took an exceptional figure (such as Prince Carlo Gesualdo) to maintain social standing while dedicating his life to composition in the manner of a professional madrigalist. Women were at a twofold disadvantage in being excluded from both the *dilettante* written tradition and a career as a professional composer, and there are no printed examples of women's compositions before the middle of the sixteenth century.

Over to the east there was an exception to the self-aggrandising northern courts. The Venetian Republic, a vastly successful trading hub with extended overseas territories of its own, was a social and artistic counterweight to the sometimes cloistered religiosity of Rome and the competitive magnificence of Florence, Ferrara, Mantua or Milan. The conventional view of a stratified society with a hereditary ruler at the top and peasants at the bottom didn't apply to a republic that was both physically and symbolically barely attached to the Italian mainland. There was a flourishing theatre scene which preferred real female actors to boys dressed up in unsatisfactory outfits, and from the 1560s the *commedia dell'arte* began to produce highly acclaimed professional female stars. Vincenza Armani (who ironically began her career as a male impersonator) died of poisoning in 1569 (the jealous lover trope), but we know from an encomium by her fellow actor and musician Adriano Valerini that she was also a singer, improviser and composer. The *commedia* also launched the careers of Isabella Andreini and Vittoria Piisimi, both multi-talented actor-singers who carved out independent lives for themselves (Vittoria Piisimi ran several *commedia* troupes over a period of twenty years). These were women with agency, visibly flourishing on their own terms in a world that history sees as male.

It is not surprising therefore, that the first complete songbook to be written and published by a woman appeared in Venice in 1558. Maddelena Casulana was a lutenist and singer whose fame had spread as far as Munich, where Lassus performed at least one motet of hers. Her *Primo libro di madrigali* was the first of three, and they presumably represent only a small part of her musical life, about which we know very little. In the preface to her first book, dedicated to Isabella d'Este, Casulana makes the point that men have got it completely wrong if they think only they have artistic and musical gifts. It's a powerful statement, and it may offer a clue as to why Casulana was drawn to written polyphony in addition to the customary but evanescent performative skills that might more usually propel women towards professional careers. Printing gave women the same exposure and opportunities as men. Publishing was a commercial transaction that had nothing to do with the clerical copying of manuscripts on which earlier generations depended. The madrigal books undoubtedly reached a broader demographic beyond both court and church; publishers sought profit, and were more concerned about the quality of the music than the sex of the composer.

Printing is the gateway to posterity, a fact clearly understood by Giulio Caccini when he published *Le nuove musiche* in 1602 (the print is dated 1601 but publication was delayed by the death of the printer). Caccini had been associated with the so-called Florentine *camerata*, his name for a group of musicians and intellectuals that had gathered at the house of Count de' Bardi from the 1570s onwards. They were all in some sense poets and wanted to recapture the essence of ancient Roman rhetoric in which the arts of music and poetry would unite in a communicative clarity unencumbered by contrapuntal complexity. Caccini's songs were mostly written in the new style which resulted from their experiments, favouring rhetorical declamation rather than metrical rhythm. This recitative-like delivery did away with the counterpoint of the madrigal and replaced it with the *basso continuo*, a bass line over which improvised chordal harmony enabled a more flexible delivery from the singer. Caccini's publication, especially the preface that preceded it, had significant consequences at the time as it represented a course adjustment in the trajectory of song, bringing it ever closer to our modern expectations. More recently it had a profound effect on the nascent early-music movement towards the end of the twentieth century.

In the 1970s and 1980s, when singers began to investigate historical performance practice, we looked around for contemporary treatises to plunder for information. *Le nuove musiche* was the perfect source: a collection of songs with instructions on how to perform them. For a generation of singers Caccini was our teacher, and we filled our previously pristine performances with his ornaments. Caccini's agenda wasn't quite what we imagined, however. We knew nothing of the fantastic virtuosity of sixteenth-century solo madrigal performance: we assumed madrigals were polyphonic pieces and that modern editions represented an ideal performance, true to the composer's original intentions (a modernist concept that would have puzzled the composers in question). The later sources rarely saw the light of day as they were usually dismissed by musicologists as corrupt, so we wouldn't have taken them seriously anyway. Used to singing only what we saw in the score, we relished the challenge of *Le nuove musiche* and began to apply Caccini's ornaments to other music of the period. It would not be the first time we would begin our historical researches in the wrong place and misunderstand the intention behind a written source: these were not exercises challenging us to be more adventurous, but Caccini's attempt to rein in the ornamental excesses of his fellow singers. We now know better, but the modern early-music movement is still living with the consequences of taking Caccini's examples as typical of the period rather than the much more elaborate style that he was railing against.

Le nuove musiche contains a number of songs and madrigals, none of which had ever been polyphonic compositions. They are written in a straightforward style to enable the text to be delivered without being overcome by the singing of it. Caccini's instructions were about reducing ornamentation to the minimum that singers could get away with while maintaining the integrity of the text. There is evidence that performers of the time ignored Caccini's strictures as heavily ornamented versions of his own songs appear in later manuscripts, and the rapidly evolving genre of opera also encouraged flamboyant display. The new songs are a hybrid art that has the simplicity of the new compositional style but is often overlaid with as much virtuosic ornamentation as a singer cared to add. It was a style which appealed to the female virtuosi as not only did it allow them to retain their signature skills, but the simpler chordal accompaniment, shorn of all counterpoint, made self-accompaniment even easier.

One of the prime exponents of the new form was Giulio Caccini's daughter Francesca. In her childhood and teenage years she was part of the family ensemble together with her brother Pompeo and sister Settimia. As a young woman she was often invited to sing with the famous virtuosa Vittoria Archilei, the two of them and Settimia at one point forming an ensemble similar to that of the ensembles created by Alfonso d'Este decades before (and subsequently fashionable in many Italian courts). She was also a skilled instrumentalist and could accompany herself on keyboards, lutes or guitars. Her book of songs, published in 1618 (the year her father died), demonstrates how subtly the old virtuoso tradition had been reconciled with the freer continuo song form, with recitative-like passages carrying the action forward but interrupted with expressive showers of notes to give the singer a chance to show her paces. There are simpler, strophic *canzonette* too, which use an alphabetic notation, showing Francesca was in touch with a wider performing community than the Medici court. Like Peri and Monteverdi, whose music inhabits the same stylistic space, she was drawn to the theatre and created ballets and music for theatrical entertainments. The songbook suggests sophisticated domestic performance at court or in aristocratic drawing rooms.

***

Francesca Caccini disappears from the record in the early 1640s, and she was presumably dead before Barbara Strozzi's *Primo libro di madrigali* appeared in 1644. Like Caccini, Strozzi had an illustrious father. Giulio Strozzi was one of the most well-connected intellectuals of his age; the various houses he rented in Cannaregio were a meeting place for the city's intellectual and artistic elite. He adopted Barbara, who was born in 1619 and may have been his daughter by a favourite servant. He was aware of her precocious musical talent and probably of her potential as a social and musical asset, initially facilitated by her extraordinarily beautiful voice. He would show her off at informal musical evenings, at one of which she probably met Nicola Fontei, who dedicated two books of songs to the teenage phenomenon (with texts by Giulio himself). In 1637, Giulio founded the Accademia degli Unisoni, an association of musicians, poets and intellectuals, primarily as a means of furthering her career. *Accademie* were cultural societies, usually all male, which debated fashionable topics of the day. In libertarian Venice these could range from abstruse philosophy to the banally superficial (such as whether or not women were the same species as men). Barbara would host these evenings on Giulio's behalf and would sometimes perform. There is a report of one gathering at which the debate consisted of a competition between singing and weeping, *la contesa del canto e delle lagrime*, at which Barbara was required to adjudicate. Perhaps this was when 'Lagrime mie' was first heard.

Barbara's upbringing, surrounded by musicians, poets and artists, gave her skills and connections that enabled her to avoid a future life in a convent and flourish as a singer and society hostess, but it was her abilities as a composer that set her apart from other singers. Francesca Caccini had had similar advantages, plus the benefit of lessons from her composer father. Giulio sent Barbara to Francesco Cavalli for lessons, and just as Francesca's music shows the influence of her famous teacher so do Barbara Strozzi's songs reflect the teaching of the foremost composer of the age. Curiously, at a time when opera was reaching beyond the exclusivity of court circles and lighting up the public domain, Barbara Strozzi wrote no operas; this despite being the daughter of a librettist and a student of the most successful living opera composer. This is unfortunate for historians; so much history of the period is dominated by opera, which often leaves a substantial trail of documentation in its wake. For Barbara there are no libretti, reports of productions, bills for scenery, costumes or stage machinery, the critical resources for modern researchers.

Instead, we have the songbooks. She published seven (possibly eight), and the dedications show her increasing confidence as a composer and musician of consequence. The first few have prefaces that draw attention to her assumed inadequacy as a mere woman, but by the final volumes she has the confidence to dispense with references to her sex. There are more than one hundred songs, almost all on the subject of unrequited love, ranging from brief arias to cantata-length pieces (she was one of the first to use the term 'cantata'). Her output compares with that of the most prolific composers of the era, and unlike those of many of her contemporaries her songs appeared in print rather than manuscript copies. Strozzi's career as a publisher is remarkable; very few prints survive but there are references to her work all over Europe, suggesting her entrepreneurial work paid off in the long term.

'Lagrime mie' is from her *Diporti di Euterpe ovvero cantate e ariette a voce sola* of 1659. Her tears come from a very different source to Dowland's of more than half a century earlier. Dowland's tears stream wearily down a fourth and then a few more are squeezed out with the same fall a little higher, still low in the voice before eventually climbing towards a terminal fall. The singer's task is mapped out by the music, with very little room for deviation from the composer's flow. Strozzi's tears are almost a shout of despair – if that's how the singer understands it. But they needn't be: with no harmonic movement and an extended rhetorical opening there are hundreds of ways to perform the first phrase; the notes in effect have durations but no rhythm. It is one of the few pieces of music before Mozart to use the descending harmonic minor scale, familiar to today's trained musicians as an exercise dulled by mechanical repetition.

After agreeing on an opening octave with the bass, the singer immediately slides down a semitone to the major seventh, one of the most dissonant and ambiguous of intervals. This can last for as long (and loud) as the singer wishes before the voice reluctantly falls, stretched by fluttering *trilli*, until it slips below the octave keynote before resolving onto it. We don't even know what the word is until the phrase is complete: the first syllable, *la* . . ., is enough to release the rhetoric and shape our thoughts. Then, having heard the words 'my tears', we discover it isn't quite what we may have led ourselves to believe: the tears are not actually flowing at all: this is a lament for tears which will not come. A further surprise is in store if you're listening for the first time to one of the many wonderfully expressive soprano recordings: the would-be lover for whose predicament the tears will not flow is called Lidia. In one of the more bizarre consequences of gender-inflected music-making, the song composed by a woman is almost invariably sung by a woman even though clearly intended for a man. It is Strozzi's misfortune to be so powerfully associated with 'women composers' that modern tenors have been reluctant to embrace her music.

The opening heart-rending refrain returns twice more. In between are exquisitely crafted phrases, recitative-like tune fragments that never develop beyond the immediate rhetorical gesture apart from long word-painting melismas on 'lagrime', 'core' and 'piangete', the key words of the poem. There are double-entendres for those who care to find them, the stock in trade of madrigal composers for generations before Strozzi, but perhaps the more effective if sung by a woman to a largely male audience; flirtation was a performance strategy (today's reviewers still talk of sopranos seducing their audience).

We probably shouldn't read too much into the rather revealing portrait that might be of Barbara (portraits of St Cecilia show her similarly endowed), but seductive Strozzi undoubtedly was. Many commentators have alluded to her possible status as a geisha-like courtesan, something we will never know for certain, but if her fame rested solely on her amatory arts we would probably know nothing about her at all. The portrait by Bernardo Strozzi, who painted Monteverdi (and who is not thought to be related to Barbara), shows her holding a *viola da gamba*, seated beside a table on which there is a violin and some music (not any of her surviving scores). David and Ellen Rosand argued that the history of the two Strozzis strongly suggests that Barbara is the subject of the painting. Barbara was a multi-instrumentalist and is likely to have been competent on both violin and the gamba, though the instrument most associated with song composers is the lute, especially the larger varieties, theorbo and chitarrone, which were ideal self-accompanying instruments. 'Lagrime mie', with its long pedal notes, seems to ask for a sustaining bass instrument such as the gamba in the portrait, in addition to a lute or keyboard.

Continuo song not only freed the accompanying instrument from prescribed harmony, it also loosened an already tenuous connection between the notes the composer wrote and those that the performer actually sang. The minimal notation used conventional staves with the occasional figure sketched above the bass to suggest intended harmony. This meant a singing player such as Barbara Strozzi no longer had to master tab and was able to focus more on what she was doing with her voice than her fingers; any piece of music could be instantly read at sight, with the accompaniment adjusted as necessary. A generation before, singers of Dowland's lute songs would have found reading tab took a lot more energy (and practice), leaving little creative space for spontaneous additions. His songs are usually performed today by a separate singer and lutenist, such is the complexity of his harmony.

The new attention given to bass lines was reflected in the development of the larger lutes. These had bass strings parallel to the neck that didn't need fingering, so they were easy to find and extended the range downwards. The acoustic volume in bigger instruments allowed a more perceptible circulation of overtones in the instrument, creating the illusion of a richer harmonic texture. There is a parallel with the late twentieth century when more powerful amplification systems meant that rock groups such as Cream, Led Zeppelin and The Police needed only one guitarist. The richer frequency spectrum of heavily amplified bass guitar obviated the need to fill out the harmony with the rhythm guitarist that had been such a feature of sixties rock bands. The new configuration freed space for the virtuosity of guitarists such as Eric Clapton and Jimmy Page, and in the seventeenth century a similar vocal virtuosity was unleashed by singers who no longer had to worry about the harmony.

Barbara Strozzi died in 1677. Her songbooks are a kind of barometer of mid-century Venetian taste outside the opera house and also represent the end of a line. In publishing longer cantata-like forms she was echoing earlier works by Salamone Rossi and Giacomo Carissimi, and hers compare favourably with both. Rossi and Carissimi had ties to Rome where opera was banned, leading them to develop the musical and dramatic aspects of opera without deploying them in the theatre. The secular cantata would in the end prove to be a musical diversion, expanded as the sacred oratorio with choir and instruments on the one hand and by the secular delights of opera on the other. The cantata flourished briefly with Scarlatti and Handel, and nineteenth-century opera spawned some memorable songs.

Although the Italian *ridotti* and *accademie* continued to provide a venue for more intimate entertainment into the eighteenth century, the Italian soul had been sold to opera. The story of the opera aria, a theatrical song requiring a vocal projection unlike anything heard before, would require a book of its own. There were intimate and less dramatic Italian songs – Paolo Tosti, sometime singing master to both the Queen of Italy and the British royal family, was one of the most widely performed song composers of the late nineteenth century, and in the twentieth century Italian composers would find altogether new ways to match words and music. But before we get there we need to look to Germany, France and England, three countries which provided the bedrock of song repertoires we still enjoy today.

Daguerreotype of Robert Schumann in conversation with his wife Clara Wieck (c. 1850).

7

ROBERT SCHUMANN
'DU RING AN MEINEM FINGER'

The song cycle *Frauenliebe und Leben* (A Woman's Love and Life) by Robert Schumann (1810–56), considered by some to be among the composer's finest works, in many respects perfectly fitted the nineteenth-century salons in which it was first performed. It has since been subjected to feminist scrutiny and often tortured defence by those who see it as abstract musical art that needn't be compromised by semiotics or sociology. Is it, as John Daverio put it, a case of 'male wish-fulfilment fantasy ... only redeemed as art through the irresistible grace, verve, and lyric intensity of Schumann's music' (in layman's terms, a rather non-pc stonking good tune)? Or is it a case of complex cultural work, as Ruth Solie's now classic feminist analysis might suggest? And does it matter anyway, if a singer wants to sing it and an audience wants to listen?

The metamorphosis of the *Lied* from amateur performances in German drawing rooms to silent worship at London's Wigmore Hall is an extraordinary story in itself, but it has also tended to obscure a remarkable history of musical enterprise by a number of brilliant women composers and performers. In this context a song cycle of poems written by a man (two men) in a woman's voice submitting totally to her husband (and, ironically, first performed in its entirety in both Europe and the USA by a man) was certain to stimulate the critical musicology of the late twentieth century. In the twenty-first century the concept of the *Lied* is once more in flux as creative performers experiment with ways to reinvent a genre that has sometimes been seen as entrenched in its own abstract excellence, far removed from the homely delights of the first performances.

Frauenliebe und Leben dates from Schumann's return to seriously productive songwriting in 1840, his *Liederjahr*. In a letter of the previous year he had let slip that he had never considered vocal writing to be great art; he had composed the odd song in the past and edited and critiqued songs by others, but instrumental music and the piano had dominated his life up till then. In January of the following year he met Felix Mendelssohn and had one of those conversations we would love to have overheard and which may have included a discussion of songwriting. Perhaps Mendelssohn asked him why he had apparently overlooked the songs of Schubert in his rather jaundiced analysis of the art. By February, Schumann had begun to write songs and even considered an opera; by the end of July he had written *Frauenliebe*, and almost all the collections on which his reputation rests were completed by the end of the year. The future of the *Lied* was about to take a remarkable turn as the fruits of this year, together with the older cycles of Schubert, brought about a step change in the middle classes' perception of song. The alignment of prolific songwriting and public concerts by cultured and charismatic performers who shared a mindset with composer and poet enabled an evolution of the *Lied* unparalleled in the history of song thus far.

Song had been an essential ingredient of German culture since the Carolingian epic and beyond, and a monophonic tradition persisted throughout the age of Renaissance polyphony alongside the secular *Tenorlied*. The old feudal top-down German society within which the *Minnesänger* had flourished gave way to a more self-consciously German urban middle-class culture in which guilds of *Meistersinger* would compete in poetry, declamation and song. This had become a rather thin thread by the nineteenth century (though it still survives in German folk culture today, resolutely ignoring attempts by the early-music movement to reinvent it); the real historical figures in Wagner's *Die Meistersinger von Nürnberg* and *Tannhäuser* would have resonated in many German households. The guilds were largely male organisations, but the competitions brought together whole communities to witness public performances.

Music also flourished in the home as entertainment and a force for moral good. In the early-eighteenth-century German-speaking lands there had been a quest for simplicity of utterance, not more than one thought at a time, as the poet Friedrich von Hagedorn put it. Italian opera had swept the continent, but was met with some resistance in Germany (and England) where a more restrained song was to be heard in middle-class drawing rooms. Simplicity of text meant a correspondingly light-touch approach to song: the message of the poet should be instantly understandable by every listener. There was no attempt to educate the audience: they already knew their poets and probably owned printed volumes of both poetry and music. To sing a song was also to harmonise it simultaneously on an instrument. In J.S. Bach's time this would more often than not be a keyboard but it might also be a harp or a lute, and the performer would read from a two-stave score giving the tune and the bass with the occasional figure to indicate the harmony. Eventually the piano carried all before it, and mass production brought one to every German household that could afford it.

Bach's two notebooks, compiled for his second wife Anna Magdalena, reveal much about domestic music-making in eighteenth-century Germany, serious and traditional but with a nod to more current and secular entertainment. The earlier of the two notebooks, dated 1722, is in the composer's hand and contains only works by Bach himself, presumably intended as a teaching aid. The 1725 *Notenbüchlein für Anna Magdalena Bach* is more substantial, with pieces by several composers transcribed in Anna Magdalena's hand. As well as instrumental pieces by family members and friends there are chorales for the family to sing, and songs and arias including one in praise of tobacco. These are personal and much-loved favourites, enjoyed by the family. We don't really have a suitable word to describe the circumstances in which the music came to life. The manuscript is not evidence of 'performances' but more an intimate resource for the sharing of private joys. A modern if somewhat banal analogy might be family evenings in front of the television, with what to watch and who to change channels being a matter for family negotiation.

J.S. Bach's son Carl Philipp Emmanuel was among the first to write out his harmonies rather than leave them for the player to guess from the bass line, and he would sometimes create alternative versions of varying difficulty. He didn't expect everyone to be able to play them: the most important thing was that as many as wanted to could access the music. J.S. Bach's sons and successors paved the way for the fully composed song, but the simple strophic *Lied* of conventional song-writers such as Johann Zumsteeg or Johann Reichardt did not appeal to Mozart or Haydn, whose art was invested in larger orchestral and choral forms. Mozart wrote the occasional song as a diversion and Beethoven brought a new sophistication with his weightier *Adelaide* and *An die ferne Geliebte*, though both these are closer to the more fashionable Italian arias than to Lieder. Like Haydn, Beethoven was perhaps sidetracked by the commercial opportunities offered by the English publisher who commissioned folk-song arrangements. The publication in 1821 of Schubert's op. 1, 'Erlkönig', with its cast of bizarre characters, and the vibrant imagery of 'Gretchen am Spinnrade', both circulated in private since their composition in 1814, marked a turning point in the history of the *Lied*.

The change in status of the *Lied* would not have happened without a far-reaching change in audience expectations. This was a multifaceted process in which publishing played a major part. Schubert (1797–1828) was not the only composer to complain about infrequent and nugatory payments for his songs, but the distribution of the music to the amateur market was hugely significant in shifting the public perception of song from entertainment to artistry. All composers' songs circulated in manuscript form among friends, and the semi-public evenings devoted to Schubert, the legendary *Schubertiades*, were part of a cultural transformation engineered by the artists, musicians, bureaucrats, students and others who attended them. They were a small minority of a prosperous middle class who enjoyed being entertained (the *Schubertiades* often ended with dancing) but also needed to feed their souls.

Towards the end of the eighteenth century, German songs would appear alongside Italian opera arias in the increasingly popular public concerts. These grew into events which might last several hours, the audience's interest being sustained by alternating choral, orchestral and vocal music with little in the way of coherent programme planning. Songs were not a major component of these events, at best a palate cleanser between heavier orchestral or choral fare, often brief displays of vocal fireworks before the next orchestral work. By the beginning of the nineteenth century the intricate convulsions of German bourgeois taste required something more than popular

Italian opera arias. An aria was, of course, a song of sorts, but decontextualised and possibly deprived of its orchestral accompaniment it was more of an instant fix than a deeper plunge into the psyche. Everyone knew the relevant bit of the plot, usually a moment of reflection between bursts of action, and at some point in its creation it would have been referred back to the composer if it didn't provide the singer with sufficient means to impress the audience. They were designed to elicit applause and were mostly too difficult to be sung round the piano at home.

The new *Lied* on the other hand did not easily present as a warm-up for greater music to come. It was emotionally complete in itself and not dependent on creative vocalism. Singers had been constantly criticised for massacring the poetic text with excessive ornamentation, and the more introspective songs of Beethoven and Schubert needed something other than impressive agility, especially as anyone could acquire the necessary technique at one of the new music schools or by reading the latest publications of the legendary singing teacher Manuel García and others. A *Lied* was about more than the singing, and to perform it in public required a completely new mindset.

Schubert was one of the first to appreciate this change in the performance aesthetic. He not only wrote what many considered the first true *Lied* ('Gretchen am Spinnrade', 19 October 1814) but he was also one of the first dedicated accompanists. He was perfectly capable of singing his own songs (and often did, accompanying himself), but in Johann Michael Vogl he found a kindred spirit who could discover things in the songs that the composer himself (and possibly Vogl) didn't know were there. The two met in 1817 when Schubert's landlord, the poet Franz von Schober, arranged for the singer to come and hear some of the young composer's songs. Many have speculated on how the meeting went, but the upshot was that the distinguished fifty-year-old singer took the twenty-year-old Schubert under his wing.

A composer himself and a former philosophy student, Vogl was the perfect musical foil and collaborator. He virtually invented the profession of Lieder singer and with Schubert as accompanist established the tradition of separate singer and pianist, enabling each to specialise and yet produce something greater than the sum of its parts. In performing for each other on stage they transformed the domestic aesthetic into professional chamber music, enabling intimate private music-making to become public event. The partnership between Schubert and Vogl surely had the same sort of complete artistic rapport and authority that Benjamin Britten and Peter Pears or Pierre Bernac and Francis Poulenc would find in the twentieth century. Pears was capable of accompanying himself and so was Vogl, but what singer would not leap at the chance to work with the composer who was also a creative and sensitive keyboard player; for a composer it could be life-changing.

Vogl was an opera singer trained in the eighteenth-century *bel canto* tradition; he would have been incapable of singing only what he saw in the score, and by elevating Schubert's songs to the status of opera arias he gave to Lieder an authority that supercharged them beyond the drawing room. He would have improvised spontaneously (compulsively, some might say) from a stock of ornaments learned over many years, but he wrote his most significant ones into a number of *Singbücher*. These versions have been much criticised by musicologists in the past and often ignored by modern performers; both have tended until recently to consider them trivial dilutions of the composer's art. Lieder singers have been reluctant to embrace the early-music movement, and the awkward reality of transcriptions by Vogl, García and others does indeed raise questions for those who believe the score is ultimately of more value than its performance.

The *Singbücher* are not prescriptions for performance; they are examples of what one singer liked to do, but they give us a priceless insight into the elastic relationship between performer and composer, the extent to which two performers shared the creative act. Many commentators who heard Schubert and Vogl perform recall Schubert being strict with his tempi. Whatever this meant, it didn't stop Vogl putting in pauses wherever he felt the unfolding narrative needed a bit of help, as any singer of the period would have done. The increased stature bestowed upon the young Schubert by the famous stage star elevated the entire process, music, poetry, performance to a previously unimaginable status. Audiences were also changed for ever, as those who heard the songs began to be aware that they were not simply being entertained but given a more nourishing and reflective experience. The *Lied* was acquiring a *gravitas* that still continues to evolve.

The song cycle is considered the peak of the classical songwriter's art, and to this day composers will often produce collections of songs linked by an overarching musical and literary narrative. In a Lieder recital from the mid-twentieth century onwards it has been the norm that performers would expect to sing the entire cycle in the published order. There is a formidable musicological literature explaining the intricacies of key relationships and textual exegesis, and a less objective discourse (often by singers or their teachers) on how the songs should be sung. This is very different from the expectations of nineteenth-century Lieder composers: the cycles of Schubert and Schumann were collections put together for publication and not conceived as an artistic whole in performance terms.

Schubert's *Die schöne Müllerin* appeared in 1824 in several volumes published months apart; Schumann's op. 25, *Myrthen* (like *Frauenliebe* also from 1840), compiled as a wedding present for Clara, consists of settings of seven different poets published in four volumes. With audiences used to hearing only a handful of songs at a time in the interminable mixed orchestral programmes, the biggest risk of adding more of them was boredom. Initially, this was mitigated by the pianist devising interludes between songs. Clara Schumann would happily insert some Bach or Mendelssohn (or something of her husband's) within a song cycle, and the practice continued well into the twentieth century. As well as giving the singer a break, it drew attention to the seriousness of the endeavour as embodied by the pianist. Of Schumann's published collections only *Dichterliebe* was described as a cycle. This was a brave move on the part of his publisher: singers worried about boring the public with long outpourings if the set had to be performed as a whole, and they were reluctant to buy complete collections.

Singers drawn to Lieder performance included some of the most famous performers of the day. Jenny Lind, the favourite singer of both Schumanns, satisfied a public demand for artistic purity with a disciplined and wholesome life. Other sopranos offered a different kind of excitement. Wilhelmine Schröder-Devrient, perhaps the most renowned German singer of the century, prolonged her ailing career by stamping her imprimatur on the songs of many composers including Schumann (she was the dedicatee of *Dichterliebe*, and 'Ich grolle nicht', which she accompanied herself, was one of her party pieces). Like Vogl, she was not above interpolating pauses and even speech or shrieks when the rhetorical moment took her. She was on the cusp of a fundamental change in the relationship between singer and composer, one of the first singers to live for their art and to live the life that many of the songs merely hinted at. She was certainly not the wife and mother that Mendelssohn expected his sister Fanny to become, whatever her considerable musical talent. Schumann, whose relationship with his wife Clara depended on a certain propriety, struggled to admit that the artist who had been there and done it all for real was not going to stay at home and look after the children. Schröder-Devrient had three marriages, many lovers and four children (custody awarded to the father), and yet she could still impress Robert and Clara Schumann with her performance of 'Du Ring an meinem Finger', having just seen off her second husband.

The daughter of celebrated actress Sophie Bürger Schröder and the baritone Friedrich Schröder, Wilhelmine had trained as a dancer and actress before coaching from her famous parents turned her into an opera singer. A forceful personality and charismatic stage presence, she cast her spell over a generation of composers including Weber and Wagner (he claimed she changed his life). Her fiercely energised performances came at a price however, and her willingness to do anything with her voice to achieve a dramatic end eventually ruled out the long-sustained lines of Italian opera. Her redoubtable rhetorical talents were perfect for the new declamatory roles that Wagner was beginning to create, but such was her speech-like delivery that opera critics began to write that she had never really learned to sing. Unable to sustain the kinds of roles she had created, she found a second career as a Lieder singer (her accompanists included Mendelssohn and Clara Schumann among others). It was Schröder-Devrient's performance of Schubert's setting of Goethe's 'Erlkönig' that convinced the poet late in life that the composer's music had merit. The Schumanns dedicated a volume of songs to her in 1848 (eleven by Robert, two by Clara). Her last years were spent applying her arts to the songs of the great Lieder composers of her generation, often accompanied by Clara Schumann.

The first complete public performance of *Frauenliebe* was given by Julius Stockhausen and Clara Schumann in 1862, though Wilhelmine Schröder-Devrient (who owned one of the copies of Schumann's manuscript) had performed it privately in 1848 and there may well have been others. Although a short cycle of only nine songs with a clear narrative thread (the only one of Schumann's cycles that has this), its earliest performances were often of three or four songs interrupted by piano interludes. Adelbert von Chamisso's poems chart the emotional journey of a young woman from youthful infatuation through engagement and marriage to widowhood. The poems read like a series of letters to herself or diary entries that reveal a surprising amount of intimate detail. The opening song could be written by a teenager of today, hopelessly blinded by love. Gender issues as we would understand them don't really surface until the fourth song, 'Du Ring an meinem Finger', which reveals her engagement and her intention to give herself entirely to him for ever, a submission that continues in song number 5. By number 6 she has been told the facts of life by her mother and is pregnant; in the seventh song, 'An meinem Herzen, an meiner Brust', she breastfeeds the baby. This is the most awkward song for modern singers to put across, especially men, but it may have had added poignancy for Chamisso's first readers, as in the higher echelons of society it was by no means certain that mothers would feed their own babies if they could command a wet nurse to do it for them. In song number 8 the husband dies, and the final song is a reflection, many years later, on a love that remained true throughout her widowhood.

Frauenliebe was one of Schumann's most popular Lieder collections and clearly played to perceived class and gender relations of nineteenth-century Germany. It was performed by both men and women, including the most ferociously liberal women such as Schröder-Devrient and Maria Malibran (who thought nothing of playing male roles on the stage, relishing a new set of vocal challenges). Audiences too were used to roles switching around (the last gender-compromised castrato roles were still being performed in the first half of the century). This is not to say that singers and their audiences did not discriminate between the sexes, but rather that they understood essential emotional tropes as common to both. Today there would seem to be little artistic mileage in anyone singing about a woman offering total submission to a man, especially if the poem is written by a man, but the affront to modern sensibilities is in the poetry, not in the music. The feminist critique of *Frauenliebe* is based on a modern listener reading the score and its text, not on a performance. The words have much further to go when filtered through first a composer's head and then a performer's voice.

From what we know of Schumann's compositional habits he would imagine a melody in his head while reading the poem (Brahms used a similar technique and would let the nascent tune gestate for a while before exploring it further). This is a performative process that musicology doesn't have access to and it perhaps explains part of the appeal his music has to singers despite any misgivings they may have about the poem. As a veteran improviser and composer of piano music Schumann must at least subconsciously have had an initial idea of key relationships and structure, but the creation of the piano part was guided in the first instance by the tune and not by the narrative. A singer starts with the tune, and then decisions have to be made about the poetry. If you want to put across the poet's meaning as closely as possible you only need to read the text (as happened in many a bourgeois drawing room). Composing the song, then the singing of it, adds layers of potential emotional and psychological response that take the process into much deeper territory. And that's before the music reaches the listeners, each of whom will have their own response.

There was nothing unusual about Chamisso's use of a ring as symbol of matrimonial commitment, though by the end of the century, as the upward elevation of the *Lied* continued apace, it had morphed into something much more sinister for poets and composers. Richard Dehmel conjured up several of them in his 1896 collection *Weib und*

Welt (Woman and World), one of which appears in Schoenberg's setting of his op. 2, 'Erwartung'; Stefan George had multiple rings in his songs from *Der siebente Ring* set by Webern. But there was still plenty of expressive potential in Schumann and Chamisso well into the twentieth century. There is a performance of Schumann's 'Du Ring' in Ingmar Bergman's 1982 film *Fanny och Alexander*, which meticulously recreates an evening in an Uppsala drawing room of 1907. We watch the monstrous Carl Ekdahl (Börje Ahlstedt) witnessing his wife Lydia (Christina Schollin) singing 'Du Ring an meinem Finger' accompanied by an aunt (pianist Käbi Laretei, Bergman's music consultant and fourth wife). Lydia manages to resist touching the ring until she kisses it at the start of the piano postlude, so the tautological gesture doesn't distract from the singing (fingering the ring is always a risk in a modern performance). The longest shot is of Ekdahl, who goes through a range of responses as the song progresses, as Dean Flower put it, 'sneering at first, and then surprised and (removing his glasses) affected, then deeply moved (as the song reaches its climax), tearful, longing for her, then uneasy, embarrassed, then (replacing his glasses) contemptuous again'. Although in Börje Ahlstedt we are watching one of Bergman's finest actors, this scene is a reminder that there is no way to predict any listener's response. Whatever meanings the singer intends, each person in the room will have his or her own interpretation. The scene also brings to life those etchings from the time of Schubert onwards of convivial entertainment in bourgeois parlours. It was in just such a room that Jenny Lind (also an admirer of *Frauenliebe*) would have begun her career as a Lieder singer.

There might come a time when men's historical treatment of women may be so far in the past that *Frauenliebe* will itself be history. But in the meantime creative performers will still attempt to mediate between ancient and modern readings. The printed page is permanent:

it embodies its own history and reception. Performance is a different process altogether: it lasts as long as a song takes to sing, and in that ever vanishing time-span singers can take the song wherever they like. A musicologist can point to the character and shape of a phrase that seems to elucidate the composer's interpretation of the poetry, but if the performer doesn't see it that way the listener probably won't either. The performer also has the luxury of a potentially infinite number of possibilities, none of which needs be definitive, unlike the historian or musicologist trapped in a written medium. When nineteenth-century performers reinvented the domestic *Lied* as great art they took a major stake in what any song might actually mean. Performers don't just reproduce the score, they extrapolate on it in the moment. Those who perform *Frauenliebe* are looking for human truths to emerge regardless of who wrote the poem and why.

There are two broad historical schools of thought about the nature of the *Lied* for performers: either the songs are suffused with a Romantic lyricism that is sufficient unto itself, or the singer is assuming a persona appropriate for the poet's vision. The distinction is a little artificial: critics at the time emphasised the lyrical, which may have made sense to amateurs buying scores to try at home, but the wider reputation of the composers depended on professional performances by famous opera singers whose own reputations were secured by their visible stage presence. The problem with not acting a role is that words still have meanings, and even leaving aside Chamisso's female impersonation, many singers today would find it hard to project the subservience of one human to another, let alone the specific intimacy of breastfeeding. And yet, women (and men) who have no children perform this, happily witnessed by a male pianist. As singers of *Frauenliebe* will quickly point out, fiction is fiction: H.G. Wells didn't have to make a time machine in order to write about it. Nor do you have to mean by your singing what the poet meant by his writing, otherwise many Renaissance and Baroque motets would remain unsung.

It was not just the singing that propelled the *Lied* into the public domain, but a new relationship between composers and their own performances. Unlike the performers of the eighteenth century and earlier, the newer generation of composers were often not singers themselves. Lieder composers performed their own songs but as professional pianists, and the evolution of the piano as an instrument and the techniques of its players gave accompaniment a new authority. Song accompaniments became so elaborate that only the most multi-talented performers were comfortable singing and playing at the same time. Songs could also take on a new life in piano arrange-ments, not just in the virtuoso hands of Franz Liszt, but as something that any talented musician could try their hand at. The upward trajec-tory of the *Lied* was confirmed by Brahms whose status as a composer was preceded by his success as a concert pianist. Accompanying his own songs, especially when the singer was a performer of the status of Julius Stockhausen, rooted the *Lied* firmly in the mainstream.

The other composer to contribute to the transformation of the *Lied* was Gustav Mahler (1860–1911). We don't think of him as a Lieder composer as his songs are more usually heard in their symphonic versions. Nearly all of them either began life as songs with piano, or were subsequently arranged as such. The association of song with the great conductor and his orchestral writing undoubtedly reinforced the legitimacy of the *Lied* as great art. More importantly, Mahler influenced the next generation of Lieder composers, Schoenberg, Webern and Berg. A Mahler piano reduc-tion of his orchestral songs is a miracle of transparency, quite unlike the density of a Brahms piano part. This economy of means resur-faces in the Second Viennese School, eventually leading to the systematic discipline of serialism.

Mahler, like Schumann and Mendelssohn, also had a significant female musician in the family. His wife, Alma Schindler, had been a pupil of Alexander Zemlinsky (with whom she had a brief affair). Mahler, as had Schumann before him, decided there was room for only one composer in the family, and it was only after the shock of her affair with the architect Walter Gropius that he relented and encouraged Alma to return to composition. It was too late: she published a total of fourteen songs before giving up composing in 1915 and embarking on an eventful life, first marrying Gropius, then the writer Franz Werfel, becoming an American citizen in 1946, and outliving her first husband Mahler by fifty-three years.

Zemlinsky was a pivotal figure in the lives and careers of both established and up-and-coming musicians. A composer, conductor and teacher, protégé of Brahms, friend and teacher of Schoenberg, his first opera was conducted by Mahler in 1900; Zemlinsky conducted the first performance of Schoenberg's *Erwartung* in 1924. At the turn of the century the older composers and the new generation were very close. Brahms had been dead for three years (at the age of sixty-four), Zemlinsky was not yet thirty, Mahler was forty (with only eleven years left to live), Schoenberg was twenty-six, and the precocious Webern only seventeen. Behind the new generation stood the ghost of Wagner, dead seventeen years, and from whom they would all claim a line of descent. In the febrile atmosphere of Vienna, famously conservative and yet home to some of the most radical artists and composers of the period, one might expect the post-Brahms *Lied* to achieve yet new artistic heights. This indeed it did: song had not only become a means by which composers could express their most intimate thoughts; in the hands of Schoenberg and Webern (Berg to a lesser extent) it became the testing ground for refashioning composition altogether.

The immediate successor to Brahms and Hugo Wolf as Lieder composers was Arnold Schoenberg. Before studying briefly with Zemlinsky, Schoenberg had in effect taught himself by close readings of Brahms and especially Wagner. His earliest published works are songs, and had his subsequent career not been so controversial (and, to many singers, a little frightening), we might celebrate these works as among the peaks of Romantic song. As Schubert and Schumann had their favourite contemporary poets, Schoenberg was drawn at first to the poetry of Richard Dehmel, especially his anthology *Weib und Welt* of 1896. The following year Dehmel was tried for obscenity (the poems appeared to promote extra-marital sex) and blasphemy (Jesus with earthly appetites), and it may have been the controversy surrounding the case that first drew the composer's attention to the poet. Dehmel was acquitted though required to excise one poem and burn the edition which contained it. *Weib und Welt* was inspired by the poet's passion for Ida Auerbach whom he married in 1901. Schoenberg was at the time infatuated with Mathilde Zemlinsky, his teacher's sister, whom he married in the same year.

In the Dehmel settings Schoenberg displays an unprecedented erotic intimacy to which he would never return, an extraordinary Romantic efflorescence, before leaving chromaticism (and most of his audience) behind. In 'Schenk mir deinen goldenen Kamm', *Jesus bettelt* (Jesus Begs) in *Weib und Welt*, Jesus combs a woman's hair in the bath. We know she's called Mary, but it is only with the last word of the song that we discover it's Mary Magdalene; this was presumably one of the poems that so exercised the censor. If you are familiar with Gregorian chant and are wondering where you have heard Schoenberg's 'Magdalene' phrase before, it is uncannily similar to the climactic phrase towards the end of the *Salve Regina* chant on the words 'O Maria', a rather different Maria. One wonders what the censors would have made of that had anyone made the connection (though as a Jewish convert to Protestantism, Schoenberg himself may not have done). Beneath the shades of sex and religion, a man is asking a woman to give herself to him entirely: 'schenken' is to give a gift, and it doesn't stop with the comb – he wants her whole self. The longings of Chamisso's woman seem positively quaint compared with the barely suppressed eroticism of Dehmel.

Schoenberg began at least ten songs in 1899, the year of *Jesus bettelt*, many of them to poems by Dehmel. His obsession with the poet reached its apogee at the end of that year in *Verklärte Nacht* (Transfigured Night), a string sextet structured around the verses of Dehmel's poem (from the early editions of *Weib und Welt*), which is not actually sung but is matched, programme-like, to sections of the music. Dehmel later wrote to Schoenberg that he was so entranced by the music that he forgot to follow along. Liszt and Mahler had helped to raise the profile of Lieder by transforming them into instrumental music; in its ironic way, *Verklärte Nacht* took the process one stage further by keeping the text but leaving any connection to melody to the listener's imagination.

Webern owned ten volumes of poems by Dehmel, the first an eighteenth-birthday present from his cousin Ernst Diez in 1901, which yielded three early Dehmel songs. In 1903, Webern was making orchestral arrangements of songs by Wolf and Schubert, but later that year he heard a performance of *Verklärte Nacht* which inspired him to ask Schoenberg for lessons. The five Dehmel settings, four of them to poems from *Weib und Welt*, composed between 1906 and 1908, perhaps represent the culmination of his Schoenberg studies. They are the last Webern songs which are recognisably tonal (just) and Webern seems to have envisaged them as a cycle (though his own programming of his songs suggests otherwise). He didn't publish them (they were rediscovered in 1961) perhaps because he felt his elaborations on the nocturnal musings of Dehmel were more appropriately expressed in his atonal settings of Stefan George that followed shortly afterwards.

Both poets' verses featured men in impossible relationships usually wandering forlornly in a moonlit landscape while the universe turned mystically against them on its axis. Both composers admired both poets and explored George's poems at the same time. Schoenberg used two poems from George's literary tour de force *Der siebente Ring* in his Second String Quartet (dedicated to his wife Mathilde, despite discovering her affair with the artist Richard Gerstl as he was finishing the piece). He used George more extensively in *Das Buch der hängenden Gärten* (The Book of the Hanging Gardens), a cycle of fifteen songs composed in 1908–09 and first performed in 1910 by Martha Winternitz-Dorda (who took part in the first performance of Mahler's Eighth Symphony in the same year). George's poems, published in 1895 and dedicated to Dehmel's first wife Paula, the poet's muse since 1892, proved to be the catalyst for Schoenberg's first venture into atonality. This was a significant step on the path to audience alienation. Tonality has audible rules which not only guide the composer but enable listeners to find their way through a song, especially one they haven't heard before. Sonata form, well worn over more than a century of use, even in its most elaborate ramblings had a beginning, a middle and an end. *Das Buch* is not like that, each short song evolving linearly with no anchor in a particular key.

Schoenberg's programme note for the first performance goes some way to explaining how the cycle differs from composerly convention. He had realised, listening to Schubert, that he only understood the song and its poem as a complete whole, the conventional correlation between music and text meaning nothing to him. This places him directly at odds with many singers, for whom conceiving of a song as a single thought is almost impossible. And yet on the surface the vocal lines are not so different from those of Brahms. More angular and less obviously melodic, the phrase shapes are more or less as you would expect and the songs can be very satisfying to sing. The bigger challenge is for the listener, who needs either to be incredibly intellectually nimble, or to accept that simply witnessing great art is enough: you don't have to understand it.

Webern's shift to atonality paralleled that of Schoenberg. He too chose poems by Stefan George for his two sets of songs, ops. 3 and 4, the two composers writing their respective atonal settings at about the same time. The final stage of Webern's journey out of the tonal solar system was provided by Hildegard Jone. Dehmel and George were public property, and their poems were available for any composer to set to music. In Hildegard Jone, Webern found a muse that was only his, and with whom he was spiritually totally at one. Jone was born Hildegard Huber, studied art, and married her sculpture teacher Josef Humplik, who went on to create portrait heads of Mahler, Webern and Berg, as well as many prominent writers and artists. Webern first met the couple at an exhibition of Humplik's work and soon became a family friend. Hildegard had given herself the name Jone after the Greek *Ion* in reference to her studies of Attic sculpture, but her art was increasingly expressed in poetry. Like the verses of Dehmel and George, her work is suffused with a quasi-religious mysticism, expressed in elegant, compressed lines which perfectly suited Webern's economy of expression. But more than that, the composer found in the poet a reflection of himself, someone who, though not herself musical, always understood what he was trying to achieve and recognised it when he got there. From his op. 23 songs onwards, all Webern's vocal works were set to her texts.

The *Drei Gesänge* op. 23, completed in 1934, manage to combine the delicacy of poetic metre with the rigour of a tone row to produce songs which some have compared to those of Schubert. The vocal lines do contain Webern's occasional rhetorical extremes at the beginning and ending of phrases, but the writing has a linear smoothness supported by filigree piano figures punctured by serial chords. In the op. 25 Lieder of later that year, the last songs Webern wrote, the tone row migrates from voice to piano and back, as delicate as a breath of wind. They are the purest expression of Webern's art and seem to take the trajectory of the *Lied* to its endpoint. He never heard either cycle performed. Both sets were scheduled for a sixtieth-birthday celebration in Basel in 1943 (Webern was stuck in war-torn Vienna), but in the event the soprano Marguerite Gradmann-Lüscher decided against op. 25, which went unperformed until 1952. It was premiered in New York by Bethany Beardslee, a singer after Webern's own heart who would later be celebrated for her recording and performances of Schoenberg's *Pierrot Lunaire*, among many other modernist composers.

There was the ghost of a performance documented by Lauriejean Reinhardt in her note to the Jone poems in the Moldenhauer archives. In November 1944 both cycles were scheduled to be performed in Vienna at a poetry reading of Jone's verse in the archbishop's palace. There was much discussion between Webern and Jone about the songs and the readings of the poetry, with each trying to persuade the other to recite. The singer booked to perform the songs pulled out so there was no performance, but instead Webern coached his friend, the poet and actor Werner Riemerschmid, to declaim the poems so that they matched the nuances of the music as closely as possible. Riemerschmid's rendering may have been as convincing as a singer's might have been, especially of the op. 25 poems which slip by so quickly there is barely time for a trained singer to deploy her full technique. It's almost as though Webern identified so closely with Jone's verses that the music, refined and reduced to its essence, had become one with the poetry and no longer needed to exist on its own. Between 'Vorfrühling', the magical first song by the sixteen-year-old schoolboy, and the final songs of his Jone epiphany, Webern lost none of his conciseness and elegance, but he did lose a potential audience (and, possibly, the need for one).

Schoenberg and Webern lifted the *Lied* beyond the stratosphere from which they could no longer see their audience. Schoenberg may not have been entirely serious when he said that he might get things thrown at him for suggesting that the score was complete in itself and didn't need the arrogant input of performers, but his comment fore-shadowed much musicology which tended to see just the music on the page. Schubert was one of the last composers to sing his own songs in public; his melodies came out of his mouth. I suspect Schumann's and Brahms's melodies came in the first instance via their pianist fingers. Once they dispensed with tonality Schoenberg and Webern's tunes became tone rows, created on paper, bypassing both instrument and voice. They gave the *Lied* new life but as an abstrac-tion, an aural expression of the art of Klimt, Kandinsky and Gerstl.

Schoenberg experimented further with *Pierrot Lunaire* and his other ventures into *Sprechgesang*, but his founding of the Verein für musikalische Privataufführungen (Society for Private Musical Performances) in Vienna in 1918 was an admission that only a few very sophisticated people would come close to understanding his music. For those who made the attempt he would write detailed programme notes trying to explain how the music worked; critics were excluded, further narrowing the potential audience. Schoenberg was certain of his own place in music history, but he never fully under-stood the consequences. That his music was performed at all in his own lifetime was due to a small but vociferous number of benefactors and supporters who recognised his genius, and to the even smaller number of extraordinary singers, mainly sopranos, who were capable of singing his music. Marie Gutheil-Schoder, the first performer of

Erwartung, also performed *Pierrot* after its first controversial premiere with Albertine Zehme; Emmy Heim was one of several singers who tried to integrate songs from the Second Viennese School into the mainstream, performing Berg and Schoenberg (including the first performances of songs from op. 4 and op. 6) alongside Schubert and Schumann. After the premiere of *Das Buch*, Martha Winternitz-Dorda went on to sing Tove in *Gurrelieder*. Webern was less fortunate in his performers. He was a busy and successful conductor and teacher, and perhaps understood that his songs were so difficult to perform that seeing them appear in print was a sufficient sign of his place in musical history.

The *Lied* didn't begin on 19 October 1814, nor did it end with Webern's *Jonelieder* or his accidental shooting on 15 September 1945, but the two dates neatly bookend a remarkable period during which song developed into an abstract musical entity and a vehicle for the most profound musical expression. The family environment had been the crucible in which Schubert, Mendelssohn and Schumann forged their art. Unlike the composers of all the title songs in this book so far, none of the three was really a singer: all were professional composers, as most songwriters would be in the future. They all died young, and had they not been struck down by syphilis, stroke and schizophrenia respectively, could have lived to hear the first recordings of their songs. All were privately educated prodigies, spared the rigours and banalities of institutional learning. Mostly, they were able to write without having to worry about earning a living and while conscious of their potential audience could focus on the integrity of their art. The careers of Mendelssohn, Schumann and Mahler overshadowed those of the significant women in their lives, leaving us with powerful examples of the relative positions of both sexes in terms of their creativity and the social environment in which they had to function. The *Lied* was able to mitigate some of the more obvious aspects of gender imbalance thanks to the magic wrought by charismatic performers of both sexes who wrenched it from the domestic shallows into the deeper waters of high art.

There are no black-and-white answers to the questions raised by *Frauenliebe*. There is nowhere on a Venn diagram where what the musicologist sees, the performer sings and what the listener hears can all be in the same space. In the end it comes down to what words may or may not mean. In nineteenth-century Europe there was no doubt: it was important that the audience understood exactly what a song was about, so translation was more important than the sound of the original language. Chamisso's text was comfortingly *innig* and its sentiments represented part of the emotional bedrock of middle-class German society. Today our needs are met by other kinds of song: by the end of the century the *Lied* had become art song and the singer duly became that mysterious and unknowable entity, an artist. Their art was subservient to that of the composer, whose genius eventually forbade any additions to the score beyond the occasional appoggiatura or trill. Finally, the phonograph, after a gloriously alea-toric start, captured the composer's notes and could repeat them *ad infinitum*. The *Lied* was marooned in its own artistry.

Today, a singer's reputation still depends on his or her interpreta-tion of the synthesis of words and music, and the constant repetition of a (mostly) very small repertoire tends to yield incremental changes which are carried forward into the singer's unique 'interpretation'. This is very much how an opera singer refines his or her roles, or how a string quartet strives towards the perfect performance on which its reputation will depend. It is a defining characteristic of classical music: both the score and its performance are freighted with a sacral quality, and this condition will replicate itself for as long as the music is valued more than its performance.

Sketch of Erik Satie playing the harmonium, by Santiago Rusiñol (1891).

8

ERIK SATIE

LUDIONS

The songs of Erik Satie (1866–1925) are some of the briefest and weirdest *mélodies* ever composed; they don't rate more than a paragraph in most histories of song. In fact, *mélodie*, the French term equivalent to the German *Lied* and usually applied to the great songs of Debussy, Duparc, Fauré and others, isn't really an adequate description of a Satie work for voice and piano. There is nothing remotely *Lied*-like about them (apart from their Webern-like brevity): they are peculiarly French, and even more specifically, Parisian. Satie cared little for his antecedents, lived a self-consciously bohemian life, and although he probably didn't think about it, anticipated both the avant-garde and minimalism of the twentieth century. In writing both *mélodies* and cabaret song he recognised (and in effect tried to bridge) a widening gap between the elite and the 'popular', and his work can be compared to some of the more radical fusions of popular and classical in the present.

Unlike most composers he had no independent means and except for a brief period of relative prosperity was not ashamed to flaunt his poverty. He invented a kind of 'poverty by conviction' as Stravinsky put it, which enabled him to engage with the bourgeoisie who provided him with both sustenance and artistic opportunity. He was, in some respects, a man out of his time whose stuttering career as a pianist and composer was supported by a number of other composers, who were very much part of the establishment and yet were fascinated by his strangeness. *Ludions* was his last set of songs, composed in 1923, two years before his death.

French-speaking courts and chapels had provided a unique source of song from the *trouvères* and troubadours through to the centuries of Franco-Flemish polyphony, which in turn generated custom-made solo songs all over Europe. The *chansons* of Janequin, Claude Le Jeune and their contemporaries had a wide currency as they could be arranged for whoever was willing to sing and/or play them. The word *chanson*, from the Occitan *canso*, has survived as a generic term to the present, although those of a certain etymological disposition will use it rather more precisely. In the last quarter of the sixteenth century the *chanson* was complemented by an elegant variety of lute song, which gained traction at the French courts. Known as *airs de cour*, these strophic songs are sometimes compared to English lute songs, but they flourished well into the seventeenth century over a period of roughly a century compared with the single generation of English lute-song composers. *Airs de cour* mark the beginning of a specifically French song culture, with tunes crafted around the quantitative stresses of the French language and a unique style of ornamentation, especially at cadences. Bénigne de Bacilly's *Remarques curieuses sur l'art de bien chanter*, which went through four editions between 1668 and 1681, is ultimately about teaching French singers how to unite the proper pronunciation of their language with the delicacy and elegance of the new songs. The eighteenth-century French drawing room heard continuo songs from Lully and Couperin (when they could be diverted from opera and dance), and by the turn of the century the *romance* was available as a simpler and more homely alternative to opera arias.

In nineteenth-century France, as in Germany, the social contexts of song consisted of the rambling public concert at one end of the performance spectrum, usually by opera singers, and at the other end the evenings at home round the piano with recently purchased sheet music. In between came a more exalted semi-public institution known as the salon, where the wealthy, literate, artistic and musical (or those who aspired to be any combination of the above) assembled by invitation for eating, drinking and entertainment. The socially prestigious would have regular days on which they would have open house for those understood to have an open invitation. Unlike the usual post-prandial ritual of women retiring to the drawing room and men remaining at the table to smoke cigars, these were occasions where both sexes mingled freely (and both possibly smoked). For performers, often invited because they were the visiting celebrity, this might need some negotiating: the most successful were courted by the social elite and handsomely rewarded; the younger or less successful were patronised and expected to sing for their supper. Estimating the social status of individual musicians was a fine art; everyone who attended a salon was there to be seen and expected their social status to be appreciated.

The term *romance*, if not Romantic when it first appeared in Rousseau's dictionary of 1767, would become so in the hands of Victor Hugo, Alfred de Musset, Théophile Gautier and Alphonse de Lamartine. The more elaborate verses of the Romantic poets inspired more structured tunes with complex piano parts, and while the *romance* continued to flourish, the more sophisticated examples began to be referred to as *mélodies*. Then, in the 1830s, Paris discovered Schubert, thanks to the advocacy of the tenor Adolphe Nourrit.

Nourrit was a highly cultured man, a friend of Rossini, Liszt and Chopin, and creator of some of the earliest dramatic roles at the Paris Opéra until he was displaced in 1837 by Gilbert-Louis Duprez. Duprez had returned from Italy possessed of the treasure that he would leave to all future operatic tenors, the *ut de poitrine* or chested top C. Nourrit, whose top notes would have been sung in a kind of falsetto, was staggered by the power of the new sound, and set off for Italy to study with Donizetti (another composer who might have been a great songwriter had his seventy operas not kept him so busy). Despite his well-documented progress Nourrit despaired of renewing his vocal powers and in a fit of depression jumped off the roof of a Neapolitan *palazzo* four days after his thirty-seventh birthday in 1839. There had been early signs of his mental decline in his letters to his wife Adèle, who had stayed behind in Paris. On one occasion he wrote of singing Schubert in French to Donizetti but being so focused on his Italian that he couldn't find his native language. At his funeral Chopin played an organ arrangement of Schubert's 'Die Sterne', which Nourrit used to love to sing, one of many Schubert songs that the great French tenor had introduced to Parisian salon audiences.

Nourrit had first come across Schubert when he heard Liszt playing his transcription of 'Erlkönig' at a salon hosted by a Hungarian banker in Paris. The tenor was transfixed on hearing it and immediately asked Liszt to play it again. You should sing it yourself, came the reply, and thus began their shared obsession with the Schubert songs which they went on to perform many times together. Nourrit commissioned translations and attempted his own, though aware that Goethe's poetry was really beyond him. The Schubert effect, even in French translation, was perhaps the biggest stimulus to the evolution of the *mélodie*. Nourrit passed on his love of Schubert to his pupil Pierre-François Wartel, who promoted not only Schubert in France but also the new generation of French songwriters abroad.

Wartel had a brief career at the Opéra. He sang small roles alongside Nourrit and in 1836 had even taken over from him in Masaniello's *La Muette de Portici* when Nourrit's voice failed him mid-performance. From the early 1840s, Wartel turned increasingly to song recitals in salons and concert rooms accompanied by his wife Thérèse (a composer and the first female pianist to be admitted to the Orchestre de la Société des Concerts du Conservatoire). By combining their salon performances with tours of public recitals the duo celebrated song in much the same way as the burgeoning German Lieder partnerships.

Wartel was the first to perform songs of Berlioz outside France and had spectacular success in Vienna singing Schubert songs in French, which he programmed alongside his native French *romance* repertoire. The early-nineteenth-century *romance* had some similarities to the earliest German Lieder: both are strophic and straightforward, tuneful and vocally undemanding. The *Lied* made a quantum leap with Schubert and changed its nature altogether. In part thanks to Schubert, some French composers began to see creative possibilities in the song form that would transcend the simplicity of the *romance*, and from about the middle of the century these more elaborate songs were increasingly considered to be *mélodies*. Other composers continued to write *romances* and both forms sat happily alongside Italian opera arias in Parisian salons.

The later composers of *mélodies* from Emmanuel Chabrier onwards today rank with the great Lieder writers as representing a peak of the song form. Their predecessors have not fared so well, and many mid-century French composers have been almost entirely forgotten. The term *mélodie*, first used by Berlioz, indicated something more sophisticated than the *romance*, and is slightly ironic in that the new elements of the *mélodie* involved more sophisticated piano parts and an expansion of the strophic form rather than having anything to do with the tunes. This is especially obvious in Berlioz's *Les nuits d'été* dating from 1840. Originally conceived as a set of songs for different voices with piano, the collection has been turned by twentieth-century performers into a song cycle, with a single soloist performing Berlioz's later orchestral arrangement. The vocal lines have the simplicity of salon songs, but enveloped in an almost Mahlerian orchestration the songs are impossible to imagine in even the largest drawing room.

The twentieth-century success of *Les nuits d'été* has eclipsed not only the other fifty or so songs by Berlioz but almost all of those by his contemporaries. Among the French composers promoted abroad by Wartel was Hippolyte Monpou (not to be confused with the much later and similarly named Catalan Federico Mompou). Monpou was born in 1804 and at the age of sixteen was briefly the organist of Tours Cathedral. He drifted into writing *romances* and his first attempt, a setting of Alfred de Musset's 'L'Andalouse', brought him considerable fame. Monpou is said to have offered it to several publishers before knocking on the door of Antoine Lemoine, who gave him fifty francs which he spent carousing with his friends Duprez, Renard and Wartel. After a convivial evening they ended up at a dance hall where the four of them spontaneously formed a string quartet and entertained the surprised clientele into the night.

'L'Andalouse' is a bold tune accompanied by plenty of root-position piano chords and it is easy to imagine the composer singing it at the piano. Monpou was a charismatic singer-songwriter much in demand in Parisian salons; he was not, as the poet Théophile Gautier proclaimed, the equal of Berlioz (both composers set Victor Hugo's *La Captive* and Berlioz's version was something of a hit), but he was very much his own man. Frits Noske, in his classic book on the history of French song, doesn't really rate Monpou's music: 'a mixture of artistic temerity, bourgeois sentimentality and forced extravagance' – all of which Satie would be guilty of at some point in his career a generation or so later. But Noske was so taken with Monpou's character that he has an Appendix devoted to quotes from Gautier and others, including a letter to an unnamed friend in which the composer sets out his Romantic credentials and declines to have anything to do with teaching or the operatic establishment. Sadly, Monpou did succumb to the lure of the stage and went on to write several operas for the Opéra-Comique, dying at the age of thirty-seven, having ruined his health while failing to complete what turned out to be his last opera, *Lambert Simnel*.

A single song could make a composer's reputation. This doesn't mean his songs are performed today, but it may earn the composer a place in music-history books. Louis Niedermeyer is another composer not quite in the Berlioz league but whose most famous song earned him praise from his contemporaries and successors. Camille Saint-Saëns considered Niedermeyer's 'Le Lac' a landmark in the evolution of French song. Niedermeyer had early success as an opera composer having studied in Naples with Rossini, and he begins 'Le Lac' in dramatic fashion before varying six Lamartine strophes with a mixture of quasi-aria and more wistful sections he called *romance*. There are hints of Schubert in the melodic writing, but the accompaniment never gets so complicated that it can't be arranged for amateur mandolin players or whatever the publisher can dream up.

The sophisticated charms of the *romance* were further enhanced by Liszt, whose mercurial presence entranced salon audiences in half the countries of Europe. He was a fluent French speaker and set poems by Victor Hugo among others. His virtuosity (and his transcriptions of Schubert songs) undoubtedly made it easier for his listeners to cope with the next steps in compositional complexity. The giant figures of Charles Gounod (more than two hundred songs) and Camille Saint-Saens (for whom Victor Hugo was a favourite) kept the sweeping melodic lines of *romance* but wrote increasingly elaborate and independent piano parts, influenced more perhaps by Schumann.

The three parallel universes in which song was performed all over Europe (the home, the salon and the public stage) become much easier to identify towards the end of the century. Singers increasingly appeared in concert halls where they could develop a public persona, performing in their own space on a stage from which their listeners were inevitably excluded. This had subtle effects on the musical activities in the bourgeois home, as 'common' stage gestures found their way from the professional stage into the domain of the cultivated amateur, even as the salon itself was giving way to the café as the creative venue of choice. If there has ever been a golden age of performing, the nineteenth-century European salon is a serious candidate for consideration: compromised by class it may have been, but it created a symbiotic closeness between those who make the music and those for whom they made it.

Social conventions aside, artistically the salon meant there was a chance to perform in an intimate, relatively informal setting, where the important thing was the perceived sincerity of the artist, so mistakes or poor choices were easily forgiven. The performers were embedded in the audience: after they had done their turn someone else would get up and take their place and comparisons were discreetly made. Even if the biggest stars were paid appearance money, the parties were usually sufficiently informal for the competent amateur (and there were many of these) to take his or her turn and be flattered by the generosity shown by the professional performers.

Salons were not just social events for the wealthy and cultured: they were centres of creative work. Choreographers could experiment with dance, painters could exhibit, and composers could try out new pieces in front of publishers, curators and businessmen. Public concerts brought fame and occasional profit, but for many musicians the salon was where they plied their trade. As a means of generating new work and raising the profile of song among a key demographic the salon was, alongside the creative partnerships between composers and performers, a crucial driver of the genre. Many of the old upper class or the newly wealthy paraded their aesthetic credentials by supporting composers and performers (though the musicians were always at risk of being fed and watered in separate quarters). The most spectacularly generous was the Princess de Polignac, who built herself a private concert hall and dedicated her life to the arts.

La Princesse Edmond de Polignac was born Winnaretta Singer, one of twenty-four children of the American sewing-machine entrepreneur, sometime actor and charismatic serial adulterer Isaac Singer and his Anglo-French American wife Isabella Boyer. Winnaretta was born in New York, but the family's upwardly mobile journey eventually took them to Paris. Isaac also built a substantial country house for them all at Paignton in Devon in the west of England, where he died in 1875, whereupon Winnaretta and her mother moved back to Paris and Winnaretta set about creating the social circumstances in which she would spend her vast inheritance on the arts.

The Parisian social scene consisted of three broad levels: the aristocracy at the top, most of whom spent their time at leisure, an entirely self-contained clique that one could only enter by marriage. Many of them were in straitened financial circumstances, which could be improved (at some social cost) by marrying into the next tier down, the *haute bourgeoisie*, successful bankers, merchants and entrepreneurs and their offspring. The *bourgeoisie* aspired to the status of those above them but as they earned money as opposed to inheriting it they were doomed to be forever *nouveaux* unless they married above themselves. Below them came a client caste of musicians, artists, writers, anyone involved in the arts. It was their task to identify patrons from the higher echelons to save them having to work for a living, a fate which no member of society wished upon themselves. Although social display and competition characterised all these gatherings, some had particular themes or clientele. Towards the bottom end of the social scale, and perhaps involving a bit of downward mobility on the part of the well heeled, were those gatherings given by and for artists and poets, the most celebrated of which were Stéphane Mallarmé's weekly *mardis* at which any bohemian artist might be spotted.

In possession of a fantastic fortune, Winnaretta needed to affirm her place in society by marrying a suitable prince. Louis-Vilfred, third son of the Marquis de Scey-Montbéliard, duly obliged, and was surprised to discover on his wedding night that his bride's inclinations were elsewhere. It was the first of two unconsummated marriages, the second of which, to the cultivated amateur composer Prince Edmond de Polignac who was twice her age, turned into a platonic success story that was a beacon of civility in the decadent Parisian social whirl. It took a while, but from the late 1880s onwards, Winnaretta's aristocratic status enabled her to create a salon that would bring together some of the Western world's most prominent musicians, poets and artists, offering them financial support in the form of commissions and performances as well as introductions to key figures who would further their careers.

Emmanuel Chabrier and Gabriel Fauré were among the first composers taken under the princess's wing. Chabrier, an indefatigable performer of his own and other composers' music, was a frequent visitor, accompanying himself on the piano. The princess had a deeper relationship with Fauré, a former pupil of Niedermeyer and Camille Saint-Saëns, and in 1891 resolved to rescue him from his tedious round of piano lessons and services at the Église de la Madeleine by offering him a princessly sum for a new work. Neither had a clear idea of what form this might take, but the two decided to ask Paul Verlaine to write a suitable text. Verlaine, the decadents' decadent, was in the throes of the absinthe and drug addiction that would kill him four years later. At first he declined Winnaretta's fee, asking instead for a contribution to his tailor or bootmaker's account, and setting in train a bizarre set of circumstances that would yield some of Fauré's most famous songs; the proposed commission would also severely test the composer's relationship with the princess and Verlaine's relationship with both of them. Fauré agreed the parameters of the piece in the hospital where the poet was being treated, but Verlaine was incapable of creative work and for several months frustrated Fauré's attempts to get him started.

To give him a bit of a break, Winnaretta decided to invite Fauré to spend some time in Venice at a *palazzo* on the Grand Canal that she and her entourage had taken for the summer. There he sat in a nearby café exploring Verlaine's previous work, and wrote the first of his *Cinq mélodies 'de Venise'*, which was then performed at a party on a boat in the lagoon. But the princess got fed up with waiting for Verlaine and conceived the idea of asking Maurice Bouchor to write a libretto on the life of the Buddha, only for Verlaine to emerge from alcoholic stupor to propose a *commedia* piece in which the three principal characters discoursed on life and love from hospital beds. Winnaretta was excited by both ideas, Fauré liked neither; Winnaretta never did get her opera. The *Cinq mélodies 'de Venise'*, dedicated to the princess, were performed at the opening of her newly enlarged and remodelled salon in January 1892 by tenor Maurice Bagès, a frequent guest who often sang Schubert and who three years earlier had premiered Claude Debussy's *Ariettes oubliées*. Fauré accompanied at the piano. Winnaretta attempted to progress the Buddha idea, and three years later managed to get a libretto out of Albert Samain, which Fauré wanted nothing to do with. Both sides were taken by surprise by each other's reaction, the princess never quite forgiving the composer for his disloyalty.

There was no typical Polignac salon: an evening might feature anything from Beethoven sonatas to piano concertos, Renaissance *chansons* to eighteenth-century oratorios or staged scenes from opera. But the thread that ran throughout this socio-musical munificence was song. The princess was an accomplished pianist and her second husband had studied at the Paris Conservatoire under Henri Reber, one of the key figures in the transformation of *chanson* into *mélodie*. Her commissions were usually for more substantial works, Stravinky's *Renard*, an opera by Milhaud, de Falla's *El retablo de Maese Pedro* (complete with puppets), piano concertos by Poulenc and Tailleferre, a symphony by Weill, but Debussy, Ravel, Milhaud, Poulenc, Auric and a host of other composers were regularly given a platform for their songs, often accompanying them themselves.

Into this glittering world walked (literally) Erik Satie. In a world where everyone was competing for social advancement of one sort or another, a composer who would flaunt his poverty rather than be embarrassed by it was, to say the least, something of a novelty. His final lodgings consisted of a bare room (to which no one was thought to have ever been admitted) containing little more than a table, a chair and a bed; there was a basin in the corridor and he maintained his fastidious cleanliness with a pumice stone and a dog brush. And yet Satie would sally forth across Paris armed with invitations to the salons of some of the wealthiest Parisian patrons, for some of whom he became a kind of mascot, their aesthetic conscience. The Princess de Polignac could invite him to dinner to discuss the commissioning of *Socrate* and yet point him in the direction of the staff catering when he was there to perform.

Satie is often said to have created himself, his life being a total immersion as a kind of method actor. If this was the case he starred in a number of roles ranging from the bohemian poet, artist and café pianist who composed popular *chansons* to the co-creator of ballets and theatre works with Jean Cocteau, Pablo Picasso and Serge Diaghilev. Satie negotiated most of these roles on foot, never having the wherewithal for a cab. His parents had both been musical, his father a shipbroker and occasional poet and, like his stepmother, a composer of salon songs. Alfred Satie reinvented himself as a music publisher, bringing out songs by his wife and the first songs by Eric (as he was christened). Eric's musical education was unremarkable, and after a short period of military service and a quarrel with his parents he left home at the age of twenty-one to plunge into the intoxicating world of cabaret.

In Montmartre, and now Erik with a *k*, he was welcomed into the society of artists, poets and musicians, none of whom were quite what they appeared to be, and in whose company Satie began to create his own bohemian persona. This process began as soon as he walked through the door of Le Chat Noir and introduced himself as a *gymnopédiste*, enchanting the resident *flâneurs* who had no idea what a *gymnopédiste* was. Satie didn't immediately enlighten them, but it eventually emerged that, of course, a *gymnopédiste* was a composer of *gymnopédies*, and Satie had indeed been working on the eponymous piano pieces while recuperating from the bronchitis that had enabled him to engineer his discharge from the army. Once the phantom *gymnopédiste* had revealed his true nature he was taken on as a 'second pianist'; quite what that meant apart from just generally gymnopedising about is unclear, but he was a fixture at Le Chat until moving to L'Auberge du Clou in 1891. It was here that he probably first met Claude Debussy, with whom he had a deep and complicated friendship until Debussy's death in 1918.

It may have been Debussy who introduced Satie to the budding *chansonnier* Vincent Hyspa. The lives of all three would intertwine over the next few years: Debussy set Hyspa's poem 'La Belle au bois dormant', and Satie would become Hyspa's accompanist and arranger as well as setting his verses. The young Debussy, an admirer of Chabrier, ambivalent about Wagner and despite his Prix de Rome disdainful of conventional composition, was far more successful than his new friend. But he was charmed by him and his music, and in 1896 he orchestrated the *Gymnopédies*, bringing Satie to the attention of the Parisian concert-going public. Satie, however, while appreciating Debussy's respect, set off on his own path, moving across Paris from Montmartre to the suburb of Arcueil-Cachan. Here he explored (and exploited) his own eccentricity, taught *solfège* and counterpoint to local schoolchildren, and continued to play for Hyspa and the celebrity *chanteuse* Paulette Darty, for whom he wrote 'Je te veux' and 'La Diva de l'Empire', among many other songs.

Darty managed to seduce Parisian audiences with her fashionable variety of love song, the *valse chantée*, the formulaic *romance* that had Paris in its grip. These songs were infinitely arrangeable and were lapped up by Darty's audiences, who could then buy the sheet music and sing or play them at home. In 1910, Darty married and retired from the stage to live comfortably in the country, but by then Satie was beginning to think beyond the capricious world of cabaret and a final reinvention was in progress. In 1905 he had enrolled at the Schola Cantorum, and just as the results of his study were about to pay off he was rediscovered by Maurice Ravel, who had been inspired by hearing Satie's *Sarabandes* in his youth.

In 1911, Debussy and Ravel promoted concerts of Satie's music, both claiming him as a spiritual forebear. Satie was bemused by his new-found celebrity but slightly rattled by the fact that it was the simple piano pieces of his youth that were suddenly all the rage. He continued to write for piano, and from 1912 onwards took to adding comments or rubrics which were not sung or spoken, but contemplated by the pianist before or during the performance. In 1914 he finally returned to *mélodies* with *Trois poèmes d'amour* to his own texts. He also began to attend the salons of Valentine Gross, and it may have been at Gross's apartment that he first met Jean Cocteau, who adopted the composer as a voice of the future. Their ballet *Parade*, a Futurist cacophony of typewriters, sirens, music hall and circus acts created for Diaghilev's *Ballets Russes*, had choreography by Léonide Massine, set design and costumes by Picasso and Balla, and a programme note by Apollinaire (that contained the first use of the word surrealism). It was another turning point for Satie: if there was anyone in Paris who hadn't heard of him before the *succès de scandale* that was *Parade*, there can't have been many afterwards. It also landed him a jail sentence (one week) and a heavy fine when he was sued for libel after insulting a critic who had panned *Parade*.

While *Parade* was being put together, the Princess de Polignac, having brought to a conclusion the commissioning of Stravinsky's *Renard*, was considering asking Satie to write something for her salon. She was intrigued by his music and its quirky titles and over a series of dinners a plan emerged for him to set a scene from Plato's *Phaedra* on the death of Socrates. She paid Satie the biggest fee he had ever received and helped him out with his fine. The piece went through various drafts; at one point it was for four sopranos then Cocteau suggested a children's choir, but the first private performance for the princess was by the go-to contemporary music mezzo-soprano

Jane Bathori with the composer at the piano. Aware of Satie's financial difficulties, Winnaretta then agreed to performances elsewhere, including the orchestral version which she hadn't yet heard. When it reached the public many were moved, most were mystified, and some thought it was a huge joke.

No Satie composition is without controversy. *Socrate* is his most substantial piece and one of his most understated; he himself was daunted by it before discovering a way through the material. He described it as a 'symphonic drama' and hoped it would be perceived as 'white', and in true Satie fashion it is neither symphonic nor a drama but he did eat only white food while working on it. It has three movements and four characters: Socrates, Phaedrus, Phaedo and Alcibiades. The vocal line has a limited tessitura, only rarely straying above or below the stave, and is often performed entirely by one voice. The score looks deceptively simple, with Satie's chuntering quavers in the left hand, often repeating the same sequence for bar after bar; the voice part is entirely syllabic, mostly in equal quavers. It was a curious work from the composer of humorous piano vignettes and a world away from *Parade*; it's no wonder some of his fans were confused.

One reason why *Socrate* was misunderstood (and continues to be) is down to a failure to see it in the context of Satie's cabaret background. The point about cabaret tunes is that they tell a story, even if they are just straightforward love songs, and a successful performance depends on projecting the tune through the charisma of the narrator. This is all the more important if the 'tune' is – as in *Socrate* – for long stretches on only one note. In practical terms it means that however strictly the accompaniment is maintained – and in *Socrate* it is relentless for much of the time – the singer's narration will be nuanced with inflections either side of the beat (jazz singers know this as swing). Satie's narrators are telling a story about a death, and if the piece was to be taken seriously it had to be performed by singers of the calibre of Jane Bathori. What Satie surely had in his mind was the storytelling of Paulette Darty and his decades in Montmartre. The music is, like all Satie, elegant and subtle, and it needs to be owned by a storyteller.

Satie was not the only eccentric to wander the streets of Paris at night. The poet Léon-Paul Fargue, lifelong friend and later biographer of Ravel, was also a denizen of Le Chat Noir and similar establishments. Satie, Fargue and Ravel all attended meetings of the renegade aesthetes club Les Apaches, and Ravel later set Fargue's *Rêves*. Fargue had been brought up by his mother in an apartment between the Gare du Nord and the Gare de l'Est (he wrote a long semi-autobiographical poem called *La Gare*) and would later become famous for *Le Piéton de Paris*, based on accounts of his nocturnal adventures (there are recordings of him reading from it). He was scruffy, never able to keep to a deadline, and enjoyed all the disben-efits of alcohol and the bohemian life. Fargue seems to have been utterly charming and his poetry, admired by Joyce and grounded in the Parisian life that confirmed the upper-class fantasy vision of those below them, touched even Winnaretta Singer. The princess thought him the heir of Villon, regularly asked Fargue to read, and even invited him to Venice on her yacht; decades later she would remember him in her will. For now, though, Satie and Fargue were brothers in poverty, and as such lived quite well on the salon circuit. In 1916, Satie set Fargue's 'La Statue de bronze', a cabaret/*mélodie* hybrid cameo about a sad bronze frog. It became the third of his *Trois mélodies* and was first performed at the extravagant salon of *couturière* Germaine Bongard (to which Matisse and Picasso contrib-uted engravings).

Satie and Fargue would meet at the legendary bookshop of Adrienne Monnier, another regular haunt of impoverished poets and musicians and where *Socrate* had once been performed to an audience that included Joyce, Georges Braque, Picasso, Poulenc, Milhaud and Stravinsky, as well as Fargue himself. In March 1923, Fargue published eight poems he called *Ludions* in Monnier's house magazine *Intentions*. A *ludion* is a children's toy which features figures bobbing up and down in a glass tube, and the poems have a mischievous whimsy verging on the nonsensical. In the spring of that year Satie was asked to write music for the annual masked ball at the salon of Comte Etienne de Beaumont, a major patron of the arts who had promoted the first orchestral performance of *Socrate* in 1920. Satie provided two works for the event: *La Statue retrouvée*, a *divertissement* for trumpet and the count's newly renovated eighteenth-century organ, and a setting of five of Fargue's *Ludions* for soprano, accompanied by piano and the famous organ. The *divertissement* consisted of seventeen *tableaux vivants* for which Satie's *Parade* team was reassembled: Cocteau provided the scenario, Picasso the sets and costumes, and Massine choreographed the dancing of the well-heeled participants.

The ball proved a great success for the count, who went on to become a serious promoter of ballet, but at the cost of his relationship with Fargue. When the names of the contributors were read out, Fargue's was unaccountably missing. The poet was extremely upset and made his feelings known to the count, who in turn challenged him to a duel. As his weapon Fargue chose spelling, so he won a certain satisfaction there, but he never forgave Satie whom he thought jointly responsible for the slight. There followed a daily series of vituperative letters, slid under the door of the apartment that no one was allowed to enter, and duly ignored by the intended recipient. *La Statue retrouvée* was presumably performed on only the one occasion and the score disappeared until it was rediscovered by Robert Orledge in the 1980s. How Satie's fifty-three bars were stretched over seventeen *tableaux* remains a mystery. *Ludions* fared rather better and entered the Satie pantheon as one of his most charming or daftest works, depending on your point of view.

Ludions are essence of Satie, short, playful and hinting at jokes that we'll never understand (and that only a select few of his friends would have got). He was in the habit of publishing his songs in groups of three until the *Quatre petites mélodies* of 1920. There are five *Ludions*, all hovering ironically on the border between *chanson* and *mélodie*; who knows how many more hybrids Satie might have produced had he lived a little longer. Fargue wrote 'L'Air du rat' (twenty-two bars of Satie) when he was ten years old as a tribute to his pet. 'Spleen' makes a brief (ten bars) nihilistic return to the park of 'La Statue de bronze' (perhaps). 'La Grenouille américaine' also features a frog, this time an American one, and is a positive cantata at forty bars long. Fargue writes the first words as though spoken by a child, making it almost impossible for anyone who isn't French to make it sound convincing. 'Air du poète' (another ten bars) is a state-ment on the burden of being a poet, expressed in a complicated play on the words Papua and poet (and similarly out of reach of non-French speakers). In 'Chanson du chat' Satie stirred himself to set two verses, a rare strophic song among his *mélodies*. Fargue's poem is another tribute to one of his pets, his cat Potasson; it's full of baby babbling and wordplay that doesn't really translate at all.

The vagabond aesthetes who met at Adrienne Monnier's Maison des Amies des Livres called themselves Potassons after Fargue's cat. 'Chanson du chat', based on a folk song improved by Satie, became their anthem. There is something touchingly Satien about the fact that this is his last song, that he remained a child to the end, and above all an inimitable Parisian. Signing the publishing contract (and receiving payment in cash) was one of the last acts of the composer as he lay dying of cirrhosis of the liver two years later.

Satie's songs are not easy to programme. They were almost always performed in the context of other music ranging from nightclub turns and home entertainment to society balls and multi media events on a grand scale. Publishing them in sets was a matter of asserting a certain status and perhaps earning a franc or two; despite his obsessive list-making it's hard to know what Satie would make of the list-like recital programmes in which his songs appear today (when they appear at all). The classical tip of the popular music iceberg also looms problematically large for the generic classical voice: there's nothing worse than a sophisticated singer appearing to be slumming it with a nod to popular music ... which raises the question of exactly what Satie's legacy actually is.

The clue is in his character. While he may have appreciated the music of his sometime friends Debussy, Ravel and Stravinsky, he allowed none of them to influence his work. Although he went back to school when he thought it might be useful, he was very selective in how he used what he learned from a conventional institution. He was essentially self-taught; more than that, he invented his entire persona, an artist who was not only out of step with whatever normality was in the early twentieth century, but who was in his way classless. His music appealed to, and was performed by, anyone with an open mind and a sense of humour.

The later advocacy of John Cage and then the British 'experimental' composers Gavin Bryars, Howard Skempton and others assured Satie of a unique place in current compositional history. Arvo Pärt's *Für Alina* recalls the hypnotic simplicity of the *Gymnopédies*, which have provided background music for countless film and TV soundtracks. Brian Eno's ambient music is Satie's domestic furniture music projected into public spaces. Simplicity, repetition, humour, reinvention, a tendency to ignore the rules, all of these were an antidote to the old avant-garde. We have gradually caught up with Satie:

we still think of him as an eccentric one-off, but so much of his life and work resonates in the present.

Despite the (mostly) affectionate acknowledgement of Satie's importance for minimalism and post-modernism, we have rarely been able to do justice to the songs. They are considered too short, too slight, too French or simply not 'classical' enough alongside those of his contemporaries and successors. The early piano pieces have inspired arrangements and performances across the spectrum, especially in the areas of electronics and dance, but the songs remain firmly in the hands of classical singers. Nobody seems to have lured Satie or his singers into a recording studio, so we'll never know what they sounded like then, but listening to other singers of the period reveals an extraordinary range of voices: you hear the person. Satie died the same year that electrical recording was introduced, in 1925, and from then on we would all know how things were supposed to go and, as classical singing became more generic, how it should sound. If we want to recapture Satie's individualism, his ability to communicate to princesses and paupers, the answer might lie in the singing rather than the songs. By over-cultivating the voice we risk losing the piquant ambiguity that Satie's songs offer us, and the chance to bring 'art' song to a much wider audience. He once described himself as 'the strangest musician of our time'; we could do with more strangeness.

George Butterworth, composer, folksong collector, dancer and soldier
(c. 1910).

9

GEORGE BUTTERWORTH

'THE LADS IN THEIR HUNDREDS'

Satie was forty-eight when the First World War broke out and its effects seem to have left no impression on him at all: he remained at its conclusion the same unfathomable eccentric that he had always been. On the other side of the Channel a younger generation of composers and poets made extraordinary sacrifices, some never living beyond the first steps into an artistic life.

Alfred Housman's poem 'The Lads in Their Hundreds' dates from 1896, when George Butterworth (1885–1916) was eleven. The composer's settings of his *Shropshire Lad* songs date from 1911, but his death in fierce fighting on the Somme in 1916 has given this particular song an added poignancy, making Butterworth, as Stephen Banfield put it, 'the perfect model of his own poignant subject matter'. Neither poet nor composer had any direct experience of the effects of war at the time; Butterworth had just moved from York to London and enrolled himself as a mature student at the Royal College of Music when he wrote the song. The poem was also set by

Arthur Somervell, Ernest Moeran, Charles Orr and Ivor Gurney among many others, and settings of Housman's verse marked a renaissance in English song compared by many to Heine and Goethe's effect on the German *Lied*.

As the twentieth century dawned, so did a renewed interest in folk music. The historical conjunction of Housman, folk song and the war would have momentous implications for the creation and consumption of song. The lad from Shropshire was everyman, and the subjects of folk songs were the sons of English soil whom the composers, reinvented as commissioned officers in the army and navy, would lead into battle. Conscription and enlistment became the ultimate engines of social change, as the officer class discovered comradeship and mutual dependency with those whose lives were only known from semi-mythical folk song and subservience at the opposite end of the social spectrum. The changes were more than musical, and they created the conditions for a final flowering of English song.

Ironically, the freshness of Butterworth's songs signalled a partial escape from the German influence that had overtaken English composition since the time of Handel, whose music still resounded in English concert halls and churches for generations after his death. Before Handel was adopted as the national composer, English song post-Dowland had flourished through successive periods of social upheaval; the Civil War, the Commonwealth and Restoration all produced great songwriters who owed their careers to aristocratic patronage. Henry Lawes, much admired by Milton, left more than four hundred songs spanning the period before Henry Purcell. Lawes's brother William left a smaller number, though his settings of poems by Robert Herrick suggest he might have been the better composer. His other claim to fame is as the first songwriter known to have been killed in battle, supporting the king and felled by a stray bullet at the Siege of Chester in 1645.

The Restoration saw an expansion of music both at court and in the theatre, but a new direction in English song was stopped in its tracks by the death of two composers whose surviving output hints at new intellectual and musical challenges. Pelham Humfrey (1647/8–74) had studied in France, possibly with Lully, and perhaps also in Italy where he may have encountered Carissimi, though the evidence for this amounts to no more than name dropping. His continuo songs show a Baroque vibrancy, suggesting a new world in which English verse would finally be matched to the dramatic waywardness of his French and Italian contemporaries. He left fewer than thirty songs, including a setting of Donne's 'Hymn to God the Father' in which he perfectly captures the expressive intensity of the poem. Samuel Pepys, himself a would-be composer who liked to sing on his roof accompanying himself on his viol, met Humfrey shortly after his return from France in 1667 but thought the young upstart too big for his French boots. Seven years later the man who might have revolutionised English composition was dead at the age of twenty-seven.

Humfrey had been Master of the Children of the Chapel Royal and may have taught the young Henry Purcell, who also absorbed French and Italian influences and left a much larger collection of songs, many written for theatre productions and later published in anthologies. His death in 1695 at the age of thirty-six brought to an end another false start to the English Baroque. Seventeen years later Handel moved to London and in 1727 formally became a British subject; for almost two centuries English composers would be inspired by (and walk in the shadows of) their German contemporaries and forebears. Johann Sebastian Bach's son Johann Christian moved to London in 1762 and spent his remaining twenty years there, the 'London Bach' who wrote songs in English. Later, visits by Haydn and Louis Spohr (who also wrote songs in English) reinforced the assumption that the best music was German, though by the end of the nineteenth century some found that Wagner's promiscuous use of chromaticism threatened the moral fabric.

As a counterweight to the rather heavier German-influenced songs, Georgian London was entertained by Charles Dibdin (1745–1814), dramatist, actor, novelist, businessman, singer and composer of more than six hundred songs. Dibdin was one of the most enterprising, shrewd and colourful figures of his age and few households would have been unfamiliar with a Dibdin song. He was an entertainer, somewhere between a stand-up comedian and a singer-songwriter who performed one-man shows, some of which he did in black-face. His pseudo-Caribbean dialect songs were not entirely at the expense of his supposed models: his character Mungo (such a success that Dibdin gave his son the same name) was a comic servant whose predicament often elicited sympathy from the audience at a time when abolition was being seriously debated. He wrote patriotic sea songs too, and his 'Tom Bowling' has been a feature of London's Promenade concerts on and off since it was incorporated into Henry Wood's *Fantasia on British Sea Songs* for the 1905 celebration of the centenary of the Battle of Trafalgar.

Dibdin's songs occupied a middle ground between those heard in pleasure gardens and taverns, and the concerts and drawing rooms of the aristocracy. All European music-making reflected the social standing of everyone, composer, performer or listener, but there was as yet no rigid division between what we would call classical music and popular. In the eighteenth and nineteenth centuries the English class system was oddly porous when it came to music, and revealed itself more in where one heard it rather than what one heard. There was a spectrum which had Handel, Mozart and Beethoven at one end and broadside ballads at the other, but a Dibdin song might be heard privately in an aristocratic drawing room, a song and supper room whose clientele might include the nobility and bohemian hangers-on, or the concert room of a tavern.

England's upper classes were no match for the Germans and French in terms of musical taste and there was little incentive for composers to produce new work. There was an understanding that music was a good thing, especially when combined with supper, but that didn't mean a commitment to actually listening to it. Spohr, on a visit to London in 1820, was shocked by the lack of respect shown to musicians in aristocratic drawing rooms where conversation continued unabated with complete disregard for the music. Below the drawing room the less exalted were drawn to royalty ballads, sentimental songs heavily pushed by publishers who would sponsor singers with small sums to promote specific songs.

More serious British composers such as Thomas Attwood, William Crotch and Sterndale Bennett were considered child prodigies, but as adults they cemented themselves into musical institutions, keeping a socially disadvantaging professionalism at bay by presenting themselves as cultivated amateurs. Many didn't need to work in any case, but enjoyed the status that came with the Royal College or Academy; the patronage of Queen Victoria (a closet Wagnerite) and her cultured German consort, Prince Albert, was not to be sneezed at. The enormous enthusiasm for the queen's favourite poets meant that in Victorian (and, later, Edwardian) drawing rooms an understanding of the text was a highly valued part of the listening experience (should the room be quiet enough to hear it). Composers expected their audience to understand the words, and translation for singers was an art in itself.

This is not generally the case today (though there have been recent creditable attempts to revive the art): one of the effects of the increasing 'artification' of song in the second half of the twentieth century was the abandonment of singing in translation. Singing

Lieder in German had become the norm for young British singers by the 1960s (though tenors were still producing English translations of Bach evangelist parts). It was yet another step in the elevation of song from a relatively simple semiotic process – the singer transmits the composer's and poet's meanings as faithfully as possible so that the maximum number of listeners get the message – to an altogether more complex transaction in which the literal meaning was displaced by a more abstract appreciation of what might be going on.

Schubert's listeners may have considered him a genius, but they identified with him as a person not unlike them, a performer of his own songs; a modern listener has to support the weight of a century and a half of his accumulated genius. Literal translation is all very well in a programme note but we expect to find deeper meanings in the magical fusion of music with poetry in a language we may not understand. We are confident when we listen to a song by Schumann that we are witnessing great art, and part of the reason for this is that we don't have to reckon with the banality of literal meanings, and whatever meaning we may assign to a song there is always the possibility of other layers just beyond our linguistic grasp.

William Sterndale Bennett (1816–75), a friend and contemporary of Mendelssohn and Schumann who spent three successful years in Leipzig, wrote two sets of songs with both English and German texts (which also appeared in German catalogues). At the time this was probably simply to maximise his potential sales, but he would want both his German and English listeners to understand the poetry. With the exception of the Latin used in church and Italian in certain operas, the vernacular was to be expected: what use were words if you couldn't understand them?

When workshopping a class of students about the reception of Lieder, I would play one of Sterndale Bennett's songs in English without telling them the composer's name. The consensus was invariably that whoever wrote it, it was trite Victorian rubbish that they needed to hear only once. The same song with its German text played a few weeks later, by which time the students knew their Lieder composers, was generally thought to be an art song by Mendelssohn or Schubert that sat happily beside the works of those German masters; as, indeed, it did in the nineteenth century.

At the top of the late-nineteenth-century British musical pyramid stood the Royal College and the Royal Academy of Music, both of which made strenuous efforts to inspire composers to rise above the easy options of balladry and the drawing room. The College in particular, under patrician composers Hubert Parry and Charles Villiers Stanford, accepted many composers who went on to become household names and who would refresh the genre. The resulting increased sophistication would have a similar effect on songwriting to that experienced in Germany. There was a heavy emphasis on the classics – Mozart and Beethoven especially, and more recently Brahms and Wagner – and the degree to which students absorbed the lessons or transcended them provided a critical creative tension. In the 1890s, Ralph Vaughan Williams, Thomas Dunhill, Samuel Coleridge-Taylor, Gustav Holst, Frank Bridge and John Ireland all began composition studies with Stanford. In 1905, Ernest Farrar joined this exclusive set, followed six years later by Ivor Gurney; George Butterworth came up to study with Charles Wood. Farrar and Butterworth, perhaps the songwriters with the most promise, would perish in the First World War; Gurney developed mental-health problems which may have been aggravated by shell shock. Bridge and Ireland went on to have distinguished careers; both would teach Benjamin Britten, and Ireland's pupils would also include E.J. Moeran and the enigmatic Peter Pope.

The Royal Academy also produced successful composers including Arnold Bax, Joseph Holbrooke and Granville Bantock, but the most significant teacher of the era was undoubtedly Stanford at the Royal College. Now known mainly for his church music, Stanford was not one of music's radical thinkers but, like all great teachers, having given his pupils a solid grounding he understood that they would follow their own path. This they did while often sharing the excitement of discovery, supporting each other's work in friendly competition. He also considered songwriting an essential pedagogical tool, and all his pupils were given texts to set. Stanford's compositions were very much of his time (or earlier), but careful stewardship of his pupils ensured that songwriting would always find a place alongside whatever more lofty ambitions they might have.

The so-called English Renaissance associated with Parry and Stanford – a return to serious composition independent of commercial considerations or drawing-room sycophancy – received a considerable shock with the onset of the First World War. The young composers were of the officer class and most felt a duty to fight; those too old to be called up responded with patriotic songs. Aviators were robustly celebrated, and composers and poets were invited to contribute to *King Albert's Book*, a tribute to the King of Belgium and his people, devised by the novelist Hall Caine and published on subscription by the *Daily Telegraph* in December 1914. It included musical cameos from Elgar, Mascagni and Debussy among many others. The English contributions are mostly heroic and masculine, even Ethel Smyth's piano 'March of the Women' (already an anthem of the suffragette movement with its text by Cicely Hamilton). A gentler contrast is provided by Lisa Lehman's 'By the Lake', written for Clara Butt to a poem by Emily Clifford. It's an optimistic expression of hope by a young mother, clasping her son to her heart as she dreams of a better world.

Inevitably, the war brought deaths, and legends of lost composers cut down before they had written the works that their reputations should have rested upon. In any discussion of the casualties of war, the 'what if' questions are always just beneath the surface; these were young men yet to develop their authentic voice, and any evaluation of their work is coloured by the cruelty of their fate.

Among the first to fall was William Denis Browne (1888–1915), a composer just beginning to make a name for himself. Browne had been a close friend of the poet Rupert Brooke since their schooldays at Rugby, and the two of them enlisted in the navy. In April 1915 their battalion was on its way to the Dardanelles on the *Grantully Castle* when Brooke succumbed to septicaemia following an insect bite. Browne, together with his fellow officers and men, buried his friend on the Greek island of Skyros. The Gallipoli campaign claimed Browne himself four months later and his body was never recovered. Until the modern rediscovery of his songs, Browne's reputation rested on his elegiac letter to Edward Marsh, describing Brooke's last days and interment in a marble-strewn olive grove. The much-quoted letter turned a banal death by blood-poisoning into a passing worthy of a poet, and it became one of the earliest threads in the many tales of Rupert Brooke woven after his death.

Denis Browne's death is particularly poignant. An intellectual still seeking his true calling, he had used his time as organ scholar at Clare College, Cambridge, to explore the arts, becoming something of an authority on lute song after transcribing tabs into staff notation. After Cambridge he tried teaching and criticism between attempts at composition; he was a perceptive critic of his fellow composers, who unlike himself were the products of institutional teaching. Also unlike them he had little interest in folk song: his musical tastes ran to Scriabin and Stravinsky. A skilled pianist (he gave the first London performance of the Berg Sonata), he had many singer friends and wrote eloquently on the relationship between the singer's melodic lines and the colour and texture provided by the piano. The tenor

Steuart Wilson had been a friend and contemporary at Cambridge (they took skiing holidays together), and their musical partnership undoubtedly created insights and opportunities for both of them.

Anticipating the worst possible outcome before enlisting in the navy, Browne had left instructions with his executor that any of his works considered not worth keeping should be destroyed. The resulting bonfire left a very small legacy, but four of the remaining songs are some of the most accomplished by an English composer of any period. His contemporaries at the Royal College of Music all show traces of their teachers; Denis Browne's best work has no obvious antecedents. Each song is unique, hinting at future possible directions and accomplishments that might have confirmed him as one of the greatest English song composers. 'Diaphenia' has something of an ironic music-hall lilt (reminiscent of Frank Bridge's 'All women born are so perverse'), despite the apparent naivety of the poem. Its intended companion piece, a setting of Ben Jonson's tongue-in-cheek 'Epitaph on Salathiel Pavy' on the death of a child actor, combines a modal mock-ceremonial grandeur with echoes of lute song.

Browne's studies of Elizabethan music really came into their own with Richard Lovelace's 'To Gratiana Dancing and Singing', the one piece together with his ballet *The Comic Spirit* that he thought worth keeping. We sweep along with Gratiana's effortless yet majestic dance as she slays her admirers with every swaying step. Browne even stealthily incorporates some Renaissance rhetoric with a quaver rest for a sigh before the sight of the floor 'paved with broken hearts', which then dissolve into an unplayed piano chord, releasing phantom harmonics to resonate in the empty instrument. Gratiana's performance builds to an exquisitely tautological top G (written for Steuart Wilson) on the word 'performed', before subsiding magnificently as the world notes that 'The Graces danced and Apollo played'. It is impossible not to feel uplifted by this song.

Browne's last song was 'Arabia', the earliest known setting of Walter de la Mare, who would become a favourite poet of Armstrong Gibbs and later songwriters including Britten. This song also has no precedent in English music. De la Mare's Arabia is a dreamscape of deserts, flowers, forests and riverbanks where time slips between day and night to the sound of mysterious instruments and voices. Eventually the poet understands that other eyes are coldly observing his reverie, but he continues to see phantom stars in the noonday sky, because 'He is crazed with the spell of far Arabia' and 'They have stolen his wits away'. Each element of this fantasy is coloured by Browne's continually shifting piano textures contrasting with outbursts of melody and short rhetorical recitatives. He enables the performers to create an entire universe in the space of a few minutes. Who knows what other magic he might have wrought had he not gone to war.

Also aboard the *Grantully Castle* with Brooke and Browne was the Australian composer F.S. Kelly (1881–1916), and Kelly and Browne played duets on the saloon piano provided by the rather well-equipped ship. Kelly's letter home also told the story of Brooke's death and burial, and in January of 1916, still in Gallipoli, he wrote an elegy for strings and harp, *In memoriam Rupert Brooke*, while recovering from the evacuation (during which he had won the Distinguished Service Cross for gallantry). It's one of the few wartime works composed close to the heat of battle. The score is inscribed with a quote from the same Greek epigram of Callimachus that Peter Warlock set in faraway England at about the same time: 'They told me, Heracleitus, you were dead . . .'. By the end of the year Kelly was dead himself, mown down by machine-gun fire on the Somme.

Kelly is one of the least remembered of the war composers. His impact at the time was muted by his international reputation as a sportsman. A precocious pianist as a child, Frederick Septimus Kelly was one of six boys sent by his Australian parents to Eton. He initially sublimated his musical urges by rowing, becoming one of the finest oarsmen and scullers of his generation. His feats on the water were legendary, from stroking the Eton eight to victory in the Ladies' Plate at Henley in 1899 (the year he went up to Oxford) to a final flourish with Leander, winning a gold medal in the 1908 London Olympics. Inheriting vast wealth on the death of his parents, he bought a substantial Thames-side manor house conveniently close to Leander Boat Club for whom he twice won the Diamond Sculls.

Like Browne and the others, Kelly was still feeling his way in the world and was content to see where his sporting and musical prowess led him, hoping to excel at both. In 1903 he began to study composition in Frankfurt with Iwan Knorr. He didn't overlap with the so-called Frankfurt group of composers but became friends with all of them, especially fellow Australian Percy Grainger. Alongside his compositions he continued to develop as a pianist, playing for Pablo Casals among others. Kelly also knew the risks of enlistment and hoped to organise his manuscripts before he went. He didn't manage it and many of his songs remain in manuscript. Of his published works two song cycles show unfulfilled promise, an Edwardian composer on the brink of something else.

The last composer to fall in the war was Ernest Farrar, who was killed on the Somme in September 1918, a mere two days after arriving at the front and agonisingly close to the end of hostilities. Like Kelly, he too has slipped off the radar, though in many ways he was never quite on it. He won a scholarship to study with Stanford at the Royal College of Music and enjoyed fraternising with his contemporaries Frank Bridge and other members of the 'Beloved Vagabonds', a club founded by Audrey Alston (who would later be Britten's viola teacher). But unlike most of his fellow students Farrar was an organist and from the north of England, and he fully expected to have to earn his living. When he was appointed organist at St Hilda's South Shields in 1910, Vaughan Williams congratulated him but added that 'it's a beastly job being organist and unless one is very careful lowers one's moral tone (not to speak of one's musical) horribly'. It was a kindly meant hint that outer darkness beckoned.

In 1912, Farrar took up a post as organist at Christ Church in the far more salubrious Harrogate, where he also taught the thirteen-year-old Gerald Finzi, and it is largely in the Finzi narrative that his name has survived, though many of Farrar's compositions were published in his lifetime. His *Vagabond Songs* include a setting of 'Silent Noon', and those who have sung it are inclined to agree with Finzi's assessment that it is a worthy equal to Vaughan Williams's more famous version. When Farrar died his songs had yet to emerge from the shadow of his teacher, and his family endowed a composition prize at the Royal College of Music (that would twice be won by Benjamin Britten). His other lasting memorial would turn out to be Frank Bridge's turbulent Piano Sonata, dedicated to Farrar, first performed by Myra Hess in 1925 and perhaps an indication of what Farrar himself might have achieved.

The deepest loss to song composition has long been thought to be George Butterworth. Of the four, he was the most fluent songwriter, the most decorated soldier, and almost certainly the best dancer. Yet another Eton alumnus, Butterworth read classics at Trinity College, Cambridge, where like many of his contemporaries he didn't particularly distinguish himself academically. He did, though, meet Ralph Vaughan Williams, with whom he shared similar musical interests, and Cecil Sharp. Sharp, something of an expert in German folk song, had recently started collecting English folk songs and notating morris dances with the aim of reviving (some would call it reinventing) the country's authentic music.

Sharp's missionary zeal was clear and he wasn't put off by suggestions that many of his rural folk songs were in fact urban compositions of a previous generation. Nor was Vaughan Williams, who would later have no problem with *ersatz* folk tunes as a teaching aid. For Vaughan Williams and Butterworth folk song meant the excitement of a music that had apparently existed for a eons without their knowledge. Questions of orality, literacy and class initially took second place to an almost childlike joy at the discovery of each new tune or variant. Decades later the mature Vaughan Williams (by then president of the English Folk Dance and Song Society) would give a series of lectures at Bryn Mawr College outlining to his American students a more reflective view of folk music. The talks were published in 1934 as *National Music* and remain a core element of the composer's aesthetic. He saw folk music as a means of mitigating the composerly dependency on 'foreign' forms and ideas but also as a brake on originality for its own sake, as opposed to creating a work of beauty which might call on pre-existing material. This decidedly un-modernist viewpoint would compromise his reputation in some quarters, but it was accompanied by a vision of 'levelling up', in which the incorporation of folk music into the composer's toolkit would shrink the difference between classical and popular, enabling the common man to access higher forms of music. It is a patrician point of view from an armchair socialist, but had more composers subscribed to it, art song might have better survived the tests of modernism and broadened its potential audience.

The well-turned folk song had been cultivated as a sideline by many composers since the eighteenth century. Londoners could enjoy English folk-song settings by Haydn and Beethoven (who found them quite profitable) and visiting celebrities such as Spohr would arrange an Irish or Scottish folk song on request. The fully composed folk-song arrangement was an urban fantasy that bridged the gap steadily opening up between monophonic street songs such as the often anonymous broadside ballads sung to any accompaniment or none, and the increasingly sophisticated song by a proper composer. The latter required more serious attention from listeners, so folk-song arrangements, often by the same composers, offered an easier kind of engagement. In many respects the fashion for setting folk songs gave composers a head start: the essential musical material and its text gave them a structure on which to work some magic. They could also reckon on audiences enjoying the result, the tunes having been successful in a previous life.

Butterworth joined the Folk Song Society in 1906 and began to collect folk songs himself, also joining the English Folk Dance Society from its formation in 1911 and making many forays into deepest Oxfordshire and Sussex, often assisting Cecil Sharp. The two societies were decidedly top-down and unsurprisingly often found it impossible to agree on what folk song or dance actually was and how to write it all down. Yet for all the organisational and notational obfuscation, a remarkable thread emerged from the English countryside via its topsoil in the form of a distinctively nationalistic modality and tunefulness that coloured the music of Butterworth, Vaughan Williams, Frederick Delius, Percy Grainger, Moeran and many other composers. Ironically, since Vaughan Williams and Butterworth had both weaned themselves off the German intoxication associated with conservatoire teaching, the effect was not dissimilar to the German experience that gave birth to key elements of the *Lied*.

Butterworth's collecting was dwarfed by the hundreds of folk songs assembled by Vaughan Williams and even more by Sharp's thousands. His attempts to perform and notate intricate dances seem to have occupied more of his time than the tunes to which they were attached. His dancing talents were considerable, as the films of his enthusiastic capering attest. He once claimed, with his tongue only slightly in his cheek, that he was a professional dancer (after his death it emerged that no one in the army knew he was a musician).

Apart from two volumes of morris dance tunes and some instructional publications on dance, both jointly edited with Cecil Sharp, Butterworth's eleven Sussex folk-song arrangements are the only fruits of his considerable endeavours that ended up in print. They have the restrained charm of a composer being very careful not to over-impose himself on his source material, but some show a distinctly artistic hand. In 'The True Lover's Farewell', for example, after a two-bar piano introduction to replicate the giving of the pitch, the singer sets off alone; under the last note of the first strophe the piano makes a surprising re-entry not on the expected tonic chord but on a second inversion of the sub-dominant (an extraordinarily bleak and transgressive effect in a repertoire characterised by root-position chords). Only at the end of the singer's journey does the expected tonic chord appear. By contrast, Vaughan Williams's more famous 'The Turtle Dove', a setting for choir of another version of the same text, amplifies the sentimentality with plenty of lush triads.

The linear transparency of folk song is never very far away from Butterworth's *Shropshire Lad* settings, though none is thought to be an actual folk song. Each song seems imbued with a halo of Englishness. Scholars have wrestled with how to describe this 'Englishness' – is it really derived from folk song, and does that make it nationalistic? Has it escaped from the age-old German musical yoke despite the songs being compared with Schumann or Wolf, or should we look for the influence of Duparc or Ravel (Vaughan Williams's teacher for a few months in 1908)? Can a composer even begin to portray the irony in Housman's verses? For singers and audiences none of this matters much: the singer rarely has anything more difficult to do than sustain a line and tell the story; the piano generally does the hard work filling in the details. That's also how the songs of Schumann and Duparc work. Housman's lines are concise, clearly expressed and euphonious; they are written in English: that's enough. When Butterworth is compared with Schumann or Housman with Heine it doesn't mean the Englishmen sound German: they're simply engaging with the *Zeitgeist* in a similar way, appropriate to their intended audiences.

Some of the early settings of Housman came in sets or cycles, an unusual format for publishers whose default understanding was that individual songs sold better. A widespread fascination with the slim *Shropshire Lad* volume encouraged composers and publishers to take a risk on a multiple-song format, though there is rarely much of a unifying thread between them. It's more a case of the composer not wanting to let his poet go. Housman's collection was originally going to be called 'The Poems of Terence Hearsay', and tell the story of a lad from London, exiled to Shropshire. The hero was a fictitious character whose creator never visited many of the places he described so colourfully. Creating the alias seems to have unblocked Housman's muse and the poems gushed out.

The Shropshire of the poems was itself almost a fiction, the 'blue remembered hills' being invisible from his Bromsgrove home, out of reach over the Worcestershire border. Several poems in the collection were written before Housman set foot in the county. But the sense of longing (the Lieder poets called it *Sehnsucht*), the melancholy suffused with a sense of loss, captivated the upper middle classes, most of whom had little understanding that their private incomes depended on the profits of the industrial revolution that was still eroding the countryside and its way of life. Later, the aftermath of war added resonance to the myth of the lost youth, bringing it within reach of a wider demographic. It's with us still, or those of us who still sing about pastoral yearnings, ploughing teams and Grecian lads.

Alfred Housman was born in 1859 into a comfortable middle-class family and had no expectation of financial gain from his poetry.

The correspondence between the poet and those who would set his verses reveals a rather spikey attitude sometimes leavened with grumpy humour. He is not thought to have been very interested in music but would always give permission for composers to set his verse as long as they didn't print the words in the programme. In this he was around a century ahead of his time: concert promoters are only just now beginning to come to terms with the infantile multitasking of audiences hearing the sung words while reading a printed version of the same text. He also expected the poem to be set complete, and famously reprimanded Vaughan Williams for omitting the footballing strophes in 'Is my team ploughing?'; Vaughan Williams replied that the poet should be grateful he'd left them out.

Vaughan Williams's cycle *On Wenlock Edge* was an early offering, dating from 1908–09. Among the first examples of songs accompanied by a chamber ensemble of string quartet and piano, it was first sung (and later recorded) by Gervase Elwes; Butterworth presumably knew his friend's songs when he was working on his own set a couple of years later. He certainly gave it the full football (Ireland was to go even better in 1920 with 'Goal and Wicket', which also had the lad playing cricket). There are very few classical songs that feature sport, and it's a measure of the trust that Butterworth and Ireland had in the context created by Housman that they were able to represent the beautiful but far from lyrical game in song.

Housman is often an invisible presence watching his hero, whether he is playing football or marching beside him as a soldier. His observations are at their most poignant in 'The Lads in Their Hundreds', where young men assemble from all over the county at the annual Ludlow fair. He wanders among them like a ghost, brushing against them and longing to meet in the flesh the stalwart and brave, some of whom will 'die in their glory and never be old'. Convention has it that he was reflecting on the fate of the naïve English soldiery called up to fight in the Boer War, but the fate in store for the handsome farm hands is a fictional one: the First Boer War was long gone when the lad made his first appearance in 1897, and the Second wouldn't start for another two years. The first performance of all six of Butterworth's cycle was in 1911 when there was no prospect of war on the horizon, but five years later it acquired an almost prophetic irony when the composer died on the Somme shortly after winning the Military Cross for conspicuous gallantry. In the chaos of trench warfare his hastily buried body, like so many, was never recovered.

'The Lads in Their Hundreds' is not a folk song, nor even modal, but its understated simplicity reflects Butterworth's debt to folk music. It's in triple time but marked *sempre tranquillo e senza rigore*, so the singer can narrate either side of the pulse with the informality of a folk singer. Between verses a two-bar dance motif appears in the piano, and when the words run out Butterworth the dancer tries one final time before almost reluctantly bringing the piece to its inevitable conclusion. The folk-like treatment enables the composer to bypass any sentimentality lingering in the poem, leaving the singer to make a judgement call.

Butterworth wrote two sets of *Shropshire Lad* songs and all eleven of them have a valedictory tone; all but two either are about death or touch on it at some point. 'The Lads in Their Hundreds' has become emblematic of the senseless losses of the First World War, where both Housman's yeomanry and their composerly officer class met their fate alongside each other. Many musicians served with distinction and survived the war; all were changed by it and all lost friends. Vaughan Williams drove an ambulance before being commissioned and ended the war with his hearing permanently damaged; Moeran was hit in the head by shrapnel with consequences for the rest of his life; George Dyson suffered from shell shock after his horse exploded under him; Arthur Bliss suffered recurring nightmares; Ivor Gurney was caught in a gas attack, which may have further complicated the mental problems that had troubled him since childhood.

Gurney (1890–1937) was among the first to seek Housman's permission to use his verse, eventually setting at least nineteen of his poems. He had developed psychological problems as a child, possibly inherited from his mother. These seem initially to have been a bipolar condition linked to eating disorders which damaged his digestive system. He loved the Gloucestershire countryside and would walk for miles, often turning up unannounced at friends' houses where he would raid the larder for cake and move on. His condition seems to have been rare and doubly unfortunate, as in adulthood these episodes manifested increasingly as paranoid schizophrenia, resulting in his incarceration in an asylum in 1922.

Gurney had won a scholarship to the Royal College of Music but he was an irascible and moody character and Stanford, though recognising his talent, found him difficult to teach. Gurney considered music to be his main calling but he had early success as a poet, his affinity with the English landscape earning praise from fellow Georgians Walter de la Mare, Edmund Blunden and J.C. Squire. At the outbreak of the First World War he enlisted as a private and in the trenches it was easier to scribble poetry than songs; his war poetry inevitably reflects a grimmer landscape but it is augmented by his love and respect for the men of the Gloucestershire regiment. It is these men who haunt many of his subsequent Housman settings and much of his own poetry.

Gurney had many supportive friends, composers and poets who stayed with him, sometimes at great personal cost, until his death from tuberculosis in 1937. His composing was chaotic, little of it prepared for publication and much of it unfinished. The heroic efforts of Marion Scott and Herbert Howells, contemporaries at the

Royal College of Music, opened windows into periods of rationality. After Gurney's death, Gerald Finzi and Howard Ferguson undertook the monumental task of editing selected manuscripts, initially in the face of opposition from the Gurney family. The first edited volumes appeared in 1938, and more followed in the 1950s and 1970s. Gurney's fastidious choice of texts and his tragic backstory make for creative programme planning, but his songs are frustrating for performers. He was not an instinctive tunesmith (and not a folk-song collector) and one can't help thinking that even with his flashes of genius and the compositional loose ends tied up by Finzi and Ferguson, his vocal lines are sometimes only just coherent. He missed not having a singer truly dedicated to his art, as Gervase Elwes was to Roger Quilter or Wilfrid Brown would later be to Finzi.

Unlike almost every other composer to date, Gurney had parents who were 'in trade', tailors who had little time for music, which was considered a decadent pastime indulged by those out of reach further up the social ladder. The young composer was always short of money and often relied on the generosity of friends and more distant family members. The Royal College and Academy offered scholarships, many endowed by previously successful musicians, but they were solidly upper-middle-class institutions in which those from working families such as Ernest Farrar and Ivor Gurney were few and far between. The provincial conservatoires had less prestige but a more socially balanced intake, though it was not until after the Second World War that composers from more varied backgrounds came to signify a change in the social fabric. The Royal Manchester College in the 1950s included the students Harrison Birtwistle, whose parents were bakers, and Peter Maxwell Davies, whose father was a foreman in an optical instruments factory. Ambitious and carried along by a modernist aesthetic, they had to make their mark with grand public gestures in order to be heard; with the obvious exception of Britten (his father was a dentist), the song with piano, a survivor from another social universe, did not appeal.

The land of lost content was a man's world, and none of the authorities on English song has much to say about the small but significant number of women who were drawn to Housman's verse in the 1920s. Many had been Stanford's pupils at the Royal College of Music, including the Anglo-American Rebecca Clarke (one of his first), Freda Swain, composer of more than a hundred songs who later taught at the Royal College, and Muriel Herbert, who was much admired by Quilter but succumbed to marriage and subsequent obscurity. Janet Hamilton was a sometime Ireland pupil whose 'By Wenlock Town' was recorded by Gervase Elwes; Christabel Marillier, daughter of artist Arthur Hopkins and niece of the more famous Gerard Manley, the American Ora Agatha Johnson and Hilda Milvain, taught by Bairstow in York and briefly organist at Rochester Cathedral – the first woman (and one of the few ever) to be appointed to such a post in England – all set Housman's poems. They tended to choose the poems that told of landscape rather than lads.

Two composers whose Housman settings have always maintained a presence in recitalists' repertoire are John Ireland and C.W. Orr. Ireland's *Land of Lost Content* is perhaps the most evocative, 'The Lent Lily' being one of his most exquisite songs and the whole cycle having a melodic and harmonic poignancy that at times comes close to a jazz-like chromaticism. Orr, like Gurney a Gloucestershire man, was obsessed with the poet, but his rich textures don't quite match those of Ireland and his melodic lines lack the deceptive simplicity of Butterworth. His finest song is a tribute to another poet, his contribution to *The Joyce Book*. 'Bahnhofstrasse' captures Joyce at the moment when glaucoma was about to strike and he feared for his sight. Orr's repeated pedal notes are sustained throughout the piece, counting down the hours until possibly permanent darkness. There were, of course, composers who didn't succumb to the Salopian muse, Peter Warlock being the most obvious; Finzi attempted a number of Housman settings in the 1920s but found the earthier colours of Thomas Hardy more to his taste.

History then moved on, and English Romantic song had a brief period of innocence before being overtaken by another world war, after which the *Shropshire Lad* songs resurfaced, classical rather than contemporary, as a reminder of the terrible cost in artistic lives. Butterworth's *Shropshire Lad* proved to be the most popular Housman cycle for most of the twentieth century, though it was Vaughan Williams's *On Wenlock Edge* that garnered the greatest critical acclaim. The latter nevertheless is an uneven work (even without the football) and the decision to set it for chamber ensemble rather than the traditional voice and piano has meant fewer performances. It's awkward (and expensive) to programme in a conventional English song recital and has often lost out to Butterworth.

Following the Second World War, the plangency of Butterworth and the composers from the earlier war added a seriousness and depth of purpose to programme planning, set alongside the coming generation of Britten, Michael Tippett and Lennox Berkeley (men, obviously, as even sopranos were socialised into the assumption of male compositional genius). No one wanted to set more Housman with the exception in the 1970s of Peter Pope, whose songs languished in manuscript. Released from the clutches of the Plymouth Brethren, he resumed a creative life preserved in the compositional amber of the interwar years.

'The Lads in Their Hundreds' is not a piece that would top a performer's list of great songs. Its very ordinariness tells the story of its time, but beneath the bitter-sweet gaiety of the doomed young men the social and musical landscape is shifting. Butterworth came to know and to die alongside the men from whom he had collected folk songs in a time of vanished innocence less than a decade before. His Housman settings would still have the sentiment wrung out of them in drawing-room renderings after the war, but songwriting itself would no longer be the preserve of the gentleman amateur, which it had in effect been since the eighteenth century. It was almost too late, as new concepts of professionalism, poetry, music and the voice, simmering away in the first part of the century, eventually coalesced into a modernist project that would question the very nature of song. Ironically, as folk music had provided art song with a fresh strand of socio-musical DNA, the status and future history of songwriting would also be challenged by a newly legitimised and sophisticated popular music in the second half of the century. The successors of the enthusiastically collected (or manufactured) folk song of the early twentieth century would achieve a worldwide currency, leaving the conventional art song disorientated in a shrinking middle-class landscape.

Perhaps it needn't have been quite like that. Butterworth died before the seeds planted in his music by folk musicians had a chance to germinate. He could reproduce and harmonise the tunes, but his only original folk-like song is 'The Lads in Their Hundreds', written before he went to war. Had he survived the conflict, would his close and often fatal encounters with the singers of folk music who served alongside him have left a deeper legacy in his future songwriting? It's futile to speculate of course, but perhaps a post-war return to folk song might have produced something that reached further into our common humanity than the charming settings of Vaughan Williams (the ambulance driver) and later Benjamin Britten (a conscientious objector). The singer of 'The Lads in Their Hundreds' has to suspend most of what they have been taught, lest the singing gets in the way of the song. Butterworth's notes on the songs he collected often mention the voices and personalities of the singers, and perhaps he

would have encouraged a more authentic voice in future performances. No song has to be sung in Received Pronunciation; it's just
what opera singers are taught to do and it surely alienates as many
listeners as it attracts. June Tabor's recording of 'The Lads in Their
Hundreds' shows that you don't need to have a classical technique to
tell a story: each of us can do that in our own voice.

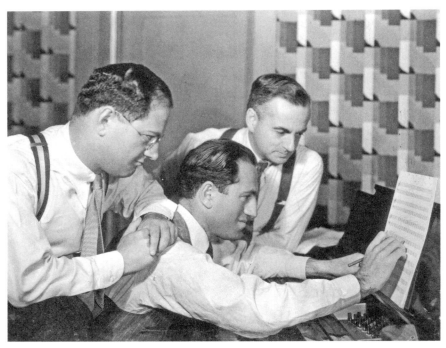

George Gershwin at the piano, with brother Ira, left, and dramatist Guy Bolton, right (1925).

10

GEORGE GERSHWIN
'SUMMERTIME'

There is no getting away from the fact that in the story so far, with the exception of a small number of women, the composers and performers have all been of the dead white male variety. It's not really surprising, given that much of the story has coincided with the rise and rise of the Western white middle class over many generations, but it does need saying. The central narrative has many gaps which might have been filled by women had they been allowed to write their own history, but we are at least aware of the problem now and are trying to put things right. The 'white' element is more problematic, and awareness of the problem in classical music has only recently begun to achieve a critical mass which should energise attempts to recalibrate our attitudes to racial diversity.

My end of the music profession (I still hesitate to use the word 'business') is certainly age-blind (my current colleagues are mostly half my age; I worked with plenty of older musicians when I was younger), and we're relatively gender-blind (nobody cares much about other people's sleeping arrangements and I have worked with a number of transgender musicians and students). I suspect we would be colour-blind too, if only we had the opportunity. I have written in the past about the lack of diversity among professional classical tenors and that is still the case, certainly in the UK. The Hilliard Ensemble only ever had one Black student attend our summer schools, and the BBC Singers had only one Black member during my youth. I have worked with only two other Black singers, the baritone Roderick Williams (in his youth) and the tenor Wills Morgan (star of *Jerry Springer the Opera*). When Wills was a member of the ensemble Red Byrd ours were the only early-music publicity photos in the UK to feature a Black face.

The lack of diversity in classical music, the elite music, is the very opposite of the scene in popular music, which is, broadly speaking, open to anyone. Perhaps that says enough about our society: we should just get on and fix it. But part of the reason that there are almost as few professional Black classical musicians working in England as there were in the eighteenth century is down to missed opportunities to embrace change and relinquish an underlying assumption of a kind of musical purity. George Gershwin's 1935 opera *Porgy and Bess*, and specifically the aria 'Summertime', crossed genres from classical to jazz and popular music, enabling Black musicians to begin to free classical song from its institutional white male straitjacket, causing considerable controversy along the way. The intertwined issues of race and genre are still being played out: the work has been claimed by opera houses and Broadway theatres as well as pop and jazz musicians and classical recitalists, and has been critiqued by both sides for its perceived positive and negative engagement with racism. When Schoenberg said you should grasp the whole meaning of a song from the music alone regardless of the text, he was only a little ahead of his time: nobody ever listened to 'Summertime' and just heard the words.

Europe had been trading with territories in Africa since classical times, though south of the Sahara was always mysterious and largely unexplored. Cultural contacts were more ephemeral, but paintings of sixteenth-century townscapes in great trading centres such as Lisbon sometimes show a surprisingly diverse population. It is possible that the first Black musician to appear in print was the Portuguese composer and theorist Vicente Lusitano (*c.* 1520–*c.* 1561). He is described as being of mixed race, though what this meant is somewhat uncertain. His fame, before music historians realised that he may have been the first Black European musician, was due to his success in a public debate which took place in Rome in 1551 with fellow theorist Nicola Vicentino; the two argued for a week about the relationship between ancient Greek modal theory and contemporary Renaissance practice. It was the kind of abstruse argument that baffles even today's musicologists and it resulted in Vicentino publishing his *L'antica musica ridotta alla moderna prattica* four years later in an attempt to justify his reasoning. This has been hailed by successive historians as a major theoretical work, though many have noted that it didn't lead him to write very interesting music, even aided by his revolutionary *archicembalo* with its thirty-one-note scale. The early-music movement rediscovered Vicentino and many attempts have been made to reconstruct his supposedly radical microtonal madrigals and the fact that he lost the debate was forgotten, as were any considerations of what Lusitano's music might have sounded like. More recently, the possibility that Lusitano may have been Black has led to the rediscovery of his music. Some of his more chromatic motets are unique, and much more appealing to the modern taste for novelty than those of his rival (think of Carlo Gesualdo dreaming of Richard Strauss). There isn't much of it, and

Lusitano never managed to find the *maestro di cappella* post that he surely deserved, which might have been because of his colour. He eventually moved from Italy to Germany, after which he is heard from no more.

If he was of mixed race Lusitano was a rare late-sixteenth-century musician of colour, and clearly his intellectual and musical prowess made a bigger impression than his skin, which seems to have caused little comment. We know nothing of his family background, but the Portuguese had many contacts with Africa. There is no hint in the admittedly threadbare sources that he was descended from slaves (the Portuguese had begun transporting Africans to Brazil around fifty years earlier), and there is a gap of around two hundred years before we hear of more Black musicians as slavery drew to a close.

The successful Black musicians who first surfaced in Europe were visible because they were colourful and exotic, and there were relatively few of them. They were also extraordinary people who often managed to make the best of their unique status. They were almost always male, the sons of ambitious fathers who strove to give their offspring the maximum opportunity to become celebrated members of white society. Ignatius Sancho (*c.* 1729–80), who published *A Collection of New Songs* in 1769, is thought to be the first Black man in Britain to vote and the first to have a published obituary. He was a friend of the actor David Garrick and Laurence Sterne and he was a key figure in the abolitionist movement. Born on a slave ship and orphaned soon after birth, he was brought to England at the age of two. His master took him to Greenwich and gifted him to three sisters who called him Sancho as they thought he looked like Cervantes' Sancho Panza. It was not a happy time for the child but he was rescued by Lord Montague, an ex-governor of Jamaica who had previously sponsored former slaves. Attracted by Sancho's spirit, Montague took him onto his staff and saw to his education. On

Montague's death his duchess, who had initially taken some persuasion to accept Sancho, employed him as her butler and left him an annuity in her will. He eventually became too obese to continue in service, but the later Montagues were sufficiently fond of him to establish a grocer's business in Westminster for Sancho and his wife Anne (who was also of African descent). Details of his life are sparse and based largely on his letters and the short biography by Joseph Jekyll that introduces the first volume.

Joseph de Bologne (1745–99), later the Chevalier de Saint-Georges, born in Guadeloupe, was also multi-talented. The son of a slave owner and one of his servants, like many offspring of colonial inter-racial liaisons in the eighteenth century, Joseph was brought to France with the expectation of a life in service. He very quickly revealed almost miraculous skills as a swordsman. Such was his prowess that in his youth his swordplay eclipsed his musical reputation with the result that we know nothing of how he became an accomplished violinist. In 1769 he joined Gossec's Concert des Amateurs (a professional ensemble despite its name) and four years later became its director. Over the next few years Saint-Georges wrote symphonies, string quartets, violin concertos and songs, and in 1776 was part of a group of entrepreneurs applying for custodianship of the Opéra. Until this point Saint-Georges seems to have lived a charmed life, his African origins less significant than his charisma and genius with sword and bow. There were limits to his acceptance, however, and his bid to run the Opéra produced an early example of institutional racism: some of the singers and dancers petitioned the queen that they should not have to submit to the 'orders of a mulatto'. Undaunted, Saint-Georges went on to compose several operas, none of which met with much success, but it's possible that his republican leanings date from this incident. He was well received in aristocratic salons where he is said to have performed *romances*, and Saint-Georges made two trips to England where he was received by the Prince of Wales. His second visit was immortalised by the artist, fellow swordsman and composer Alexandre-Auguste Robineau, who captured the exhibition fight at Carleton House in 1787 between Saint-Georges and the Chevalier(e) d'Eon, a transgender fencer and sometime spy, who fought in a silk dress and bonnet.

The fall of the Bastille in 1789 brought an end to the old European order and (temporarily) the comfortable round of salon visits; Saint-Georges joined the National Guard, eventually leading a 'mulatto' regiment against the Austrians. In 1796 he went back to the West Indies with fellow musician (horn virtuoso) and fencer Lamothe as part of a mission to abolish slavery. Saint-Georges disappears from view in the chaotic savagery of the colonial wars on Hispaniola (later to be divided into Haiti and the Dominican Republic), reappearing two years later to reinvent himself for a final time as a violinist before his death in 1799. Most of his compositions are instrumental, many for the violin, but a collection of songs and a number of individual songs and arias have survived.

George Bridgetower (1778–1860) was born in Biała Podlaska, Poland, the son of an 'African' (possibly West Indian) father and Polish (possibly German) mother. Members of the Radziwiłł family, for whom his parents worked, stood as godparents. The family moved to the Esterházy court where George's prodigious talent on the violin almost certainly attracted the attention of Haydn (whose pupil George subsequently claimed to have been). Bridgetower's father was very ambitious for his son, and moved the family to Germany where there was the opportunity for his seven-year-old offspring to give concert tours. Bridgetower senior was fluent in several languages and moved to England with his son when George was ten, the father describing himself (and dressing for the part) as an African prince. After playing to the king in Windsor, the young George performed in Bath, the country's second cultural capital and summer resort of the aristocracy. The concert, a huge success, was promoted by the city's resident composer, the castrato Venanzio Rauzzini, who was amazed by the young boy's talent. Perhaps the distinguished castrato also had in mind the grim parallel between the musical sons of African slaves and the Italian boys selected for castration to preserve their voices: those who made it could be very successful indeed; those who didn't vanished from sight.

The Prince of Wales opened many doors for George Bridgetower and paid his father's costs back to Germany when the latter's reputation as an over-ambitious foreigner began to be harmful to his son's career. In Vienna in 1803, Bridgetower had his famous encounter with Beethoven, who dedicated his A minor Violin Sonata to him, the *Sonata mulattica composta per il mulatto Brischdauer gran pazzo e compositore mulattico* (Mulatto Sonata composed for the mulatto Brischdauer, big mad mulatto composer). The two apparently fell out and the published version emerged with its dedication to Kreutzer (for whom it proved too difficult). While he was in England, Bridgetower studied composition with Thomas Attwood and published a collection of songs, now lost, which presumably served him well in aristocratic drawing rooms; his one surviving ballad, 'Henry', was dedicated to the Princess of Wales. Bridgetower's colourful heritage gave rise to exotic and largely fictional backstories, which were incorporated so firmly into the family history that his grandson made a claim to the Abyssinian throne.

Sancho, the Chevalier de Saint-Georges and George Bridgetower had the good fortune to be co-opted into the posh end of a society whose sense of self was measured by cultural as well as financial and social enrichment. It's no coincidence that all these musicians were in the first instance talented instrumentalists from a very early age: their patrons were impressed by the sheer skill and the novelty of such talent in a child from an unknown continent; *kudos* came with creating someone in your own image who did not actually look like you. From a very young age the children knew nothing but aristocratic service and patronage, and they exploited their circumstances in the only way open to them. Musically, they had no option but to become pillars of the establishment and any 'Africanisms' that may have found their way into their music would have been perceived as charming or quaint by their audiences and patrons.

At the moment there are few visible successors to these three charismatic figures later in the century, though future historians will surely enhance the narrative. The Brazilian Antonio Carlos Gomes had some success in the theatre (including a Verdian opera performed at La Scala), but in the British Isles it was not until Samuel Coleridge-Taylor (1875–1912) astonished the Anglophone musical world with *Hiawatha's Wedding Feast* in 1898 that the question of a composer's colour reasserted itself. Coleridge-Taylor's father was from the new post-slavery Black middle class in Sierra Leone and had come to England to study medicine. He qualified as a doctor and after what seems to have been a brief encounter with a white English woman called Alice Martin he returned to Africa, perhaps not knowing she was pregnant. Coleridge, as the family would know him, never knew his father and was brought up by Alice and his grandfather in what is now the London suburb of Croydon, encouraged and supported by well-connected local musicians. He sang in church choirs and, like so many musicians of African heritage, developed an early and precocious talent for the violin. Having enrolled as a violin student at the Royal College of Music, he made the change to composition and became one of Stanford's star pupils. Edward Elgar, whose works would later eclipse those of Coleridge-Taylor, was among many more senior figures to recognise his talent. Elgar later came to have a somewhat jaundiced opinion of Coleridge-Taylor's music, but he passed on to the younger composer a significant commission with the Three Choirs Festival which helped to launch Coleridge-Taylor's career.

Coleridge-Taylor was a prolific and obsessive composer who made an extraordinary impact on the British and American musical establishments. His secular cantata *Hiawatha's Wedding Feast* made his reputation on both sides of the Atlantic when he was only twenty-three, and although Longfellow's poem is a Native American epic, it stimulated Coleridge-Taylor's interest in his own racial heritage. His subsequent tours of the USA were a landmark in raising the profile of Black musicians (he even managed to conduct performances by all-white orchestras) and were an uplifting contrast to the casual racism revealed in the memoir by his wife, the former Jessie Walmisley, who had been a fellow student at the Royal College of Music.

History hasn't been kind to Coleridge-Taylor's music. His death in 1912 from pneumonia at the age of thirty-seven was a shock and produced tributes from across the social and musical spectrum, with multi-racial crowds lining the streets at his funeral. Elgar and Vaughan Williams would dominate the interwar years, and Coleridge-Taylor's potential position in the national music hierarchy is one of the great 'what ifs' of English music. He wrote a large number of songs; they are distinctive but have generally been considered slight through the lens that also sees the composers who succeeded him. The songs are not alone in their neglect: almost all English vocal music of the period has disappeared into the black hole that is late Victorian and Edwardian taste. 'Onaway! Awake, Beloved!', the tenor aria from *Hiawatha* that became something of a hit, still survives as an occasional music diploma test piece, but Coleridge-Taylor's choral music has even dropped out of that refuge of forgotten anthems, the English cathedral repertoire.

His reputation also doesn't quite fit the modern binary Black/white narrative of identity politics. His background was more conventionally middle class: he was an English Black success. The texts of his most famous song cycle, *Sorrow Songs*, are not the sorrow songs of W.E.B. Du Bois's *Souls of the Black Folk* but poems by Christina Rossetti ('When I am dead my dearest' was sung at his funeral). There is the problematic fact that Longfellow's poem has always been controversial, as has any work by a white man purporting to represent the voice of a different race. The race in question is a further awkwardness: although Coleridge-Taylor's work inspired both African Americans and Native Americans, the depressed and repressed position of the latter in American culture is seen from Europe as beyond rescue: Black lives matter, but Native Americans nonetheless seem in public consciousness to remain Indians. Coleridge-Taylor's music resists recovery because of its essential Englishness (and perhaps because there is too much of it). He never really made it in Germany, the English composers' Mecca (his half-hearted attempts to get there invariably ended at Dover). He moved freely between English and African communities in London and knew key figures such as Du Bois and Frederick Loudin of the Fisk Jubilee Singers, but discovering the music of his African heritage came too late in his short life; it seems in retrospect more like an add-on to his Stanfordian inheritance and Dvořákian aspirations. His hopes for his own music were that it would do for 'his race' what Grieg and Dvořák did for their national folk musics and Brahms did for the profile of Hungarian gypsies, incorporating them as colourful melodic and rhythmic tropes into the Eurocentric mainstream.

With the death of Coleridge-Taylor, Britain lost the first (and so far last) African-English classical composer to capture the public imagination, and with no successors the chance of recolouring the musical landscape faded to white. The twenty-year period in which Coleridge-Taylor's star briefly dazzled the musical scene has remained in a historical limbo, overshadowed on both sides of the Atlantic by the First World War and in the United States by the Harlem Renaissance of the following decades.

Almost lost in the fog of the first few decades of the twentieth century was the only English composer actually to have had direct experience of an American plantation, the enigmatic Frederick Delius (1862–1934). The son of a German wool merchant who settled in the north of England, Fritz Delius (as he was christened) was born in Bradford. He was a talented violinist and pianist as a child and grew up in the cultured atmosphere of a wealthy middle-class home. He was expected to join the family firm, and his father sent him to Germany, Sweden and France to familiarise him with the business, which yielded little business acumen but much musical enquiry. In 1884, perhaps as a last attempt to stimulate the young Delius's commercial instincts, his father took a lease on an orange grove in Florida and sent the young Fritz to manage it.

Sitting on his veranda beside the St Johns River at Solanto Grove inland from the port of Jacksonville, Delius heard the songs of Black labourers drifting across from the plantation on the opposite bank. Smoking cigar after cigar, idling away the warm evenings, the wealthy, musically talented Anglo-German was inspired to write music of his own, and later would often reminisce about those evenings on his porch. He had heard American minstrel shows in Bradford in his youth, but his Floridian experience, immersed temporarily in Black culture, was not the regularised harmony made safe for white audiences; it was something altogether strange and untranscribable. Many of Delius's own pieces would have traces of American or Afro-American music at a micro-level, rhythmically and harmonically, though his music often defies conventional analysis. He studied briefly in Leipzig and eventually settled in France, and his music never quite fitted the conventional musical narrative despite being championed by Thomas Beecham. His profile as a composer is unique: a largely self-taught Anglo-German musician who lived most of his life in France, a truly European composer inspired in the first instance by the music of Black Americans.

After the First World War, Stravinsky, Hindemith, Milhaud and a raft of composers engaged selectively with jazz, in the main seduced by what many considered a transgressive harmonic language. The more obvious elements of Debussy's cakewalking or the invented Africanisms of Poulenc's *Rapsodie nègre* obscure more subtle influences of Black culture which musicologists continue to speculate over. Is Ravel's *Chansons madécasses*, commissioned by Elizabeth Sprague Coolidge in 1926, the result of a real understanding of Madagascan music or are the songs just a composer spectacularly fulfilling a rather exotic brief? There are subtly tangled threads here: what might have been perfectly obvious as benign and sincerely meant African influences at the time may have gathered other connotations in retrospect, and most of the African-influenced white composers would subsequently be accused of cultural appropriation. A less controversial but no less significant observation we can make is that a music beyond the European tradition momentarily enriched the music of some significant classical composers, especially in France.

The Europeans of African descent had almost invariably flourished in the national music of the country they ended up in, success measured by how far they were integrated into the onward march of European musical history. This was never going to happen in the USA, with its fractured history of a European master race almost obliterating the native population and subsequently transporting countless numbers of people from Africa in order to enslave them. Inevitably, North American classical music and much of its popular music were influenced by (or actually were) European music. The native population remained a cultural mystery to most white Americans; in 1900 there were less than a quarter of a million Native Americans (and

almost 9 million Afro-Americans, just over 11 per cent of the population). The chances of the continent's original inhabitants making any
sort of impact on the national music were very slim indeed (and remain
so, despite more recent attempts to bring the two cultures together).
The thirteenth amendment to the US constitution abolished slavery in
1865 but segregation lingered on for almost a hundred years until the
Civil Rights Act of 1964, and genuine emancipation seems even now to
be a long way off. There were nineteenth-century Black composers,
living in a parallel and segregated universe, and there were white
composers who were influenced by Black music, but the hesitant glances
from one side towards the other needed more substantial encounters to
shift the cultural inertia. Coleridge-Taylor would provide one such
stimulus, but before him America briefly adopted a Czech composer.

Nobody, Black or white in turn-of-the-century America, could
possibly have envisaged the musical revolution that would unfold
as the twentieth century progressed and Black music planted the
seeds which grew into the world's popular music. One European
composer who believed an American national classical music could
evolve from the bottom up was Antonín Dvořák (1841–1904), who
began a three-year stay in the USA in 1892, directing the National
Conservatory of Music in New York. The Conservatory, founded by
Paris Conservatoire-educated philanthropist Jeannette Thurber in
1885, was an extraordinarily enlightened institution which not only
was racially integrated but gave special consideration to women and
to those with disabilities. Thurber's aim was to kickstart an American
classical music that was independent of its European heritage and
recognised the ethnic diversity of the continent's own music. Crucially,
her vision ensured scholarships were available, so the most talented
need never be turned away.

Dvořák was the perfect match to Thurber's vision, though his
conviction that the future of American classical music would be

based on African and Indian folk roots now seems naively optimistic. Nevertheless, his Ninth Symphony ('New World') was a landmark attempt to reflect the country's mixed heritage. As would be the case with Coleridge-Taylor a few years later, Dvořák was sufficiently impressed by Longfellow's *Hiawatha* epic to consider using it himself. Like Coleridge-Taylor, his interest in the continent's original inhabitants led him sideways to the music of former slaves. He had been deeply moved by hearing spirituals sung by Harry Burleigh (1866–1949), a second-year student at the National Conservatory that the composer took on as his assistant and copyist. The two shared similar histories and aspirations, Dvořák determined to acknowledge his Czech inheritance in a basically German cultural landscape, and the young Black student seeking to find a place for the music of his forebears in the musically Eurocentric environment of the Conservatory. Burleigh was primarily a vocal student and studied composition with Rubin Goldmark (whose students would later include George Gershwin and Aaron Copland). During Dvořák's first year in New York, Burleigh spent many hours in the company of the composer, singing and discussing the slave songs he had learned from his grandfather. Their sessions together created the well-spring from which the Czech composer would draw the inspiration for the first great work celebrating African-American music, the 'New World' Symphony.

Burleigh's fellow students included Will Marion Cook (1869–1944), who like Burleigh went on to make a significant contribution to the profile of Black music. Despairing of making any impact in the classical sphere, Cook turned his talents to musical theatre. His *In Dahomey* from 1903 was the first African-American Broadway production and the following year his *The Southerners* was the first Broadway production with a completely integrated cast. Cook was from a middle-class background but collaborated with the poet Paul

Lawrence Dunbar, both of whose parents had been slaves and who wrote in dialect. This turned out to be a mixed blessing as attitudes to dialect later changed among both Black and white communities. Cook would mentor Duke Ellington, encouraging him to go his own way and not allow himself to be drawn into institutional conformity. Burleigh stayed within the classical domain, becoming a notable composer of songs and choral music, and the country's first successful Black baritone (his fame rivalling that of the Black tenor Roland Hayes). More importantly, encouraged by his time with Dvořák, he brought the slave songs to both Black and white communities with arrangements that are still performed today. He also established an instant rapport with Coleridge-Taylor, singing in the first American performances of *Hiawatha*, touring with the English composer as a recitalist, and later working with him in England.

Burleigh's arrangements of spirituals were an attempt to vitiate the pseudo-authenticity of the minstrel shows by finding a style that retained the original aesthetic and yet would enable the songs to stand comparison with the songs of Schubert and the great European composers. This was a difficult balancing act, and like so many aspects of the race question it was far from a binary problem. The Fisk Jubilee Singers, founded in 1871 to raise funds for Fisk University College (formerly Fisk Free Colored School for the education of freed slaves), were among the first to bring Black music to white audiences with an authenticity and respect that bypassed the indignities of black-face minstrelsy and coon songs. The singers had great success, especially on European tours (Coleridge-Taylor heard them in London), but from the moment they began to bring slave music out of the Black cultural ghetto and into mixed-race concert halls they not only encountered the white elitist trope that Negro music was inherently inferior (sub-human, even), but they began the journey into what we now call identity politics, on the jagged rocks of which the entire debate about Black and white music still comes so close to foundering. Attempts by early-twentieth-century white composers to engage with Native American composers are still dogged by accusations of appropriation, yet we will happily listen to Brahms or Vaughan Williams incorporating folk music into the European aesthetic.

The Fisk Jubilee Singers' repertoire included music by Stephen Foster, whose songs also featured in black-face shows and who was considered by many to be the father of American music. For all the cultural appropriation that may have occurred (in whatever direction), the one thing we can say with reasonable certainty is that audiences could tell the difference between black-face and the real thing, and were capable of being moved by a performance sincerely meant. The bizarre and ultimately unknowable melting pot that was turn-of-the-century inter-racial music-making even saw Burleigh and others blacking up for fun: musicians did (and do) what they needed to do to make things work for themselves and their audience. Beneath the turmoil the future was being created by musicians such as Will Marion Cook and Harry Burleigh, whose empathy and steadfastness could bridge what so often seemed like an impossible divide. Cook said of Burleigh, 'I know of no Negro (not even Coleridge-Taylor) during the last fifty years, so loved and who has done so much to lift his and my Godforsaken Race out of the mire – as this grand old man – Harry T. Burleigh.' It was a sentiment often expressed by those who knew him, Black and white.

Then, in an unlikely and magical example of historical synergy, one of the most remarkable examples of Black music came to be written by a white man. George Gershwin (1898–1937) was already one of America's most successful composers when he composed *Porgy and Bess* in 1935. As a teenager Gershwin was a gifted pianist, and although he had many classically inclined teachers he succumbed to the lure of song promotion, soon writing his own songs in collaboration with his brother Ira. By his mid-twenties he had written huge hits as well as groundbreaking concert music such as the Piano Concerto in F and *Rhapsody in Blue*. While continuing to produce highly successful Broadway shows he turned to European composers in an attempt to expand his technique, but both Nadia Boulanger and Maurice Ravel declined to take him on, on the grounds that he already had a unique voice and should continue to follow his own path. Gershwin sometimes gave the impression of never quite knowing exactly what that path was, and he seems to have finally discovered it when he read DuBose Heyward's 1925 novel *Porgy* about the life and community of a disabled Black beggar.

Gershwin called it an American folk opera, and together with Heyward researched the backstory of Porgy with extended visits to the Gullah communities in South Carolina. The Gullah Negroes were the most authentically 'African' of all the post-slavery communities, retaining their own language, a creole that featured many elements of African grammar and vocabulary. In 1934 on Folly Island, not far from Charleston, the two immersed themselves in the local culture; Gershwin became so adept at the complicated footwork of the 'shouting' dances which accompanied spirituals that he was hailed as the only white man in the country capable of being a champion shouter.

If the libretto was informed by a folk tradition, the music was going to rest on operatic foundations so could only be performed by trained singers. The cast that Gershwin assembled, hand-picked from the best Black opera singers he could find, knew little of the South and nothing of Gullah dialect. They had to be coached, and the more the production was accepted by white audiences, the more the language was neutralised to make it more acceptable to opera-goers. The successful afterlife of 'Summertime' beyond its original context is partly due to the universality of its language, the small dialect elements being easily modified.

'Summertime' is the work of a singer-songwriter. Gershwin wouldn't have admitted to the singer part (he mostly sang only to entertain friends in private), and his brother Ira wrote the words, but the song has the intimate connection between voice and accompaniment that allows you to stretch time between the two; in the process you elongate the image of summer itself. More conventional composers would assume the stress to be on the first syllable of 'summertime'; a student composer putting the stress on the third syllable would raise a tutorly eyebrow. It has the upbeat feel of waiting to establish the key, but instead of moving off further into the harmony it returns to the first note, keeping the listener in a state of suspension. In fact, the singer keeps everyone waiting: this is going to be a long, lazy, hot summer, all indicated in the first three notes. It is not the calculation of a composer thinking about technique and form, but that of a songwriter empathising with his audience.

It moved its earliest hearers. Todd Duncan, the first Porgy, and Rouben Mamoulian, director of the original production, both had cathartic experiences in the Gershwin apartment on first hearing 'Summertime'. Mamoulian had directed the original stage play and agreed to direct the opera without knowing anything about the score. Putting his Hollywood career temporarily on hold, he arrived in New York to be entertained by George and Ira with an informal sing-through over drinks. He was captivated, describing the two brothers' ad hoc rendering of 'Summertime' as beatific, summoning up the Southern sun as they busked their way through it, eyes closed, each taking over from the other when they could no longer resist joining in. The two sang late into the night, singing all the parts and half the orchestra, and were voiceless the next day.

Todd Duncan had been summoned to the Gershwin apartment to a three-way audition session, Gershwin needing to persuade Duncan that he should play Porgy, and both Gershwin and Duncan having to convince the producers of the Theatre Guild that he could do it. Duncan and his wife had encountered the Guild's Lawrence Langner ('a foppish man in striped pants') in the lift and not been very impressed, but Duncan won over the assembled company with a mixture of opera arias, Lieder and spirituals. Then, after some refreshment, George and Ira started their *alternatim* rendition of 'Summertime'. Duncan, an operatic baritone who would go on to perform Porgy close to 2,000 times, thought neither of them could sing in tune, but by the second verse was ready to weep.

The similar reactions of Mamoulian, a white Armenian immigrant filmmaker, and Duncan, a Black baritone fresh from performing *Cavalleria rusticana* with a Black opera company, were early indications that Gershwin had got it right with 'Summertime': on a basic human level a song in a minor key, in which optimism shines through the oppressive Southern heat, has everything and nothing to do with race. Unlike its signature song, *Porgy and Bess* the opera would often turn out to be everything to do with race, with Black musicians and activists either welcoming it or denigrating it according to the socio-political wind. The best intentions were often a casualty of the culture war: the Royal Liverpool Philharmonic's intended performance in 1989 using local Black choirs was eventually cancelled as Black arts organisations found the prospect offensive; too often the work has been seen simply in black and white.

The first version of 'Summertime' to escape from the opera house/ Broadway dichotomy was by the twenty-one-year-old Billie Holiday in 1936. It's a long way from an operatic lullaby and encapsulates the exponential interpretative power of a pop song as opposed to an art song: the performers don't simply interpret the music, they recreate it and then become it. There are countless recordings of the song (currently thought to be more than 30,000), each of them unique. Billie Holiday's is strangely disengaged, the tune oddly compressed as though she doesn't quite know what to do with it, letting Artie Shaw's clarinet and Bunny Berigan's trumpet share the limelight. She was famous (notorious to some) for adding her own contribution to any arrangement and she would never have sung any song the same way twice, so perhaps the recording doesn't really tell us much. But it was a hit, and it set a precedent: this was not just an operatic lullaby, it was anything you wanted it to be, and anyone could leave out swathes of Gershwin's notes and add their own. The Gershwin estate got the royalties, but the performers owned the music.

Gershwin didn't live to see the long-term consequences of his creation, dying three years later at the age of thirty-eight. *Porgy and Bess* underwent many changes, always attracting controversy except when performed instrumentally; jazz musicians quickly took the songs on board and classical musicians arranged concert suites. Decontexualised, 'Summertime' became the world's most popular tune, stimulating musicians to ever greater heights of whimsicality and celebration. There are too many to name, but we could make a start with Joe Pass on guitar duetting with Oscar Peterson playing clavichord for the first time (thanks to encountering the one owned by British Prime Minister Edward Heath); Joni Mitchell singing almost none of Gershwin's notes powered along by Herbie Hancock, Wayne Shorter, Stevie Wonder and Ira Coleman; Peter Gabriel and Larry Adler, Paul McCartney (both in Hamburg with the Beatles – a recording now lost – and his own version with Mick Green), Janis Joplin re-harmonised in a rock-baroque extravaganza ... It would take a book longer than this one just to list them all. Listening just once to each one would take you more than a year at a rate of around eight hours' worth a day, and you would hear performances by some of the finest musicians of their time.

The list would include many wonderful versions of 'Summertime' sung by Lieder recitalists and famous opera singers from Leontyne Price to Harolyn Blackwell. These tend to respect (or at least acknowledge) Gershwin's original orchestration and treat the song as the lullaby first heard in the opening scene of the opera. This is classical music doing what it does best, the conductor representing the dead composer and facilitating the best possible performance from a classically trained singer. And yet many will find the insistent vibrato and carefully calculated tempi over-stylised and stilted, even though this was what Gershwin apparently wanted when he chose his first cast. He was trying to persuade American society that there was a uniquely American music to be unleashed, and that it would involve all races on equal terms. In a culture so racially lopsided his Black cast had to be the best, and in vocal terms had to equal whatever a white cast might have done with the songs. But those first iterations in the composer's apartment were sung by the two brothers who famously couldn't sing. It was pure music, and in retrospect Rouben Mamoulian thought the blissed-out rendering they did for him was the best performance he ever heard.

*Benjamin Britten and Peter Pears rehearsing, observed by Ronald
Duncan and Arthur Oldham (1949).*

11

BENJAMIN BRITTEN
'O MIGHT THOSE SIGHES AND TEARES RETURNE AGAINE'

Towards the end of the twentieth century the song recital declined in the United States and much of Europe. In England music clubs vanished altogether and this lack of opportunity combined with the increasingly esoteric nature of modernist composition reinforced the growing disconnect between composer and audience. The tradition was kept alive by creative composers in Europe and America, most obviously in the UK by Benjamin Britten and his collaboration (as composer and pianist) with the tenor Peter Pears. Britten's relationship with literature continued the symbiotic links begun with the English lute-song composers and in his hands song arguably reached its apogee.

Britten was born in 1913 and his formative years were spent in the aftermath of the First World War, a period when English song finally flourished before eventually beginning what some would see as a slow decline as the century wore on. It's tempting to see the war as a dividing line between the insipid drawing-room offerings or royalty ballads so excoriated by most critics and the more poetic and lyrical material of the 1920s. For many composers the war was indeed a psychological *caesura*, but the change to a more experimental and sophisticated concept of song had begun decades earlier and continued with only a brief interruption in the lyrical flow.

Not a little ironically, given the failure of nineteenth-century composers to deliver the hoped-for *Liederisation* of English song, it was study at the Conservatorium in Cologne that inspired some of the most dynamic songwriters from the 1890s onwards. Both Cyril Scott and Balfour Gardiner first went to study piano with former pupils of Clara Schumann (Gardiner was seventeen, Scott only twelve), later returning to take in composition lessons with Iwan Knorr. Knorr's students would also include Roger Quilter, Norman O'Neill and Percy Grainger (briefly, as the two didn't get on). Famous in the first decade of the new century as members of the Young British School of composers, these five later became known as the Frankfurt Group. They didn't all coincide at Frankfurt but became lifelong friends united by their mutual experiences with Knorr; they also shared a love of Delius and complex chords, and a loathing of Beethoven and counterpoint. All had a strong inclination to avoid the institutional mainstream despite their sometimes conservative inclinations.

They were a privileged lot (Scott, less so), and with little time for the musical establishment and no need to earn money from their music (unless they over-plundered their allowances) they were able to produce music on their own terms. In practice, this often manifested itself in song, with private and public performances in manuscript before publication was sought. With the possible exception of Quilter, their stubborn individualism, and a tendency to write songs that sometimes diluted their purity with popularity, meant they would ultimately be doomed to long-term critical failure. But the precedent of personal creativity regardless of the mainstream would always be there for classical songwriters of the future to acknowledge. And they were not the only ones: the cantankerous Josef Holbrooke (not himself wealthy but often well supported), the eccentric and multilingual Lord Berners and the enigmatic Belgian-born Régine Wieniawski (who became the English Lady Dean Paul and composed under the pseudonym Poldowski) all wrote songs on their own terms with only a nod to current styles and idioms.

Cyril Scott (1879–1970) was probably the most talented of them all. Lauded by Debussy, courted by Stefan George, he was a prolific songwriter who found early success on both sides of the Channel, but unable to focus on a unique contemporary idiom he suffered an eclipse as great as that of Coleridge-Taylor (without the excuse of having died young). His butterfly intellect led him into the occult, alternative medicine and esoteric musical commentary, and it is only very recently that his reputation has begun to thaw. Norman O'Neill (1875–1934) became a successful theatre composer and left a large number of songs in several languages, but he died of blood poisoning following an accident in 1934 (the same year that claimed Delius, Holst and Elgar). Balfour Gardiner (1877–1950) wrote some two dozen songs but really found his voice with his 1908 cathedral anthem 'Te lucis ante terminum'. He used his considerable wealth to promote concerts of new music; his support for his less fortunate friends included buying Delius's house so that the ageing and sick composer could spend his last years without financial worry. Always diffident about his own musical worth, he gave up composition in 1925 to devote himself to forestry. Grainger arrived in Frankfurt at the age of thirteen, a talented pianist who would go on to charm society drawing rooms in England and give the first performance of Delius's Piano Concerto in 1914 before emigrating to America. Grainger wrote the quirkiest of songs, many of them based on folk tunes that he collected himself and would sing in an appropriate accent. The most enduring of the group, and possibly the only one whose songs receive more than the occasional performance today, was Roger Quilter.

Quilter (1877–1953), son of Sir Cuthbert the 1st baronet, like Gardiner often used his wealth to further his musical aims and those of his friends and acquaintances. A sickly child and rarely in good health at any point during his whole life, he discovered an early talent for songwriting. The exquisite 'Now sleeps the crimson petal' was one of his first successes, and is still sung today. Although he shared the group's love of Delius, his skills as a pianist enabled him to weave wonderfully transparent piano parts, expanding the harmony into a linear cushion on which a singer could float the poem. He frequently accompanied his own songs and was fortunate in collaborating with the sensitive and highly intelligent tenor Gervase Elwes at the start of each of their careers. Both were from aristocratic stock and used their society connections to enrich a vibrant musical and artistic life. Elwes' death in 1921 at the age of fifty-four (on tour in the USA when he fell between railway carriages) was a huge shock for the composer whose songs had been shaped and finessed by Elwes' artistry. The great tenor had premiered many works by Quilter, Vaughan Williams and a host of other living English composers.

The Elwes and Quilter circle also included Maude Valérie White (1855–1937), whose songs Quilter grew up with and who accompanied Elwes in performances of her own songs, famously becoming so excited that Elwes would sometimes find it hard to keep up. Maude Valérie White left some 150 songs, many of which, like those of her contemporaries Lisa Lehmann and Amy Woodforde-Finden, have come in for criticism on the grounds of excessive sentimentality or simply being too popular. Woodforde-Finden's songs were recorded by tenors as distinguished as Richard Tauber and Frank Titterton,

Lehmann's by John McCormack, Mario Lanza and Webster Booth among many others.

Popular success and art song are uneasy bedfellows, a wider audience somehow implying a dilution of their art (a sad assumption that still compromises some reputations today). For society women, whatever their musical activities, their primary role was still assumed to be the running of a household. This meant plenty of opportunity to display their talents at evening salons (as long as they didn't upstage their male colleagues), and they never forgot that they had an audience to appeal to; Lehmann also wrote children's songs, something that few male composers were inclined to give time to. Ironically, Ethel Smyth, their more forceful contemporary whose song output was dwarfed by her larger-scale works, was considered by many male commentators to be too masculine.

The tendency of composers to neglect song in favour of larger forms as they climbed the compositional ladder had a parallel effect with performers. English song was not a great export, and those aiming at an international career would make their mark through opera. There was a porous middle ground occupied by Clara Butt, whose international stardom depended on a potent mixture of oratorio (she was one of Elgar's favourite performers) and recital programmes which might begin with the national anthem and finish with fairies at the bottom of her garden.

Roger Quilter was fortunate to discover the singing of Mark Raphael, a similarly sensitive baritone, two years after the death of Gervase Elwes, and the two of them developed a partnership that lasted till the composer's death in 1953. Quilter first heard Raphael at the Wigmore Hall where he was accompanied by the Black pianist Lawrence Brown. Quilter's letters reveal a fascination for black musicians and their music (which wasn't quite how he put it using the colourful vocabulary of the time), and he entertained Brown and later Paul Robeson, Marian Anderson and Roland Hayes, supporting them as their careers got under way (and mitigating, where he could, the quotidian racism they inevitably experienced). The jazz-inclined Brown, the son and grandson of slaves, became Robeson's main accompanist and coach (replacing the too classical Harry Burleigh whose spirituals they would perform together). Quilter accompanied both Roland Hayes and Marian Anderson at Wigmore Hall recitals, though his graceful and elegant music seems impervious to influences beyond Fauré, Debussy and to a lesser extent Delius. He was one of the few composers of his time whose artistic persona was expressed almost entirely through songwriting.

Quilter was a key influence on the young Philip Heseltine, whose songs written under the pseudonym Peter Warlock (1894–1930) have proved to be the most enduring of any of the composers who flourished between the wars. Born in the Savoy Hotel in 1894, he died in 1930, possibly by his own hand (their mid-thirties were dangerous years for composers from Mozart and Mendelssohn to Coleridge-Taylor and Gershwin). His family had been wealthy landowners and he was sent to Eton which he did not enjoy, but eventually followed up with brief periods of study at Oxford and in Cologne; to all intents and purposes he was musically self-taught. He was uninterested in the larger forms that ambitious composers invariably turned to, and his legacy is a collection of more than a hundred songs and a legend that still intrigues nearly a century after his death.

It was an encounter with Delius's music at the age of sixteen that triggered Warlock's life-changing release of what until then had been a rather dormant musical talent. A later meeting with Bernard van Dieren led to a more linear sparseness to some of the early songs in contrast to the dense Delian harmonic textures, but the only other significant influence on his music was Elizabethan and Jacobean song and verse. His family's ties to Wales and a year in Ireland gave him a taste for Celtic poetry, and like many of his contemporaries he had a passing interest in folk song, but with one notable exception neither of these potential influences left much of a trace in his songs.

The first Warlock songs were published in 1918. There have been many fanciful explanations for the pseudonym, but three facts may have a bearing: he liked pseudonyms and enjoyed the mystification they caused, he had discovered an interest in the occult during his time in Ireland, and he had had a row with the leading song publisher Winthrop Rogers to whom he sent this first batch of songs. Rogers had rejected some songs by Bernard van Dieren commended to him by Heseltine, who reckoned their subsequent row was sufficient to jeopardise the publication of his own songs which he then decided to submit under a different name.

Warlock had been introduced to van Dieren by the sculptor Jacob Epstein whose biography van Dieren was to write, and who in turn sculpted a head of van Dieren. Van Dieren's life is still poorly documented, but he had been living in London for some years when the two composers met. The Dutchman was a charismatic polymath, fluent in several languages and, like Warlock, musically self-taught. Both were vehemently anti-establishment, and the establishment has remained consistently anti-van Dieren ever since. Very little of his music has been published, and many singers would agree that the best van Dieren is to be found in Warlock's *Saudades*, the outer two songs of which have the van Dieren chromatic linearity and lack of bar lines but actually make musical and rhetorical sense.

Saudades is a Portuguese concept meaning an inexpressible longing, melancholy or regret, and this atmosphere penetrates each of the three poems. 'Along the Stream' is Warlock's only venture into Orientalism, a Cranmer-Byng translation from the Chinese of Li-Po (a poet favoured by Warlock's friend Constant Lambert). The piece is a tribute to Bernard van Dieren (to whom it is dedicated) but, unlike the formlessness of the model, Warlock's recitative-like lines beautifully shape the text. The middle song is a more conventional setting of Shakespeare's 'Take, O take those lips away', which merely serves to point up the radicalism of its companion pieces (he would try again later with the Shakespeare – twice). 'Heracleitus', also stylistically in the van Dieren orbit, is a William Cory translation of an epigram by Callimachus (Warlock's only foray into the classics). Both outer songs are exquisitely sad, the poems distant in time and geography, but the voices of the stream and the nightingale ensure that this is not the stagnant bleakness of his cycle *The Curlew*, but a remembrance of a past to be quietly savoured.

The Curlew also dates from around this time, though it was not published until 1924 owing to the composer's ongoing row with the poet whom Warlock had met in Dublin in 1918. W.B. Yeats had been loath to let composers loose on his poetry since being traumatised by hearing his poem on solitude, 'The Lake Isle of Innisfree', given an *al fresco* rendering by a thousand boy scouts. As was his wont, Yeats duly refused permission for Warlock to set his poems, greatly angering the composer who complained vociferously in the *Musical Times* in a letter of February 1922, which only made matters worse. The cycle was eventually published but the two never resolved their differences: Warlock set no more Yeats and destroyed other existing settings; Yeats only considered the argument settled when Warlock was safely in his grave.

The song cycle, a form much loved by some German composers, was for British composers rarely more than a collection of songs set to the same poet. Perhaps for this reason Warlock did not consider *The Curlew* to be a cycle so much as a piece of chamber music. It eventually coalesced into his most extended work, a setting of four poems linked by instrumental interludes, unfolding over a period of more than twenty minutes. The poet wanders, apparently aimless and barely coherent, through a desolate marshy landscape meditating on lost love, his emotional agitation amplified by the bleak interjections of cor anglais and flute hovering over a sombre string quartet. For many there is no sadder music, Yeats's weeping, withering images of despair transformed into the instrumental calls of curlew and peewit. It is also sublimely beautiful, and considered by many to be one of the greatest English song cycles of the twentieth century.

There are more than twice as many Warlock transcriptions of sixteenth- and seventeenth-century songs as there are original compositions by the composer himself. His book on lute song, *The English Ayre*, confirms his love for verse either side of 1600, and such was his understanding of the genre he may have been tempted to write songs with lute, had there been any lute players around. Presumably to keep the risk of pastiche at bay, Warlock generally avoided poems that were set at the time, and his most 'Elizabethan' pieces never come close to aping a Renaissance model, though the word-setting and occasional affectionate archaisms leave us in no doubt about his intentions. John Fletcher's 'Sleep', which also received a ravishing setting by Ivor Gurney, is perhaps Warlock's most eloquent expression of a deep understanding of seventeenth-century verse. In 1927 he worked on a Matthew Locke manuscript in the British Museum and the following year set Thomas Wyatt's 'And wilt thou leave me thus?'; it has bar lines but an instruction to ignore them, and a recitative-like rise and fall that may well have been inspired by Locke (and is very different from the more Dowland-like 'Sleep').

From 1925 to 1928, Warlock and E.J. Moeran shared a cottage in the Kent village of Eynsford, where they famously received the great and the bad in the literary and musical world, many of whom had such a fantastic time that they couldn't remember much about it. It's from this period that the myth of the split personality originated.

Warlock/Heseltine may have been bipolar but, with the exception of his biographer and friend Cecil Gray, few of his contemporaries thought of him as anything more than a brilliant personality who played hard and was subject to occasional bouts of depression. The Eynsford period produced plenty of great songs between the naked bike rides, copious drinking and much miscellaneous roistering, but over the following two years Warlock increasingly felt that his muse was deserting him. The market for songs was still in a state of flux and he found his songs difficult to sell, but he remained a prolific researcher and supporter of other composers' music.

Most of Warlock's poets were long dead, but in Bruce Blunt he found a living kindred spirit, and what turned out to be his final years produced some of the composer's most memorable work. Like Warlock, Blunt was a serious toper (he spent his final years in the 1950s importing burgundy). We don't know when they first met, but there is a 1927 record of the two of them being fined for shouting and singing while being drunk and disorderly, and by December that year they had co-written 'The First Mercy' and 'Bethlehem Down'. The latter was published in the *Daily Telegraph* on New Year's Eve, Blunt claiming to have concocted the verses walking one moonlit night in Hampshire between The Plough at Bishop's Sutton and The Anchor at Ropley. In 1929 came two of Warlock's finest songs, the first of an intended set of several Blunt settings. 'The Frostbound Wood' appeared in a Christmas edition of *Radio Times*; 'The Fox' was Warlock's last song, and such was the state of the market that neither piece found a commercial publisher until the shock of Warlock's death in 1930 from coal-gas inhalation (allegedly a suicide) suddenly made him publishable.

'The Fox', inspired by a fox's head on the wall of the eponymous inn at Bramdean, near Ropley, is Warlock in complete control of his material, its haunting piano horn-calls and minimal voice line that never goes above *mezzo piano* perfectly conjuring up the death mask. The song that might have signposted the way to a compositional future, however, is 'The Frostbound Wood'. No composer until Benjamin Britten would have the audacity and confidence to write a vocal line that made use of only four notes. As in *The Curlew*, the poet wanders through a mystical landscape, this time a winter woodland in which he meets another silent wanderer, Mary, 'the child's mother'. In a parallel universe Bethlehem celebrates a saviour's birth, briefly disturbing the quiet. Here in the frostbound wood the protagonist is revealed to be the spirit of everyman, 'the sower of the woodland' responsible for the mother's grief. The sparse accompaniment eventually resolves into thick chords as we become aware of the identity of the wanderer, and these in turn dissolve almost to nothingness as the voice repeats the opening stanza, almost empty of harmony. Wilfrid Mellers compared it to the final song of the hurdy-gurdy man in Schubert's *Winterreise*.

The Second World War had a less traumatic effect on composers' lives than the First. Many of the household names were too old for conscription and many of the younger ones managed various forms of conscientious objection, most famously Michael Tippett who was briefly imprisoned. The post-war years brought significant song cycles. Tippett, of comfortable upper-middle-class stock (briefly a Trotskyist between the wars), wrote song cycles which, despite the influence of Purcell, have proved challenging for singers. Lennox Berkeley, of aristocratic Anglo-French ancestry, studied with Nadia Boulanger from 1927 to 1932, and wrote songs in both English and French, coming into his own in the 1940s and 1950s. His Auden settings, like Britten's, are miniature masterpieces of the genre.

Another Boulanger pupil was Peter Pope (1917–91), whose story, most of which remains to be told, is one of the most tantalising and tragic in the history of song. His studies in Paris were brought to an abrupt end when he had to flee the German occupation in 1940. Pope had been a pupil of John Ireland at the Royal College of Music (one of the few who found Ireland a congenial teacher) before gaining a scholarship to study with Nadia Boulanger at the American Conservatoire in Paris in 1939. He made quite an impression on the doyenne of composition teachers, who introduced him to the Princesse de Polignac. The princess supported many musicians by giving them performance opportunities at her salons, and also commissioned a small number of composers, an exclusive list that included Stravinsky, Manuel de Falla, Poulenc and Satie. Peter Pope's String Trio was one of only two British works commissioned by Polignac (the other was *Deux poèmes de Pindare* by Lennox Berkeley, who became a lifelong friend). Polignac had hoped to commission a piano trio from Benjamin Britten whose *Variations on a Theme of Frank Bridge* she had heard the year before, but Britten was in the USA and the commission fell to Pope, whose work would take its place as a Polignac commission alongside those of his illustrious contemporaries.

The String Trio was a success in Paris and subsequently had several festival performances. Then came the war, and Pope as a conscientious objector was sent to Italy to serve in the medical corps. He had converted to Catholicism during his studies, but after returning home to begin composing again he and his new wife Noreen were persuaded by mutual friends to join The Brethren, a strict Protestant sect that split into ever more extreme subsects (of which the Plymouth Brethren is the most well known). All secular creative activity was forbidden. Members of The Brethren attended a Wigmore Hall concert of Pope's work, after which the publisher Augener offered him a contract which would have secured his future as a composer. The Brethren persuaded Pope not to sign it, and to burn his music.

Peter Pope was lost to music for the next two decades, but the rest of the story has something of the fairy tale about it, his art dormant until awoken in 1970, when the composer left the sect to find that musical life had gone on without him. To listen to the songs that he continued to write, unpublished, until his death in 1991 is to hear the lyrical hand of John Ireland, guided perhaps by Debussy, painting on an almost Britten-esque canvas.

Benjamin Britten and Peter Pears began working together around 1937, just seven years after the death of Peter Warlock and two years before Pope went to Paris to study with Boulanger. The twenty-seven-year-old tenor was still a member of the BBC Singers and had recently made his first recording (Warlock's 'Corpus Christi'). The composer, three years younger, was one to watch and soon to write his first major song cycle, *On This Island*, settings of five poems from W.H. Auden's collection *Look, Stranger!* This, like the vast majority of Britten's songs, would be written for Pears. They were both learning their respective trades and their musical adventure and intuition evolved in parallel with their personal relationship.

Britten thought that talking about music was a waste of time, and Peter Pears had a distaste for musicological analysis; readers should feel free to skip the next bit and just listen to the song (or, better still, sing it). Many singers would agree with both sentiments, and there is plenty of musicological and literary analysis of both Britten's music and Donne's sonnets out there for those who need it. Anyone who takes on Britten's songs, especially the great song cycles, will even now, decades after the death of these two extraordinary musicians, sense their spirit somewhere in the ether. So complete was the partnership between singer and composer-pianist that singers who came after them risked being compared unfavourably with Pears if they sounded like him, or the music not sounding like Britten if they didn't. In fact, each score is a miniature masterclass in interpretation: Pears's idiosyncratic delivery is built in. The staccato marks that feature so often to create particular emphasis, for example, are not to tell Pears what to do but to tell future performers how he did it.

Britten had been working on his Purcell transcriptions before setting the Donne sonnets and the first performance of the sonnets took place at Wigmore Hall in 1945 as part of the 250th commemoration of Purcell's death. Earlier in the year Britten had accompanied Yehudi Menuhin in a recital for survivors of the Belsen concentration camp, an experience which cannot but have influenced his musical thinking. There is no simple musical connection between the music and Belsen beyond the themes of death and redemption, but turning to Donne accessed an emotional perspective on the human condition that transcended the horror of the immediate past. Working on Purcell and performing his editions with Pears had enabled Britten to get to grips with projecting the text in a stylised way that also did justice to the original spoken language of the poem.

If Pears's Purcell sounds over-stylised in retrospect the same cannot be said for his Britten: the Donne sonnets make a perfect case for the rhetorical delivery of darkness in the form of song as embodied by Pears. There's a quasi-recitative looseness in 'O might those sighes and teares returne againe', the third song in the set; it's a perfect mode for a singing actor and is absolutely geared to Pears's unique rhetorical talents. The minimal material and the space around and below the vocal line allow time for reflection (which, after all, is what the poem is about), and this in turn creates the illusion for the listener that the singer is making it all up as he goes along. Singers tell stories, and a composer that gets out of the way just enough for them to be able to do that is a great gift to performers. It's quite possible that the Donne settings were Peter Pears's idea and he knew that it would result in a perfect unity of their two arts. The contrast with the song composers of early in the century is stark: gone is the obsession with harmony, which in many Britten songs barely exists (though he is a master of colour and timbre when it is needed). For Pears's biographer Christopher Headington, it was the tenor's spiritual intensity and vocal virtuosity that enabled Britten to write the sonnets, sounding 'a new note in British music, or at least one unheard since Purcell'.

'O might those sighes and teares returne againe' is an object lesson in how to replicate the sonnet form musically. Britten's predecessors and contemporaries tended to avoid setting sonnets, their hybridity and potential ambiguity presenting unique compositional challenges. Britten uses the structural ambiguity of Donne's form – dividing the poem into three quatrains and a final coda rather than the strict Petrarchan division into an octet and a sestet. The first quatrain sets out the basic material, about as minimal as any composer of the period could have contemplated, around half the notes consisting of alternating Bs and Cs. Britten had little time for the sometimes cloying harmonic indulgence of Warlock, but the reduction of the piano texture to its bare essentials surely comes from a similar mindset to the composer of 'The Frostbound Wood'.

From the late nineteenth century onwards, composers have had the option to add layers of meaning that may or may not be grasped by listeners (or even performers). This is sometimes a tortuous process as words and music can only be fused up to a point; the songs of Schoenberg and Webern, for example, despite an empathy with Symbolist poets, are ultimately determined by a strict compositional logic. By convention, harmony requires at least three notes (two notes are just an interval) – for the first quatrain of 'Oh might those sighes' the piano part has no 'harmony', with only one pitch in each hand at any one time; harmony is only created when the pianist is joined by the tenor. For those that wish to see it, this is much more than a composer setting a text, but a shared expression of love and guilt.

The poet bewails his condition, hoping his weeping will bring relief. In the second quatrain the singer repeats the music, adjusted for the new text which reaffirms his past sin, suffering and repentance, with an amplified and agitated commentary from the piano, arpeggios hinting at harmony. The climax is reached in the third quatrain as the singer breaks into recitative with new music over an increasingly brutal piano *tremolando*; functional harmony (for the only time in the song) batters the poet as he complains that at least thieves, drunkards and lechers can enjoy their sins in retrospect whereas he didn't enjoy his idolatory in the first place. Britten follows Donne's enjambment, running the sense of the text over the rhyme scheme and metre before recalling the original material for the final bleak two lines in which the poet finds no redemption. For that, we have to wait till the last line of the last song in the cycle, where death itself dies.

Britten possessed a copy of the complete works of John Donne but most of his textual choices were made from anthologies, often in consultation with Pears. They both enjoyed the richness of language itself, and one of Britten's supreme achievements was to understand the sonic potential of a text from the micro-level of a word to the shape and structure of a whole phrase. With the exception of Auden, his poets were all from the great (and mostly dead) poetic canon, and more than any of his predecessors he married music and text with a literary intelligence that made him the equal of his poets.

Creative musical partnerships, as we have seen in the case of Vogl and Schubert, Pierre Bernac and Francis Poulenc or Elwes and Raphael with Quilter, can open up new horizons in songwriting. Pears and Britten did more than that, helping to keep alive a flagging tradition of earlier song (rather more selectively in the case of Britten, whose compositional path saw dead ends in the works of some of his forebears). The coming of recording and radio had been a mixed blessing for composition and live performance. The availability of song at the flick of a switch led to choices of what might be sung and what might be listened to. The music you bought in the form of recordings or via your radio licence had a certain value, and although sheet-music sales tended to decline as the music became impossible for amateur performers at home, composers still found a market for more sophisticated music on record or radio. With each technological upgrade – 78 to LP, LP to CD – potential audiences were able to maintain a connection with song even when the song recital became increasingly rare.

Britten and Pears both connected deeply with the music of Dowland and Purcell, but the reputations of many twentieth-century song composers were considerably enhanced if they were endorsed by Pears and fellow performers such as Janet Baker, Kathleen Ferrier, Benjamin Luxon and John Shirley-Quirk, all of whom produced major recordings of the English repertoire. Pears and Britten's *Twentieth Century English Songs* LP of 1964 includes music by Ireland and Bridge (Britten's teacher) and two Pears commissions: Priaulx Rainier's *Cycle for Declamation*, which he used in recitals as a foil to a group of Pérotin conductus (long before the early-music movement rediscovered the twelfth century), and Richard Rodney Bennett's wonderfully theatrical 'Tom O'Bedlam's Song' for tenor and cello. The pair recorded all of Britten's cycles and the albums stand as a remarkable testament to a late blossoming of twentieth-century song.

As the century progressed, the public and the critical press began to take women composers much more seriously and the post-war years saw a more even gender balance in performance and composition. There could be no return to the salon and the idea that a woman's place was in the home, and music colleges, populated largely by young women during wartime, ensured that gender was no bar to a complete musical education. There was, for the first time, a 'music profession' which didn't depend on private wealth, but on a curious mixture of market forces and state subsidy, and from the 1970s onwards many composers were able to take university positions to facilitate teaching and composition. Female composers could compete (at least in theory) with their male colleagues for more substantial commissions. Inevitably, perhaps, this meant a focus on larger-scale works. Elizabeth Maconchy, her daughter Nicola LeFanu, Thea Musgrave and Elizabeth Lutyens, though all drawn to the voice, found their own voice in chamber music or the theatre rather than the conventional song with piano. This is not so much a gender issue as a measure of the contemporary *Zeitgeist*: dedicated song composers such as Elaine Hugh-Jones, Trevor Hold and many of those who preferred song to symphony rarely heard the performances they hoped for.

The composition of a song is just the start of a process that begins with the composer and ends with the listener. To get from one end of this process to the other requires an infrastructure that enables opportunities for competent performers to sing the work to people who want to hear it. In the Britten/Pears bubble this procedure operated with a miraculous circularity – in the Snape Maltings in Suffolk they had their own concert hall in which to present the songs to an adoring audience. Sometimes it seemed as though the two were maintaining the classical song tradition all by themselves.

In many respects they were. Post-war publications that considered the song repertoire were increasingly pessimistic. Arthur Jacobs ended his chapter on song in the British Isles in Denis Stevens's 1960 *History of Song* by reminding readers that there were plenty of undiscovered songs from the past to compensate for the prospects of future English song, which were 'not bright'. Peter Pears, in his 1983 contribution to the *Yehudi Menuhin Guide to the Voice*, 'Text and Voice in English Song', acknowledges the problem of composers being apparently unable to write songs that are good to sing and to listen to, challenging but still within the reach of an 'average trained singer'.

He mentions only Britten and Tippett among his contemporaries. By the beginning of the new century Stephen Varcoe is still calling the problem 'an unanswered question' in his chapter on European art song in the *Cambridge Companion to Singing*.

It doesn't help, of course, that these publications are reluctant to discuss songs other than those composed by the two English heavyweights. There were (and still are) song composers, many of whom wrote no operas or large-scale orchestral works with the result that their reputations never gained critical mass (literally and figuratively). Some achieved recognition through the advocacy of the indefatigable soprano Jane Manning. Manning's *New Vocal Repertoire* volumes discuss dozens of songs, each one analysed and graded according to five levels of difficulty. Her assembled cohorts of classical songwriters are an astonishing testimony to the affection in which the art was held by so many composers at the start of the twenty-first century (even though some of those chosen have written hardly more than a handful). The rehearsal and performance advice from a near-legendary practitioner is an invaluable aid to students, though a non-singer reading it would immediately understand that finding more than a token place for them on today's concert platforms might be problematic.

The penultimate chapter will explore some of the ways in which composers and performers are redefining song in the post-Britten landscape. Before we get there, my final choice of song will look at a parallel compositional and performative track, in which composers from the twentieth century onwards have mined the creative potential of language itself and the physicality of the poetic voice.

Luciano Berio rehearsing (1960s).

12

LUCIANO BERIO
SEQUENZA III

I f you've read this story from the beginning you may think it a little
odd that my choice of songs began with an iconic piece written by
and for a woman and ends with 'a few words for a woman to sing' by
two men. Not much to show for the best part of nine centuries? Perhaps the short answer is that history is largely what it isn't (or perhaps wasn't) and there is no straight line from one end to the other.
A better answer might be that, as Luciano Berio put it in an interview with Bálint András Varga, music is '. . . a miraculous gift. The
gift of becoming aware of questions that can be answered with other
questions.'

One of the first pieces Swingle II performed after Ward Swingle
had got us together in 1974 was Berio's *Sinfonia*. In a rehearsal break
we had a coffee with the great man, whom we would eventually get to
know quite well over many performances all over the world. We were
hanging on his every word and trying to ignore the music blasting
from the café's sound system. There was a lull in the conversation and

on came Gilbert O'Sullivan's 'Alone again'. Luciano looked up, and we waited for a composerly excoriation of café music. But he listened, and none of us dared say anything for a second or two, and then he said rather wistfully, 'I wish I could write tunes like that.'

He could, of course, and sometimes did, but as in much of *Sinfonia* he often chose to rewrite other composers' tunes, a process not dissimilar to the *contrafacta* of his medieval predecessors. The carefully crafted chaos that is *Sinfonia* in many ways sums up the philosophy of a certain sort of late-twentieth-century avant-garde composer: push the boundaries but don't trash them, celebrate the past, even incorporate it, and move on. There is also a sense, especially in Berio's works, that vocal music is more about the word than the tune, and more than that about the voice and its connection to the self. Berio's most eloquent expression of his relationship to the voice, to text, and to the poets and singers who generate it, was *Sequenza III*, dating from 1965–66. It was the latest stage of a process that had begun with an electronic piece, *Thema (Omaggio a Joyce)* in 1958, and continued through *Circles*, *Epifanie*, *Passaggio* and *Laborintus II*. Or, to continue Berio's question-and-answer metaphor, it was the piece that might have answered questions raised in his Joyce piece, but which generated further questions that would be partially answered and continually reformed in each of his subsequent vocal works through *Sinfonia*, *Cries of London*, *A-Ronne*, *Coro* and beyond . . .

A key aspect of the by now almost totemic status of song has been the parity between composer and poet. We're used to songwriting partnerships in rock music, but many early-twentieth-century composers and poets began searching for a new kind of synthesis, driven by the poetic exploration of the nature of language itself. The demise of pre-Wagnerian virtuosity coincided with a new sensitivity to text on the part of song composers. Although the words were inevitably subservient to the music (they were musicians after all), the ultimate aim was to discover new meanings in a fusion of both elements. Until the end of the nineteenth century (roughly), composers set poetry on the understanding that their songs would be sung by conventional singers in bourgeois drawing rooms or concert halls. Although the texts were carefully chosen and integrated artistically into the song, it was the singer that audiences mostly came to hear, hopefully well served by the composer. No one came for the poet unless it was a poetry reading.

Poets, the other half of this equation, often approached the whole question of music from a rather different literary and intellectual perspective. Many wrote words for music in much the same way as Renaissance musicians wrote *poesia per musica*, but some were reluctant to have their poems set at all. Others approached the whole question from the music inherent in the poem itself or the voice of the person reading it. Yeats liked to recite to the psaltery, and he sought to recover 'the old music that was half speech', as he put it in a letter to Arnold Dolmetsch in 1902. In 1899 he had overseen the performance in Dublin's Antient Concert Rooms of a revised version of his play *Countess Cathleen* and had gone to considerable lengths to get the actors to chant rhythmically like 'bards and rhapsodists', supported by flute or violin. Yeats had been drawn to Homeric epic as a child and as a teenager would compose verse aloud to the accompaniment of an imaginary harp. Later, wealthy lady admirers, such as his patron Lady Augusta Gregory, would hear Willie chanting to himself in the middle of the night.

This rhetorical declamation intrigued some but was ridiculed by others; William Morris was a fan, but George Bernard Shaw thought it ridiculous. Nevertheless, Yeats persisted, experimenting with the actress Florence Farr, accompanying recitations with piano or harp. He didn't want the poetry to become music, and one of his solutions was a one-stringed Eastern European lute which was primitive enough to keep the music at bay, relegated to a basic pitch and rhythm. In his 1902 paper 'Speaking to the Psaltery', Yeats tells the story of his attempts to create a mode of rhetorical delivery that is a kind of heightened speech, initially inspired by his notions of Arabic and Tibetan and finally brought to fruition with the help of Arnold Dolmetsch. Dolmetsch was able to transcribe Yeats's reading and made an instrument that would cover all the pitches generated. It was a creation of their joint imaginations (often described as a cross between a lyre and a psaltery), and Florence Farr would deploy it to support pitched readings.

Yeats was grasping at something that did have historical precedent. The permeable borders between the two modes of delivery had been a part of literary and musical culture for hundreds of years (Pietrobono in the fifteenth century and the Petrarchian recitalists of the sixteenth), and until the nineteenth century poetry everywhere was as likely to be declaimed as read silently. But Yeats, consumed by a semi-mythical pre-Raphaelite mindset, and defending his ownership of both text and its performance, was often doomed to frustration when composers and performers wanted to extrapolate from his published work. He disliked singing; he loathed Peter Warlock's *The Curlew*, considered by many to be a deeply moving setting of his verse, and one can imagine the kind of baleful apoplexy that Frank Bridge's 1919 setting of 'When you are old and grey' might have induced. Despite his and Florence Farr's attempts to teach fellow poets to chant (Robert Bridges and Roger Fry among them), Yeats's obsession never quite gave him the satisfaction he sought, and without Farr's advocacy after her move to Ceylon in 1912 the chanting community reverted more to Yeats's own rhythmic monotone.

At the time, his influence among a group of younger poets inter-ested in the sound of poetry was profound. In the audience for the 1899 performance of *The Countess Cathleen* was the young James

Joyce, who was so impressed that he set one of Yeats's lyrics to music (presumably he hadn't quite understood the point of the chanting). Joyce was a tenor with enough talent to compare himself to John McCormack. His interest in declamation was more inclined to the innate and liberating musicality of the human voice, a connection that the charismatic but curmudgeonly Yeats never quite made. Joyce's position in the kaleidoscope of 1920s and 1930s artists, writers and musicians was more mellow and collaborative than that of his mentor. *The Joyce Book*, a collection of thirteen items from *Pomes Penyeach* published in 1931, is a glorious celebration of the poet and his aesthetic by thirteen prominent composers. As a trained singer he could not but enjoy his poetry interpreted by like-minded composers, though *Pomes Penyeach* was hardly the revolutionary catalyst that *Ulysses* would turn out to be for later twentieth-century musicians.

Ezra Pound, a friend and promoter of Joyce, was also part of the Yeats circle and like him looked to the past for the future of poetry. He initially fell under the spell of Yeats's quest for ancient declamation, but by 1918 he was advocating poetry as musical phrases rather than metronomic recitation and was seeking the help of professional musicians to fill in the gaps in his limited musical education. He too was an admirer of Arnold Dolmetsch (who made him a clavichord), and he became a music critic (writing as William Atheling) partly to explore the relationship between musical and poetic expression in song.

There was much talk in Paris of Antheil operas set to libretti by Joyce and Pound. Joyce and Antheil, then flirting with Futurism, failed to complete their *Cyclops*, but Pound and Antheil did collaborate in the 1920s on an opera celebrating the fifteenth-century poet François Villon. In *Le Testament*, Pound attempted to reproduce the poetic rhythms of medieval poetry by using extremely complex time signatures (later simplified by Antheil) which he called fractional metrics, and which were close to unperformable at the time. In its seriousness of purpose it was the very opposite of his contemporary Satie's playful and self-deprecating humour, and a world away from the refined elegance of *The Joyce Book*. Yet Pound's music was not all relentless rhythm, and sometimes showed a closer connection to his troubadour soul: the violin solo *In poco giorno* has no time signature and realises Dante's text in the form of pitches derived from the reading of the poem (which is not itself sung). Pound had researched troubadour song in European libraries and the romance of the past gripped him as it did many of his fellow poets, but though he could read, transcribe and then arrange the songs of Gaucelm Faidit, Arnaut and others, he was reluctant (or unable) to sing them himself. Like Yeats, he seems to have lacked a certain sort of instinctive musicianship and was ultimately unable to realise his sonic vision in music.

Le Testament went through various drafts and was performed in concert versions before being reimagined as an experimental performance for BBC radio (making it one of the first operas to be broadcast). Pound and his producer Archie Harding thought radio could circumvent print as a medium for poetry by delivering musical rhetoric straight into people's ears. It was a revolutionary notion that anticipates today's smart speaker in the kitchen. For his second attempt at opera he turned to the poems of post-troubadour *dolce stil nuovo* poet Guido Cavalcanti whose poems he had translated in 1912, and having completed *Le Testament* he spent some ten months in 1931 converting *ballate* and *canzoni* into songs, duets and trios. The score was finally completed two years later, but Archie Harding having cooled on the project all trace of it vanished until its first performance in 1982. Pound began work on a third opera and composed microtonal settings of Sappho and Catullus, but that too was overtaken by events and never completed.

Pound is a difficult poet for modern performers to engage with because of his antisemitism and support for fascism, but his attempts to fashion poetry as a Dante-esque fusion between music and rhetoric make him a compelling pivotal point between the medieval and the modern. His poetry was set by 'proper' composers (including Josef Holbrooke and Granville Bantock) but he never really made it work for himself, not least because his amateur musicianship was continually outstripped by his poetic imagination. But together with Yeats and Joyce he was among the first poet-musicians to explore the physical vocality of song and its wider connection to music and meaning; he was also one of the few twentieth-century composers of art song who was also a poet. Joyce's own experience as a tenor *manqué* (or perhaps not so *manqué*) chimed well with the more lyrical expression that would become English Romantic song, but the symbiosis striven for by Pound and Yeats would be further explored by Futurists, Dadaists and sound poets through to the post-war avant-garde, before reappearing in the work of Luciano Berio.

Some years before these poetic excursions into the musical unknown, Schoenberg was pondering similar problems from the opposite end of the spectrum. The idea that singing had some way to go to match the rhetorical power of speech had troubled progressive composers since Wagner's speech-inclined declamation broke the link with the traditional Italian purity of line. The subject exercised composers, critics and singers, though audiences for grand opera resisted further modifications to the singing that they had become addicted to. Other less formal theatrical genres had no such compunction when it came to delivering meaning in whatever way worked: heightened and stylised speech were routine in cabaret and the *Singspiel*. The melodrama, a musical and theatrical hybrid, used speech in the context of music. Unlike a modern television drama or film where actors speak 'naturally' over background music, melodrama required an actor's theatrical declamation. Pitches were not normally notated until Engelbert Humperdinck experimented with crossed noteheads to indicate non-sung pitches in his *Die Königskinder* of 1897, in much the same way as Schoenberg was to do a few years later. Humperdinck was unable to convince his singing actors, who probably felt that spoken pitches were their domain not his. The audience didn't like their efforts anyway and Humperdinck gave up the struggle, eventually rewriting it as an opera.

Schoenberg may or may not have known *Die Königskinder* (both composers were sometime Wagnerians) but he certainly felt the *Zeitgeist*, as did an actress-turned-singer called Albertine Zehme who was also exploring new ways to unite singing and speech. As Albertine Aman she had a career as an actress before marrying the successful society lawyer Felix Zehme, after which she gave up the stage as convention required but kept her artistic interests alive by organising cultural salons at her home in Leipzig. In 1891 she went to Bayreuth and studied singing with Cosima Wagner and Julius Kniese, the composer's disciple and interpreter of his vocal vision. Returning to Leipzig, Zehme reinvented herself as a Lieder singer. It's hard to fathom what she actually learned from Kniese and the progression from actress to mezzo-soprano must have been in some respects a backward step. By some accounts Zehme's career was sustained largely thanks to her husband's social and financial clout, which gave her access to opportunity. We will never know how good she was at either singing or speaking, but her experience at both ends of the vocal spectrum gave her cause for considerable creative thought. In her search for a singing-speech hybrid Zehme introduced spoken recitation into her recitals and corresponded with Richard Dehmel on the difference between the declamation of actors and poets. In 1911 she sang, or possibly spoke, settings by Otto Vrieslander of Otto Hartleben's translations of Giraud's *Pierrot Lunaire* poems.

Zehme knew the poems well, but touring with the Vrieslander pieces, conventional songs for voice and piano, convinced her to seek out a composer who might capitalise on her own experience and ideas about musical and poetic declamation. She discovered Schoenberg's music, presumably intrigued by its abstraction and tonal ambiguities which would not be compromised by age-old musical forms, and organised the commission. With a commissioner and composer of like mind in so many ways, there was the potential for a ground-breaking song cycle (in the first instance with piano). The ground has continued to be broken anew ever since, as neither Zehme nor Schoenberg arrived at a definition of what *Sprechstimme* actually was.

Schoenberg's notation specified pitch and rhythm; his concession to speech was to have only one note per syllable, none of them sustained longer than might be the case in a rhetorical delivery. The pitches are integrated into the tonal framework of the accompaniment (now augmented to five players wielding a total of eight instruments) and would make musical sense if actually sung. This means (somewhat perversely) that if the pitches are approximate, they risk becoming, in effect, mistakes which might compromise the harmonic framework. Schoenberg saw pitch as an aspect of tone colour, and he was looking for a vocal delivery that would first produce a speech-like sound but not one that sounded like the generic voice of a trained singer. He expected the audience to understand the effect as a whole, rather than literally following the words. The problem for many people has been understanding it at all, though the first performances by Zehme (who also went on to perform *Gurrelieder*) were mostly very successful.

For the rest of his life Schoenberg made successive failed attempts to clarify what he meant; Zehme also muddied the waters with her 1920 book on singing, *Die Grundlagen künstlerischen Sprechens und Singens* (The Fundamentals of Artistic Singing and Speaking). The problem for conservatoire-trained singers is not so much learning the pitches, challenging though these are, but that it is very hard for them to perform without vibrato. Vibrato does not occur in speech, so Schoenberg's required delivery (whatever he actually meant) is more likely to be achieved by a singing actor than an acting singer. Perhaps musical notation is never going to be sophisticated enough to give more than basic information about pitch and rhythm, and we should celebrate the interpretative possibilities that flow from that.

In 1922, at the suggestion of Alma Mahler, Schoenberg and Darius Milhaud conducted a double performance of *Pierrot* in German and French versions respectively. Erika Wagner, an experienced Schoenberg singer, spoke the German text, dramatic and intense with little respect for pitches. Marya Freund (who decades later would briefly teach the young Cathy Berberian) performed in French, sensuous and subtle according to Milhaud, whose conclusion after such widely different interpretations, both sanctioned by the composer, was that the problem of the 'recitative' would never be solved. A decade later Constant Lambert still thought that *Pierrot*, though undoubtedly a masterpiece, had 'a slight touch of a *Lieder* recital that has taken the wrong turning', that it was where 'the ghost of the German *Lied* meets the ghost of French decadence'.

Recitation of poetry to music was a favourite of the salons and focused the listeners' attention on the personality of the speaker, making the poet's meaning more directly understood. This would never be the case with *Pierrot*: critical reception would always home in on the mode of delivery before anything else. *Pierrot* didn't have any obvious successors, though William Walton's *Façade*, first performed in 1922, shares some attributes: both are for reciter and instrumental ensemble and were commissioned by the women who first recited them. The speaking roles in both works appear almost to sabotage classical performance by introducing elements from cabaret and music hall. In both works the players may be hidden from view so that the focus is firmly on the singer and her voice.

Façade was the brainchild of poet Edith Sitwell, the eldest of the three Sitwell siblings whose well-publicised artistic endeavours lit up London from the middle of the First World War until the 1930s. At the time, many commentators found Edith's collaboration with the young William Walton bewildering, and with hindsight it is still hard to know whether it was intended as serious art or simply a bit of *haute bourgeoise* fun. There were many revisions and rearrangements over the years including a version of three of the songs for a real singer with piano and orchestral suites with no voice at all, suggesting Walton may not have been entirely confident himself (and you can recite your own version by turning to Edith Sitwell's 1950 collection, *Façade and Other Poems, 1920–1935*, accompanying yourself with highlights from one of the recordings of the *Façade* suites).

Façade was billed as an 'entertainment', so a certain ambiguity was built in from the start; in order to subvert the idea of the artistic ego the performance took place behind a screen displaying a giant mouth. The reciter (Edith herself at the first private performance) was amplified by a megaphone, the famous *papier-mâché* Sengerphone which covered both nose and mouth and so produced a (slightly) less robotic sound than the industrial model. The Sitwells and their circle were familiar with both Giraud and Schoenberg and may conceivably have known of Josef Holbrooke's 1907 'Illuminated Symphony' in which orchestra and chorus had been hidden behind a screen with part of Herbert Trench's poem sung but large sections projected onto the screen and illustrated by the orchestra alone. Constant Lambert's critique of *Pierrot Lunaire* in his *Music Ho!* quotes an extract from Sitwell's 1918 poem 'Clown's Houses', and he was rumoured to have introduced quotes from the Schoenberg in his own performances.

Edith Sitwell's preoccupations were different from those of Albertine Zehme, and the result is as English as *Pierrot Lunaire* is German. Her attempt to fuse music and text meant dispensing with melody and literal meaning, whereas Schoenberg hoped, a little optimistically, that audiences would leave humming his tunes. Sitwell's poems are abstract nonsense verses which toss out multiple images as Walton's polkas, tangos and foxtrots dance along on a magic carpet of onomatopoeia and alliteration. Like the Schoenberg, the rhythms are those of the music-hall entertainer (albeit with a cut-glass accent) and it's as light and joyous as the Schoenberg is dark and sinister. Schoenberg may have enjoyed operetta (he orchestrated an inordinate number), but Zehme's experience included cabaret. Schoenberg was charismatic and he had a fantastic ear, but he was not a singer or an actor; Edith Sitwell had performed her poetry since childhood and could entrance audiences, even if speaking in a monotone.

Zehme/Schoenberg and Sitwell/Walton had all been familiar with Symbolist poetry since their teenage years and none of them expected their texts to make anything so banal as literal sense. Symbolism has been claimed as the founding spirit of modernism, a reaction to the comfortably elegant, unquestioning verse of the nineteenth century in which, in musical terms, a composer found a poem and tried to replicate and enhance its sentiments. Reading Symbolist poetry liberated composers from literal word painting, and accompaniments became more like canvasses on which the singer could paint a melody. Schoenberg had set Dehmel, Webern chose Stefan George, and Debussy, Ravel and Milhaud set Mallarmé, all of them exploring the expressive potential of symbolic poetic landscapes.

Symbolism didn't just mean colourful imagery and gnomic pronouncements, and Mallarmé's attempts to dissolve the borderline between text, page and sound were a step too far for traditional composers. It was his *Un coup de dés* that would propel the Symbolist project into a future fuelled by Futurism, Dada and sound poetry, and that would finally be claimed by Berio and the late-twentieth-century avant-garde. Mallarmé's twenty-page collage of inverted syntax, bizarre punctuation, onomatopoeic imagery, random capitals and typefaces and unpredictable layout is a visual attempt to realise a literary concept in sound. It's almost untranslatably French and full of pitfalls for the unwary, and shocked and amazed the literary world when it first appeared. Its influence hovers over the *Parole in libertà* of the Futurist founder Marinetti (who as he drifted into fascism became embarrassed by his debt to Mallarmé). Above all it was Dadaists Raoul Hausmann, Hugo Ball and Kurt Schwitters who, in attempting to turn the page into sound by reinventing language, were the direct descendants of *Un coup*.

Since the invention of Esperanto in 1887 there had been many attempts to invent a universal language (including at least one based on musical tones), but the Dada sound poets preferred straightforward nonsense. Hausmann's *fmsbw* is one of his *Poèmes phonétiques* first performed in 1918. In 1921, Hausmann and Schwitters made a Dada (or, more Dadaistically, an anti-Dada) trip to Prague where Hausmann's rendering of *fmsbw* in an anarchistic cabaret made a deep impression on his friend. The freeing of performed poetry from the tyranny of meaning sometimes triggered a profound emotional response; the poet Paul Valéry had wept the first time he encountered *Un coup de dés*, and Schwitters was so struck by *fmsbw* that the next day on the journey home, much to Hausmann's amusement, he repeated bits of it constantly, riffing on the first few lines. Over the next few years, alternately improvising and extending the text, Schwitters morphed it into the most famous piece of sound poetry, the *Ursonata*, structured (much to the disgust of Hausmann who thought it a very retrogressive step) as a kind of demented textual sonata. The *Ursonata* is Schwitters's most elaborate creation, in marked contrast to his most minimal work, a poem reduced to the single letter **W**. This is recited according to a series of instructions, beginning almost imperceptibly with a breath and climaxing with an insane *fff* before subsiding with a final gentle exhalation.

Can we really consider these extrapolations from poetry as song? Schwitters's declamation does have sustained vowels which inevitably have a pitch, and many of his exclamations can easily become melodic cells. Although there were many examples of sound poetry with more than one voice and therefore potentially with a kind of harmony, the creations of Schwitters and his generation are essentially monophonic. In parallel with the rich tradition of twentieth-century accompanied song, another strand of performance was returning to a solo aesthetic last used by the troubadours and *trouvères* almost a thousand years before. Hildegard or Bernart would have been frustrated by the apparent lack of a coherent text, but they would probably have recognised the performance as song. They would also probably recognise the creative unity between composer and performer, though the extent to which the early-twentieth-century composer-poet embodied the song may have taken a bit of getting used to. In a further divergence from the increasingly institutionalised recital mainstream, the evolution of this alternative voice turned the song recital into a one-man (or -woman) show.

In the second half of the twentieth century the one-man Dada or Futurist cabaret (both genres were heavily male) would be replaced by the one-woman show in a radical rebalancing of the gender profile of contemporary song. Much of the credit for this must go to Cathy Berberian, in whose footsteps followed Joan La Barbara, Meredith Monk, Diamanda Galas, Laurie Anderson and a host of female composer-poets on both sides of the Atlantic. Berberian was born to Armenian parents in Massachusetts in 1925 (the same year as Luciano Berio). Multi-talented as a teenager, she made her first visit to Europe in 1948 to study briefly with Marya Freund in Paris. Freund was, like Berberian, a cultural nomad with a very long pedigree. She had studied with Julius Stockhausen and sung for Mahler, Schoenberg (the premiere of *Gurrelieder* and the first performances of *Pierrot* in French and English), Satie (the premiere of *Socrate*) and almost every other significant composer of the early avant-garde.

Although she was only with Freund for a short time, Cathy Berberian must have been aware of Freund's extraordinary past, and its connection to a possible future for herself. A year later she moved to Milan to study at the Conservatorio di Musica Giuseppe Verdi with Giorgina del Vigo. It was while searching for an accompanist that she came across fellow student Luciano Berio, still playing the piano after an accident with a gun had injured his hand during military service but thinking of himself increasingly as a composer. It was a fateful encounter: the two married in 1950. So began one of the most spectacular and intriguing musical partnerships which lasted (despite their divorce in 1964) until Berberian's death in 1983.

Berio's love of song and singing came via his father, an organist who taught singing, loved opera, and filled the house with chamber music. Hearing *La Bohème* on the radio as a thirteen-year-old surprised him with its emotional impact (for Cathy Berberian it was *Lakmé*). Perhaps part of the legacy of Puccini was the idea that music could relate to real-time human experience, and despite his formidable intellect Berio never lost touch with a wider audience. His musical education was no different from that of other aspiring composers of the time, but he had a fascination with language that seems to have come out of nowhere. It was not just literature (though his reading was prodigious) but, with the elements and structures that enabled meaning and interpretation, language as a creative tool. In the Studio di Fonologia Musicale that he founded at Radiotelevisione Italiana (RAI) with Bruno Maderna in 1955, Berio was able to explore these fundamental elements in new soundscapes created by electronic sounds.

Two years later, with the studio up and running, Berio was introduced to Umberto Eco, also working at RAI and wrestling with James Joyce. The composer and the proto-linguist discovered a mutual interest in onomatopoeia, which they would explore over dinner with Cathy Berberian reading extracts from *Ulysses*. Berberian had helped Berio choose the texts for his *Chamber Music* of 1953, but this was engagement of an entirely different order, and over the following year their explorations developed into a radio programme, *Omaggio a Joyce: Documenti sulla qualità onomatopeica del linguaggio poetico* (Homage to Joyce: Documents on the Onomatopoeic Quality of Poetic Language), investigating onomatopoeia in English literature from Anglo-Saxon verse to Edgar Allan Poe, Dylan Thomas, Auden and Joyce.

The programme was never broadcast (it was released on CD in 2000), but it was in effect a research project from which Berio salvaged *Thema (Omaggio a Joyce)*, using only the voice of Cathy Berberian reading Joyce. It's a tape piece celebrating the musical and structural use of onomatopoeia in *Ulysses*, merging text and music into one element and channelling the fugal structure that is the point of departure for Joyce's own text in Chapter 11, 'Sirens'. Berio manipulates the voice to produce a texture that shifts between music and speech to the point where it is no longer possible to distinguish between the two. The flurry of hisses and squawks, no longer words, takes Joyce's sound world into the vocal unknown; at the time it seemed the end point of the composerly obsession with Joyce that had lasted for decades; were Joyce to hear it, one wonders if he would consider *Omaggio a Joyce* to *Ulysses* what *The Joyce Book* was to *Pomes Penyeach*.

Berio also consulted Berberian on his choice of e e cummings texts for *Circles*, which he wrote for her two years later as a live iteration of his attempts to fuse sound and poetry into a single element. Berio selected instrumental textures to match the phonetic qualities of the poems and the two elements become ever closer, finally merging to the extent that the voice becomes an instrument and the percussionists become singers. *Visage* from 1961 took the partnership with Berberian and the quest for musical and poetic synthesis a stage further. Another tape piece, it features Berberian's voice in a devilish dialogue, a competition even, with electronic sounds. Nothing makes sense; it's full of vocal gestures substituting for speech and which still resonate, even though the electronics sound very much of their time. Berio originally conceived it, like *Omaggio a Joyce*, for radio ('the most widely used means of spreading useless words', as his programme note put it). RAI, however, had a fit of the vapours and refused to broadcast it on the grounds of obscenity. It's hard now to imagine what the fuss was about; it's one of two Berio pieces (the other being *Sequenza III*) that the composer thought children enjoyed listening to.

John Cage, working in the studio at the invitation of Berio on what would become *Fontana Mix*, was also a frequent guest at the Berio apartment. It was hearing Cathy doing an impression of the rapid splicing of tape montages that gave him the idea for *Aria*, which basically gave her licence to show off every style and technique in her vocal and paralinguistic armoury for a period of ten intense minutes. *Aria* has a huge significance for both composers and performers. It recovers something of the pre-Wagnerian relationship between the two as well as offering post-Webern freedoms and a release from 'interpretation' in favour of creative collaboration. It also was a marker of Berberian's potential as a vehicle for composers, and something of a challenge to Luciano Berio, which he answered with *Sequenza III* in 1966.

The professional and personal chemistry between the two began to come apart as each of them developed their separate public personas, Berberian initially combining her burgeoning career with bringing up their daughter Cristina, born in 1953. Berio moved to the United States, and in 1965 received a commission from the Bremen Festival for a work for Cathy. Aware of the apparently limitless vocal hinterland of Berberian, he built the piece on the raft of Cathy-isms that had carried him along since *Thema*, *Circles* and *Visage*. He had already written *Sequenzas* for flute and harp (two of his favourite instruments), each one a virtuosic tour de force devised for a specific player. Berio's compositional persona was in many ways defined by his explorations of Cathy Berberian's voice, and the Bremen commission gave him the opportunity to celebrate the success and survival of their musical partnership despite their divorce.

Berio referred to the voice of a classical singer as being like a venerable instrument that once used would be returned to its case: it was nothing like the voice they used for communicating in real life. It was this quotidian voice that Berio mined in Berberian, and which almost never surfaced in the generic classical recital. The spoken voice is highly personal, no two sound the same, and reveals aspects of ourselves that we may not even be aware of. Berio decided that his third *Sequenza* would be not just *for* Cathy but *about* her, using her virtuosity as a means to extract her vocal DNA and recreate aspects of her character. The performer comes on stage already muttering and then goes through some forty emotional states, segmented into laughter (several varieties), coughing, tics, cries, and whispers and babbling, many of them transitioning extremely rapidly. It's like a live realisation of parts of *Visage* or *Thema*, created in the light of Cage's *Aria*. The score is a template: when Berberian sang it, it was about Cathy (or, as she put it, about Cathy acting the role of Cathy); when another soprano sings it, it becomes about them.

As was the case with all of Berio's vocal work to date, his interest lay not in literal meanings but in devising paralinguistic gestures that would excavate new ones from the guts of the language. He never 'set' a text, which meant that whoever provided him with words never quite knew how they would end up. In this case he called on the relatively unknown Markus Kutter, perhaps thinking that his more high-profile collaborators might baulk at the wrecking of their text in order for it to be reborn. In fact, the text is heard in its entirety, escaping in fragments from the centrifugal vocal whirlwind, though it is never heard as Kutter wrote it:

Give me a few words for a woman *to sing a truth allowing us* to build a house without worrying before night comes

Nor does it appear in this form in the score, so the performer is part of the extraction process. Berio cut it up and reorganised its elements for Berberian to reassemble.

Berberian only saw the complete score a few days before the first performance, and she road-tested it over several more until she was happy with its final form. It was a huge success, audiences and critics dazzled by it. For academics it provided reams of future analysis, musical, linguistic, psychological and feminist. For performers it was a unique challenge, asking them to use extended vocal techniques to bare their souls. Audiences can't fail to be impressed by the virtuosity needed if the performer is in the zone; having heard a few performances he didn't like, Berio considered a version for three voices, such are the technical demands. The risk is that the virtuosity subsumes everything, and both the craft and the underlying point of the piece are lost in what appears to be a series of technical challenges. Ironically, the real-life sounds do not aggregate into a real-life experience that is in any way normal: this is a snapshot of a life lived in fast-forward.

For the composer *Sequenza III* was, as were his previous Berberian pieces, a resource that would yield more explorations in the future,

281

most obviously in *A-Ronne* which broke down an alliterative text by Edoardo Sanguineti into many different emotional states. For Berberian the *Sequenza* was a point of departure, enabling her to transcend the avant-garde and make sideways moves into compositions of her own and to discover a new repertoire that would include Monteverdi and the Beatles. She continued to perform the repertoire created by her ex-husband, the two of them maintaining a mysterious and sometimes uneasy friendship until her death. She performed and recorded many of the songs in this chapter including both *Pierrot* and *Façade*. From previous chapters she sang Gershwin's 'Summertime' and salon songs by Satie; her virtuosity was that of the singers of seventeenth-century division madrigals or eighteenth-century castrati.

Berio's last extravagance for Berberian, *Recital 1*, might have made an ideal title for this chapter. A singer arrives on stage to discover that her accompanist hasn't turned up, and over some forty attempts to recreate pieces from her repertoire she descends into incoherence. The published score, after a lot of wrangling over copyright, became a fully prescribed programme chosen by Berberian (it includes an extract from *Pierrot* in a list spanning 400 years from Monteverdi to her ex-husband). As originally conceived in 1972 it was an 'open' theatre work into which a performer could insert their own choice of repertoire. As a synthesis of monodrama, opera, recital and spoken word it brings together many themes that had preoccupied twentieth-century composers.

Berio was not alone in his exploration of the human voice, though his contemporaries Kagel, Xenakis, Ligeti and Stockhausen were generally without a Berberian at their back and tended to write ensemble pieces rather than solo songs. If there was a male equivalent to Cathy Berberian it was Roy Hart, or there would have been had he not been killed in a car accident in 1975. In 1969 he premiered both Henze's *Versuch über Schweine* (Gaston Salvatore's 'Essay on Pigs') and Maxwell Davies's *Eight Songs for a Mad King* (Randolph Stow's reimagining of George III's descent into madness). Both works were written around Hart's remarkable talents; the Maxwell Davies piece has been successfully performed by other singers and actors, but few performers have exposed themselves to the ferocious vocal requirements of the Henze. South African-born Hart (he was a year younger than Cathy Berberian) was a RADA-trained actor who became obsessed with the potential of the human voice after meeting the Jungian voice therapist and singing teacher Alfred Wolfsohn. While studying with Wolfsohn, Hart developed his own personal repertoire of extended vocal techniques that ranged from whispering to screaming, all of which he could express multiphonically. As an actor with a fine conventional baritone voice he could move easily between the two modes (and would have made an ideal *Pierrot*).

Georges Aperghis, born in 1945 in Greece but living in France, did have the kind of collaborator who inspired him to write for solo voice. Aperghis' father was a sculptor and his mother a painter; he was largely self-taught as a composer and at first divided his time between music and painting. Significantly, his formative musical experiences were entirely oral, in the form of *musique concrète* and radio broadcasts. His marriage to the actress Edith Scob stimulated a latent interest in the stage, and his *La Tragique Histoire du nécromancien Hieronimo et de son miroir* of 1971, for puppets, actress, mezzo-soprano, lute, cello and tape was his first excursion into music theatre.

Aperghis' most well-known work among singers is *Récitations*, composed in 1978 and first performed in 1982 by singing actress Martine Viard, a performer of the calibre of Cathy Berberian who collaborated with Aperghis on several theatre works. It is tempting to listen to *Récitations* as a French successor to *Sequenza III*, but the underlying psychology of the two pieces is completely different. Both require a similar virtuosic technique as both actor and singer, and both were worked up in collaboration with specific performers. Aperghis, perhaps conscious of the Berio precedent, deliberately keeps his protagonist within a very precise set of parameters that are very much an oral realisation of the graphically arranged score. In contrast to the worldliness of Cathy Berberian, Martine Viard often displays the innocence of a child trying to learn her lines. The fourteen sections, many of which involve cumulative rapid repetitions and can be performed any way up, allow the performer to create multiple personas from syllables and letters. Most sections surf along on waves of uncontextualised words, though *Récitation* 3 has a line from Théodore de Banville's *Malédiction de Cypris* (notated on a single-line stave but with a grid of possible moods), and in number 9 the repetitions gradually reveal a complete sentence. There is no obvious reason for the Banville reference, though Aperghis was surely aware that Mallarmé quoted the very same verse in his tribute to Banville in his *Divagations* of 1897. Once again, the long shadow of Mallarmé's *Un coup de dés* reveals itself a century later.

Berio's *Sequenza* was a milestone in the history of song and singing technique because it was summative: it showed, for the time being at least, a complete repertoire of vocal sounds compiled from one woman's voice. All of the techniques, including Cathy Berberian's previously unheard dental trill, are part of the standard armoury for her successors. *A-Ronne*, which took Swingle II months to learn, can be rehearsed in a week. The peripheral areas of the human voice are no longer uncharted territory, and voice and music collide in ways that we now take for granted. The use of extended or non-standard vocal techniques perhaps only ever had a niche appeal, but the more stylised integration of speech and music for its own sake has continued to inspire composers and performers from Sergei Prokofiev's 1936 children's story *Peter and the Wolf* to Gavin Bryars's 1992 *A Man in a Room Gambling*, in which the hypnotic voice of Juan Muñoz reads the sculptor's texts describing how to cheat at cards. *A Man in a Room Gambling* was originally conceived for BBC Radio 4, as the last programme before the shipping forecast, the nightly recitation of rain, wind speeds and visibility in each of the thirty-one designated weather areas surrounding British waters, itself a performance any Dadaist would be proud to recite.

We need music like the *Sequenza*, *Pierrot*, *Façade* and *Récitations*, and even Yeats's aggravated monotone, if only as a counterbalance to the ubiquitous banality of film and television speech over background music (much of which is melodrama without the singing). But conceiving of a vocal line as speech-related rather than the domain of a generic trained voice has more problematic questions for classical music. Cathy Berberian, hugely versatile singer though she was, never shook off her generic training when she left the avant-garde for pastures old, and Luciano Berio, when it came to writing proper operas chose proper singers. Those who came later, especially singer-composer-poets like Meredith Monk and Laurie Anderson, were not beholden to the pedagogical past. For their journeys into their own musical psyche they chose not to retrieve a voice from its classical instrument case and instead opened up song to a potentially infinite number of possible performers: we all have a voice, and it is the poet's voice, the voice of the singer-songwriter, that would re-define the art of song in the twenty-first century.

HISTORY AND FUTURE SONG

The history of song is often an afterthought in the grander scheme of musical things and tends to start with Schubert, with the rest of history given just a paragraph or two, the songs created in earlier centuries only becoming art song when we incorporate them into our own present. The chapters in this book don't represent a consistent pattern of evolution and change, but each one could be construed as a snapshot of an era or phenomenon with a beginning, a middle and an end. The decision to include *Sequenza III* as the final song was made in the context of a move away from the traditional song recital as composers, poets and performers struck out into new territory – still with a singer performing on stage but increasingly disconnected from the age-old ecosystem of the voice and piano of the traditional recital.

There are infinite ways to tell the story of song, and many would argue that the tradition still continues, evolving to keep pace with changing times. Schumann's *Frauenliebe und Leben* is still guaranteed performances and audiences, and commentators continue to debate whether classical music is or is not elitist (while musicians just get on and do it). Any history runs into problems when it closes in on the present; the historical focus won't be resolved until it becomes the past at some point in the future. There will be as many forecasts about what lies ahead as there are constructions of the past.

Looking back over the story so far, one could make a case for musical textbooks being right, in that we have made the post-Schubert song a very different confection from any that preceded it. The conventional assumption is that the genre will continue to evolve, and that successors to the famous songwriters of the past will emerge in due course (despite a certain post-Britten pessimism). But could it be that the Britten and Berio threads represent the ultimate expression of their respective contributions to the song narrative, and that post-Romantic song will seem from the future to have been a diversion from the path that song has taken over count-less previous centuries? Perhaps its future nature will much more resemble the songwriting performers of the pre-Romantic era. While both generic singing and extended vocal techniques continue to attract performers and audiences, the creative spark that inspired musicians to write songs in the past may be burning more fiercely elsewhere, and managing quite well without institutional pedagogy, dead poets or pianos.

One of the threads that connected Berio with Britten was the fact that the music of both was influenced by extraordinary singers: Berio and Berberian, Britten and Pears, these are partnerships that defined the genre, a great composer and a dedicated performer/muse. They were the inheritors of the keys to the genre since it coalesced as *Lied* from Schubert onwards. Hildegard, Bernart, Josquin, Cipriano, Dowland (possibly) and Strozzi sang their own songs. They were singer-composers for whom the two arts were almost indistinguishable. The classical singer-songwriter had a late flowering with Dibdin, but as the roles of composer and performer went their separate ways, songwriting lost the umbilical connection between creation and performance. We now treat earlier music simply as composition, in much the same way as we treat Satie or Schubert. The embodiment of the song by its creator has become (perhaps inevitably) a casualty of the way we reduce music history to a list of great composers.

The late-nineteenth-century professionalism brought new skills and new relationships between composers and performers. A significant number of great song composers were pianists able to finesse their compositions in collaboration with dedicated singers; they were the first composers who by and large couldn't sing. In Germany, Schubert and Vogl, Brahms and Julius Stockhausen; in France, Poulenc and Pierre Bernac; and in England, Quilter and Gervase Elwes, Denis Browne and Steuart Wilson, Finzi and Wilfred Brown – all were partnerships of musical passion and expertise which developed the genre and its audience. There was nothing like the music profession as yet – many (if not most) of those early duos were sustained by inherited wealth with no need of patronage or monetary gain. At the beginning of the twentieth century there simply wasn't much in the way of cultural infrastructure to support careers for musicians without independent means.

It was a comfortable life for many song composers, with time to polish their art on their own terms. Public performances were in any case relatively rare and the gramophone was still new and expensive; the largest audience for their works was often other composers, honouring each other with dedications and sharing transcriptions of their larger works in versions for piano duet. As the century progressed a more coherent economic model in Britain enabled the formation of concert clubs and music societies, by subscription initially and subsequently with some state funding. These provided opportunities for performers and audiences to meet, the former by this time properly trained professionals, and the latter also from the professional middle class for whom concert-going was part of their social round.

It was not just composition that evolved – singing itself has contributed to a change in the perception and creation of song. In this book there are no examples of song between the time of Purcell and the first Lieder in the eighteenth century. It's not that singers were silent, but the fashion was for opera arias, which always required a particularly public form of singing, Performance with a capital P. The seventeenth- and eighteenth-century castrati who drove the operatic repertoire created a hyper-stylised singing elevated beyond the reach of ordinary mortals. Genital mutilation was a high price to pay, but those who survived and succeeded could become international stars, and their feats encouraged the genitally intact to greater heights. Two things then happened which changed the vocal landscape: somewhat late in the day the mezzo-soprano voice was found to be a musical and ethical alternative to castration, and in order to sustain spectacular singing in all voices a much more rigorous pedagogy was needed. Singing was becoming an elite professional skill, with profound consequences for performers, composers and audiences.

Napoleon's wish to ensure the future of Italian operatic singing in France was a contributing factor to the founding of the Paris Conservatoire in the last decade of the eighteenth century. England eventually followed suit with the Guildhall School of Music in 1880, the Royal Academy of Music in 1822 and the Royal College in 1883. The fortunes of these institutions fluctuated over the years (including two world wars which emptied them of young male students). In the last quarter of the twentieth century the conservatoires, now joined by provincial institutions in Manchester and Birmingham and national equivalents in Scotland and Wales, began to reinvent themselves as centres of excellence, which in singing terms meant a focus on opera.

There were many British singers in the earlier twentieth century who performed both opera and song (John Coates, Heddle Nash and Kathleen Ferrier, for example), but none of the singers associated with the Butterworth-Warlock-Ireland-Gurney decades was an opera singer. Songs often had their first performance in front of friends before more formal outings in recital programmes; it was an intimate medium in which the singer could make eye contact directly with the listener, still in essence a domestic transaction.

In my youth the singers I looked up to had learned on the job, mostly taking private lessons, sometimes followed by a postgraduate year at a music college (they weren't called conservatoires then), but this was by no means considered essential. Kathleen Ferrier, Janet Baker, Peter Pears and John Shirley-Quirk, four singers who promoted the song repertoire through concerts and recordings, all developed their careers while taking lessons whenever they came across a suitable teacher. But towards the end of the century opera came to dominate the singing teaching in music colleges (now upgraded to conservatoires, which would have delighted Napoleon). The principal of the college at which I studied told me it was his duty to ensure that I did the opera course (as opposed to old or new music to which my voice was much better suited), as within a decade no one would be singing anything else.

Today, almost all music colleges have examination syllabuses that require singers to perform a selection of songs and arias, mostly from historic repertoire, in a recital format. This doesn't preclude other types of singing, and some conservatoires allow for a much broader approach, but the public face of most music colleges tends to be opera productions which require a particularly robust and stylised voice production. I once spent a memorable three years as an external examiner, listening to 'final recitals' at one of the leading British conservatoires. The standard was ridiculously high compared with what I remembered from my youth. It wasn't difficult to make comparisons as the repertoire was much the same (and indeed very similar to what my father would have studied). I also had to look at the students' written work, and was impressed that they were asked to write about how they hoped their career would develop. The students were surprisingly realistic – no one automatically assumed an inevitable rise to fame, most expecting to be keeping themselves alive by teaching and perhaps some chamber music while auditioning for operas or orchestras and keeping their fingers crossed for a lucky break; I never encountered a student who expected to be a recitalist. At the end of my three-year stint I asked why the students' final recital bore little relation to the music that they were likely to perform in the real world. After some hesitation (I suspect the question wasn't asked very often) came the reply, 'It's the only way we can measure their excellence ...'

Excellence as an end in itself is a curious criterion for creative institutions. It's something you can require of a craftsman: your plumber will do an excellent job according to agreed criteria with predictable outcomes. No composer, no singer or anyone involved in the creative arts works quite like that. A Centre for Excellence in Singing was proposed while I was at York; I vetoed the E word – who would want a centre for mediocrity? In judging song performance in terms of excellence we may be acknowledging that the genre has reached its ultimate peak, and possibly its resting place. Abstract excellence also insulates musicians from needing a wider dissemination of their art. Since Schoenberg (an excellent composer if ever there was one), the creation and consumption of new songs has been sorely taxed by the refusal of many composers to acknowledge an audience beyond a very small (and often academic) bubble. Successful songs of any sort depend on a degree of familiarity, which can make extraneous cleverness hard to cope with. Writing songs that are a challenge for professionals to sing yet have instant appeal to an amateur listener is an awkward conundrum. The song-recital format is sustained by some remarkable singers and pianists, but no song composer seems to have been able to claim succession to Britten, a composer who mastered the medium by developing his craft at the piano in partnership with his chosen singer over many decades.

The past has inevitably weighed heavily on classical music, but even as Bach, Mozart, Beethoven and Wagner became fixtures in the classical firmament, the Romantic composers had ensured that song was a living thing, created in the present. Once the thread between the living composer and the listener was compromised by complexity, audiences increasingly stuck with what they knew. The Lieder recital became the platform to which twentieth-century singers would aspire, ideally with nothing composed after about 1910. At home listeners also looked backwards, and as the technology moved forwards, 78 becoming LP, LP replaced by CD, CD displaced by streaming, they had the opportunity to invest in the same repertoire all over again.

The new transmission technology also coincided with the early-music movement, a hugely successful phenomenon that meant we could acquire even more of the past, giving us more reason to postpone the future. All of this activity generated public concerts and we continued to maintain an illusion of music as a living phenomenon that happened in real time, whereas it had in fact returned to the living room, consumed on an industrial scale via recordings. At the present time (things may have moved on by the time you read this) you are more likely to listen to songs in your kitchen via your personal assistant or on headphones while out running, rather than at a concert.

In the aftermath of the Second World War, with the demise of music clubs and the ascent of subsidised opera, the 'oratorio singers' who also did song recitals if they got the chance retreated from the musical landscape. The evolution of the genre depended on performers being able to cope with an increasingly difficult repertoire and to convince promoters and public that they would enjoy it. At the sharp end, singers such as Cathy Berberian and Jane Manning did exactly that, often very successfully. But the *Lied* evolved a museum-like afterlife in festivals, the same repertoire expertly performed again and again. Enterprising performers continually sought to refresh the genre with imaginative programme planning (ranging from video to puppetry) and contemporary music festivals also occasionally feature song, but many composers moved on from the conventions of the genre. The recording industry introduced audiences to a different kind of composer-performer from beyond the classical sphere. The art of the 'hydroptic drunkard, itchy lecher and self-tickling proud', so eloquently expressed on Donne's behalf by Britten, was as likely to be found in the songs of David Bowie, Leonard Cohen, Joni Mitchell or a host of younger singer-songwriters for whom abstract excellence is a meaningless term.

Which brings us to the matter of texts. Composers from the twentieth century onwards have tended to seek out poets of the past (Housman and the Symbolists are notable exceptions). Britten, Tippett and their contemporaries were not averse to setting contemporary verse, but their default choice was to trawl the existing literary canon. The folk-song revival of the early twentieth century didn't revive the singers' voices, just their tunes and their texts which were then sung with immaculate Received Pronunciation, an accent that stripped the songs of their geography and relocated them in a socio-linguistic no man's land.

Complaints of elitism in the traditional arts always invite a response that points to examples of classical song flourishing in unexpected places, successful outreach programmes or a wider demographic attending prestigious concert halls. This is all often true, but it is the right answer to the wrong question. Performers are not sociologists; not many of us step onto a stage wondering about the social composition of our audience; we're just there to perform the music. If there's a problem, it's that an over-cultivated voice limits what composers can write, and how we sing it. Put simply, Received Pronunciation, which we are trained to articulate so precisely, sounds daft if you're trying to sing in the vernacular: the language of art song, regardless of wider considerations of elitism, is sung in a class-based accent. The stylised delivery of the classically trained voice was ideal for metaphysical poetry and more, bringing a certain gravitas and depth to the genre, but the formality of a generic voice singing a text by a dead poet makes it very hard for living composers to sound truly contemporary, especially to a younger, more diverse audience.

The clichéd split between the classical and popular, never entirely a binary phenomenon, was muddied for good after the Beatles' *Sergeant Pepper* and the progressive rock phenomenon that followed it. Investing popular music with aspects of the classical has involved reimagining what singing is, reinventing the concept and nature of repertoire, and discovering a new relationship with words. At the centre of this potential paradigm shift is the voice: does song depend on the enhancements developed since the castrato watershed, or can we go with something more like the 'natural' voice that singers used until that point? The songs of Dowland and his predecessors were elite in that they were the result of complex musical processes aimed at a sophisticated and literate audience, but their place in the social spectrum wasn't defined by the voice that sang them: there is no reason to think that sixteenth-century singers sounded very different from a ballad singer out in the street. But since the eighteenth century, art song has absorbed a generic voice into its DNA: if we return to a pre-Baroque voice, we end up with a voice not unlike that of the jazz, folk or rock singer.

The crucial difference between a classical singer and an untrained voice is that the latter is identified by a unique vocal persona: you hear the person. A classical singer is identified by voice type – variants of soprano, alto, tenor or bass reduced even further for opera singers by the constraints of their *Fach*, which confines them to a set of prescribed roles. Classical singing lessons result in a generic voice, retaining as much individuality as possible, which is sometimes not very much. For an opera singer to perform something as intimate as a song recital considerable adjustment is needed. Many make this adjustment with no problem at all: Peter Pears, Janet Baker or Dietrich Fischer-Dieskau were equally convincing on the operatic stage and as recitalists, and many of today's opera singers will do recitals when their schedule allows. The problem for the genre is not the performers themselves but, in part, the reach and relevance of a generic voice with an elitist image and history in a world where audiences are able to get their song fix in many different forms. In the fragmented and commercially aware arts scene of today, a medium associated with a historical middle-class repertoire, however excellently performed, may not be the first choice for today's songwriters (not least because the potential audience may be uneconomically small). This means that the chances of a composer choosing to power a performing duo from the piano are also very small.

From the early twentieth century onwards popular music has had significant input from classically trained musicians, and the increasing sophistication of rock music and jazz later in the century has legitimised the blurring of boundaries between the two. The academically trained composer now has to compete with composer-performers, often themselves classically trained, such as Elton John (Royal Academy alumnus Reg Dwight), Radiohead guitarist Jonny Greenwood or Jacob Collier, who find more creative opportunities in the collaborative world of commercial music. Here the composer may no longer be the unique genius but a provider of crucial source material in much the same way as their medieval, Renaissance and Baroque predecessors, and their vocal delivery matches their speech. Laura Mvula, an alumna of the Birmingham Conservatoire, has used her classical education to create songs that expand the genre, finding a sophistication that appeals to a much more diverse demographic than would have been the case had she stuck to a traditional post-conservatoire path. Errollyn Wallen, Belize-born but educated at Goldsmiths College and King's College London (a former student of Nicola LeFanu and David Lumsdaine), is both singer-songwriter and opera composer. She acknowledges a compositional debt to Britten and yet there is little trace of him in her songs. Polymath Kerry Andrew sings and composes across many genres from alt-folk with their own band to Juice Vocal Ensemble.

The historic classical song has yet to find a comfortable place within this mix, and it may be as much to do with the singing as the songs. The porous boundaries between 'classical' and 'popular' were highlighted by Sting's recording of Dowland. Dowland's songs are emblematic of the early-music movement, revived in the 1920s with piano accompaniment, then taken up by countertenor Alfred Deller with guitar and subsequently with lute. So convincing were Deller's performances and the turbo-charged male altos that followed him, that the countertenor became one of the key voices associated with the early-music revival. Subsequently almost every tenor (and many sopranos) in the early-music world aspired to perform and record Dowland. Sting's Dowland, sung with few concessions to classical singing, also began with piano – the fortepiano of Katia Labèque for an informal performance of a handful of songs – and came to fruition with the lute playing of Edin Karamazov on *Songs from the Labyrinth* of 2006. It is the only modern recording by a voice that might conceivably sound like a performance Dowland would have expected (and it is nothing like a 'historically informed performance' as taught to conservatoire students). The classical world was suspicious; after all, if Sting could sell thousands of copies without having had a singing lesson what was the point of all those expensive early-music courses? The point many commentators missed was that to Sting, Dowland is simply music, and when he sang the songs he made them his own; it was Sting that his audiences came to hear rather than Dowland. It's no different from eighteenth-century opera-goers turning out for their favourite singers regardless of the composer; Mozart's letters are full of his whingeing about singers for whom he had to write the arias they wanted, otherwise no one would come to hear his music.

This was not Sting's first foray into classical music. In 2000 he took part in Steve Nieve and Muriel Téodori's theatre piece *Welcome to the Voice*, recorded by Deutsche Grammophon in 2007 with Robert Wyatt, Elvis Costello and opera singers Barbara Bonney, Sara Fulgoni, Nathalie Manfrino and Amanda Roocroft, accompanied by the Brodsky Quartet augmented by jazz musicians. Although described as an opera, the work is essentially a narrative of songs about a foundry worker's obsession with opera (hence the two sorts of singer), culminating in a duet between Sting and Barbara Bonney on the nature of the voice. The boundary between commercial and 'art' music dissolves musically, but vocally each singer remains true to their voice; Nieve's music is 'classical' in intent (both Berio and Satie are name-checked in the accompanying booklet) but has popular music's lack of boundaries and slips in and out of pastiche. I suspect the album didn't convert many from one to the other but there is some impressive singing from all of the participants and it does raise profound questions about the nature of singing and voices. Classical singers may be reassured by the ability of Barbara Bonney's 'Opera Singer' to turn off the full *bel canto*, a skill which is (thankfully) not matched in reverse by the rock singers, a reminder that there is much more to the question than a simple binary conversation.

In 2009, Sting returned to the classical song repertoire with *If on a Winter's Night*, an album of songs including music by Praetorius, Bach, Schubert, Purcell and Warlock, among others. The German songs are sung in English, as they would have been in nineteenth-century England, and are arranged for the musicians Sting invited to perform them, a throwback to the sixteenth- and seventeenth-century practice of making the music your own with whoever is there to make it. Particularly instructive is Sting's acoustic version of his own 'The Hounds of Winter' in which he calibrates his voice according to the new context. He continues to experiment: in the uncategorisable space on the edge of art song is his 'Bury me Deep', written at the piano and intended for Russell Crowe to sing in the movie *Robin Hood*, but ending up as a song for me and two lutes.

Jeff Buckley's recording of Purcell's 'When I am laid in earth' almost screamed in a searing falsetto shows an emotional intensity that classical singers cannot come close to expressing: with the constraints of a generic voice, repression and restraint are the only means available in such a context. His falsetto version of Britten's 'Corpus Christi Carol' is a miraculous example of a countertenor voice deployed in a non-generic way. A different kind of engagement can be found in June Tabor's singing of Butterworth's 'The Lads in Their Hundreds'. Here her simple and supple delivery is all that a classical singer might aspire to but which a generic voice rarely allows. As with Sting's Dowland you are drawn primarily to the words and don't really hear the singing at all, just the song. The classical and the non-classical are very close here, paralleling Maria Pia de Vito and John Taylor's recording of Cipriano's 'Ancor che col partire'.

The untrained voice has also had an appeal for some classical composers. John Tavener wrote 'Prayer of the Heart' for Björk in 2001 and Gavin Bryars has written for some fifty non-generic singers from Adelaide Hall to Father John Misty. The other way round – pop musicians creating classical pieces – has had mixed results. Pop music is a collaborative process, and although the 'composer' gets the credit, the arrangement and orchestration is often done by someone else. It was natural, for example, for Paul McCartney to collaborate with Carl Davis, who would handle the orchestration and shaping of his *Liverpool Oratorio*. The oratorio form (it's actually a secular work) collides with McCartney's music and the piece lacks a solid foothold in either classical or popular camps. The lute songs of Genesis keyboardist Tony Banks, on the other hand, manage to combine an instinctive feeling for the form with the essence of Banks heard in many Genesis songs. John Paul Jones, a sometime teenage church organist before joining Led Zeppelin, has also been drawn to the seventeenth century, writing fully composed songs and songs with figured bass.

Also successful have been those musicians working in the area sometimes defined as avant pop, a portmanteau term that doesn't really do justice to the extraordinary individuality of the musicians involved. As with the old classical avant-garde the singer-composers aspire to originality and experiment, but in drawing on styles and genres that the audience already knows (often from popular music) the challenge to their audience is a generous and elastic one, inspirational rather than confrontational. Three pioneers stand out: Laurie Anderson, Meredith Monk and Björk, who have successfully navigated the potentially compromising waters between commercial and classical worlds and inspired a younger, yet more liberated generation of song composer-performers. All three are multimedia artists with a background in literature and the visual arts that informs and often transforms their music. None of the three had a generic institutional education but each would acknowledge the value of classical music, perhaps best expressed as a musical toolbox from which they can select only what they need. Unlike the historic art-song composer-genius they work best in collaboration with other artists, a lesson that many in the wider field of classical music have yet to learn.

The three have little in common musically beyond their compulsion to explore. Laurie Anderson is known to many through her 'O Superman' which became a worldwide hit, and performs with instruments of her own devising or electronics ranging from banks of synthesisers to a simple laptop. Meredith Monk became in her own way a folk-influenced vocal laboratory comparable to Berio's perception of Cathy Berberian. Björk's career is one of the most tempestuous and idiosyncratic in the world of celebrity songwriters and one of its threads involved a collaboration with the Brodsky Quartet. As a teenager she discovered Meredith Monk's 1981 ECM album *Dolmen Music* and she went on to record and go on tour with 'Gotham Lullaby', a song Monk wrote for herself. It transcends language with apparently random syllables and paralinguistic shrieks and gasps. It's an intensely expressive vocal tour de force whether sung by Monk to her own piano accompaniment or by Björk with the Brodskys, recalling the work of the Roy Hart Theatre, an art song at the interstices of language, song and theatre. 'Gotham Lullaby' appears on the Brodsky Quartet's album *Monk Mix* – a remix in this context being the modern equivalent of a seventeenth-century continuo version of an intabulated original.

Keyboards and quartets are not the only instruments available to today's songwriters. In a throwback to the accompaniment by lute or viol, especially the latter, the cello has emerged as the instrument of choice for some singers who play or players who sing. This may involve arrangements of the classical canon such as the American tenor Nathaniel Pierce singing Schubert (his repertoire includes 'Erlkönig') while accompanying himself on the cello. Others take the singer-songwriter route, such as the German former orchestral cellist Mara or the sometimes explosive incantations of Laura Moody. Some have used the medium to create an entirely new genre: Polish cellist Ashia Grzesik (who also reinvents Schubert among her multimedia creations) writes for voice, cello and electronics; the South African Abel Selaocoe, an alumnus of the Royal Northern College of Music, fuses an African heritage with European classical music and a sideline in Tuvan throat-singing. Ayanna Witter-Johnson's influences range from Bach and Berio to Nina Simone and Sting. For these musicians, essentially born in the post-art-song era, live performance is their life-blood, but the World Wide Web is their primary venue, the space where the performer has a simultaneous one-to-one intimate connection with an unknowable number of listeners at home.

The early-music movement is also beginning to reinvent its songs. Performers now feel less at risk from what many used to think of as the musicology police and increasingly see history as a resource; we can use the *lacunae* in the historical record to generate new compositions. In the various extrapolations on early music by the Hilliard Ensemble with Jan Garbarek, Red Byrd, the Dowland Project and Alternative History, I made frequent use of the lack of surviving material; lutenist Jacob Heringman has arranged Peter Pope's songs and choral music as lute song, just as his sixteenth-century predecessors would have done. The more distant past has provided a different kind of opportunity. The realisations of early medieval epic by Benjamin Bagby have created plausible new worlds in which ancient art regrows, and Sam Barrett has made speculative reconstructions of songs from late antiquity to the early medieval period. The concept is taken a stage further by the investigations into the music of antiquity by Stef Conner, Barnaby Brown, Samuel Dorf and others. We are never going to know what Babylonian epic sounded like, but there is a huge amount of intellectual and artistic mileage in using the paucity of the surviving evidence as a point of departure for new compositions, extrapolating from what we know. By its nature, early music stops being early once it gets within range of an audible present. By looking in the opposite direction, and replacing academic competition for the surviving scraps with creative opportunities provided by what we don't know, there is room for a vivid multi-media new music that can flourish in a world of hybrid performance.

The examples above, the American and Nordic singer-songwriters, the pop singers who stray across the divide into classical song, the singing cellists, the creative early-music singers and researchers, the classical composers who write for pop and jazz singers, are all predicated on a non-generic voice, a voice that retains and even amplifies the personality of the singer. They defy genre but they are artists and they create songs, reinventing the medium for the twenty-first century. There is, of course, a commercial element to contend with here, but classical music also comes at a cost and we all, composers, performers and audiences, discreetly collude in our own exploitation.

I'm wary of drawing conclusions about the present based on the past: an evolutionary thread is only there if we decide to look for it; every musical act is of itself and not on the way to something else. But looking back at how the songs touched on here have been created over the centuries, it's tempting to ask if perhaps the extraordinary energising of song-making from Schubert onwards may be a historical anomaly which is close to running its course. In looking for successors to Britten we may have been looking in the wrong place:

perhaps the new song composers are the successors of Satie, the classless multimedia artist who invented himself and saw all music as art, whether popular or otherwise, or of the troubadours and *improvvisatori* of the Middle Ages and Renaissance whose art pre-dated the classical–popular divide.

I began this art-song odyssey by making excuses for how difficult it is to choose a route through the history of song, citing the deliberations of the *Voyager* committee when trying to compile an Earth anthology for the benefit of any aliens the spacecraft might encounter on its journey into the unknown. Since I started writing the book, *Voyager II* has travelled an unimaginable distance (something close to 25 billion kilometres if my calculations are correct). It is still in touch with us, but the time will come when we won't hear from it anymore; history has moved on from the contents of the musical cargo uploaded nearly half a century ago. The Golden Record remains a kind of objective product of much research on the part of its contributors, but an alien arriving here from the other direction would find that musical Earth is made up of billions of individuals, each of whom has a different take on their own history, and few of whom would have chosen the Voyager's cargo. I wonder how different the track list would be if a number of individuals with different musical tastes had simply suggested their favourite music. History is continually in motion, remade and reinterpreted by each generation, and perhaps a subjective and personal account may tell us things that an objective view will not reveal.

This narrative has been based on the experience of one person, taking as its starting point a piece of Gregorian chant. It then identified a number of way stations over the next thousand years or so when 'song' morphed into something else until it finally arrived at the conventional voice-and-piano definition which saw us through to the end of the twentieth century. Inevitably, much of it has been about the pre-history of song as we would eventually come to define it. It may have seemed to many at each of those historical points that the genre had reached its apogee, whereupon the following generation consigned it to history. But then the process started all over again, reinventing itself with a new set of attributes appropriate to its creators and consumers; to quote John Donne's famous pun, 'when thou hast done thou hast not done, for I have more'. My granddaughters, educated as classlessly as possible, are currently summoning up Taylor Swift and Lin-Manuel Miranda from Alexa (musicals are another story . . .). They will write a different history of song should they feel inclined to do so in fifty years' time. That history might show that the early twenty-first century, far from seeing the end of art song as we knew it, marked a shift from elite excellence to a more diverse celebration of the human condition that all who wanted to could subscribe to.

Songs did get into space but only as far as the Moon, popular songs enjoyed by the Apollo astronauts (including, inevitably, Frank Sinatra and 'Fly Me to the Moon'). For the curious left on Earth, Laurie Anderson, former NASA artist in residence, created a virtual Moon in her collaboration with Taiwanese artist Hsin-Chien Huang, *To the Moon*. 'Art' song eventually made it into space when Steve MacLean took recordings of Errollyn Wallen to the International Space Station, where they travelled 7.84 million kilometres completing 186 orbits of the Earth on NASA's STS115 mission. That's Errollyn Wallen, the Black Belize-born British woman composer and singer-songwriter influenced by Benjamin Britten, Schumann, Stravinsky and the human-rights movement.

Onwards and upwards . . .

BEYOND THE NOTES . . .

The journey of the *Voyager* spacecraft with its cargo of artistic artefacts was a metaphor in many senses. The tiny representatives of our humanity will never arrive anywhere: they are in a state of permanent progress. They are also infinitesimally small in the context of the vastness of space. The story of song is also one of a never-ending journey, and any attempt by a historian to capture it is never going to do more than identify a few footprints. This final chapter should enable readers to follow up on some of the topics, chapter by chapter, that the twelve songs may have hinted at, some of which I have only just touched upon. I have deliberately kept the narrative free from footnotes, but quotations are referenced here, as are all the sources I used. The suggestions for further exploration are written by historians, performers and musicologists, who are authoritative but – equally importantly – love their subject. There is a great deal of information available online; I have generally not given web addresses as these can be accessed easily with a simple search.

Points of Departure

The story of the *Voyager* is told by Carl Sagan *et al.* in *Murmurs of Earth* (Random House, 1978; *repr.* Ballantine Books, 1984). The chapter 'Choosing the Music' is by Timothy Ferris. Ozma Records produced a vinyl box set in various formats. The NASA JPL site relays the distances travelled by the spacecraft in real time, so my vague figures can be immediately updated.

1: Hildegard von Bingen: 'Columba aspexit'

Both the musicology and ideas of medieval performance practice have changed considerably since Hildegard's re-emergence in the 1980s. Many scholars now acknowledge the over-dependency on written sources and the skewed historical perspective that can result; there is also a much greater awareness of the gender imbalance of the written record. So-called historically informed performance practice has changed too: the musicians featured on all the recordings mentioned below would probably create very different versions today, and an increasing number of performers are thinking beyond the early-music paradigm.

The medieval interchange between orality and literacy has a parallel in the technical changes sweeping the publishing world. The study of medieval monophony, solo song both sacred and secular, has benefited from groundbreaking publications, and almost all major research projects have an open-access web presence which may be regularly updated. Most will feature at least one significant print publication and the physical artefact still has (for the moment) an important place in an increasingly digital world.

For a compendium of more or less current scholarship see *Poets and Singers: On Latin and Vernacular Monophonic Song*, ed. Elizabeth Aubrey

(Routledge, 2009/2018), which contains chapters excerpted from several of the books mentioned below. For a single-authored account that fills more holes in the oral narrative of the earlier period (and includes a revealing Appendix of quotes condemning medieval singing), see John Haines, *Medieval Song in Romance Languages* (Cambridge University Press, 2010/2016). Two publications that almost redefined modern scholarship in their respective areas are Sylvia Huot, *From Song to Book: The Poetics of Writing in Old French and Lyrical Narrative Poetry* (Cornell University Press, 1987/2019), and Walter J. Ong, *Orality and Literacy* (Routledge, 1982/2002). The online version of Margot Fassler's *Music in the Medieval West: Western Music in Context* (Norton, 2014) is a useful resource for anyone new to the topic and considering studying the period in depth. Christopher Page's authoritative and beautifully produced *The Christian West and Its Singers: The First Thousand Years* (Yale University Press, 2010) gives a vivid picture of musical life in the first millennium, focusing on the literate Christian world.

There are several iterations of Benjamin Bagby's *Beowulf* on YouTube. Bede's *Historia ecclesiastica gentis Anglorum* is available in a Penguin Classics translation as *Ecclesiastical History of the English People* (Penguin Books, 1990).

Dobson & Harrison's pioneering *Medieval English Song* (Faber, 1979) is of its time but still has much to offer performers, especially on textual considerations such as pronunciation. Helen Deeming's *Musica Britannica 95* volume *Sources of British Song c. 1150–1300* (Stainer & Bell, 2013) and its associated website are state of the art. Her 'The Songs of St Godric: A Neglected Source', *Music & Letters* 86/2 (2005), includes transcriptions of the songs and is similarly useful reading for students of the period. For those interested in Godric's backstory, Frederick Buechner's *Godric: A Novel* is a fictional stream of consciousness as narrated by Godric himself that extrapolates on the known 'facts'.

The University of Cambridge Digital Library page 'Compilation of Classical, Late Antique and Medieval Poetic Works (Including the "Cambridge Songs") (MS Gg.5.35)', has a facsimile with a history of the Cambridge Songs and extensive bibliography. A hard-copy reprint of the 1915 facsimile with commentary by Karl Breul (Cambridge University Press, 2009) is also available. The university website has pages and video of Sam Barrett's work on reconstructing Boethian *metra*, which resulted in a CD by Sequenzia, *Boethius: Songs of Consolation: Metra from 11th-Century Canterbury* (Glossa – GCD922518). Sequenzia have also recorded material from Gg.5.35 as *Lost Songs of a Rhineland Harper* (DHM 82876 58940 2).

John Stevens's *The Later Cambridge Songs: An English Song Collection of the Twelfth Century* (Oxford University Press, 2005) is a rare example of an elegant modern edition that is as useful for performers as it is comprehensive for scholars. There is a CD based on Stevens's edition: Gothic Voices, *The Earliest Songbook in Britain* (Hyperion CDA67177), with a note by Christopher Page.

Manuscripts and Medieval Song, ed. Helen Deeming and Elizabeth Eva Leach (Cambridge University Press, 2015), is an invaluable collection of case studies including the Reading Abbey ms GB-Lbl Harley 978 (Helen Deeming), the *Carmina Burana* (Gundela Bobeth) and both Cambridge codices (Sam Barrett, Jeremy Llewellyn), which look at the wider context of manuscript production.

There is an extensive literature on all aspects of Hildegard's life and work. Two earlier publications are still worth consulting: Fiona Maddocks, *Hildegard of Bingen: The Woman of Her Age* (Headline Books, 2001) is a compelling and elegantly written introduction; Sabina Flanagan, *Hildegard of Bingen: A Visionary Life* (Routledge, 1989/1995) has a more specific focus. *Symphonia* is edited with a translation, Introduction and Commentary by Barbara Newman, 2nd edn (Cornell University Press, 1998); *Scivias* is translated by Columba

Hart and Jane Bishop with a Preface by Caroline Walker Bynum and an Introduction by Barbara Newman (Paulist Press, 1990). Anna Silvas's *Jutta & Hildegard: The Biographical Sources* (Brepols, 1998) is a critical translation and analysis of all the relevant biographical material. Jennifer Bain's *Hildegard of Bingen and Musical Reception: The Modern Revival of a Medieval Composer* (Cambridge University Press, 2015) charts the rise and rise of Hildegard's reputation as a composer; Bain is also editor of *The Cambridge Companion to Hildegard of Bingen* (Cambridge University Press, 2021), an updating of the Hildegard story by many noted scholars.

The Sequenzia website has details of the ensemble's thirty-year Hildegard project, which culminated in a nine-CD box set of the complete works, released by Sony in 2017. The site also has a link to a pdf of the complete lyrics with English, French and German translations.

Christopher Page's recording of Hildegard's sequences, *A Feather on the Breath of God* (Hyperion CDA66039), with his ensemble Gothic Voices, dates from 1981; 'Columba aspexit' is sung by Emma Kirkby. Page's edition of the music was published in 1984 (Antico Edition MCM1), with an English translation and an authoritative note.

Medieval.org has a complete discography of Hildegard recordings by song, subdivided into categories (saints, antiphons, etc.); 'Columba aspexit' has fourteen entries. The Hilliard Ensemble's *Mnemosyne* album with Jan Garbarek (ECM 1700) features Hildegard's 'O ignis spiritus'.

The Meredith Monk reference is to her 'Notes on the Voice' in Sally Barnes, *Terpsichore in Sneakers: Post-Modern Dance* (Wesleyan University Press, 1977/1987): 166–7. Her fourth note in full is 'The voice as a direct line to the emotions. The full spectrum of emotions. Feelings that we have no words for.'

2: Bernart de Ventadorn: 'Can vei la lauzeta mover'

The most straightforward introduction to the history of troubadour and *trouvère* song is the first chapter of John Haines's *Eight Centuries of Troubadours and Trouvères: The Changing Identity of Medieval Music* (Cambridge University Press, 2004); subsequent chapters deal with reception up to the present day; the modal rhythm duelling incident is described in his 'The "Modal Theory", Fencing, and the Death of Aubry', *Plainsong and Medieval Music* 6/2 (1997): 143–50. *A Handbook of the Troubadours*, ed F.R.P. Akehurst and Judith M. Davis (University of California Press, 1995), is a wide-ranging collection of scholarly articles on *fin'amor*, women troubadours, the diffusion of Occitan song, and much else. Elizabeth Aubrey's *Music of the Troubadours* is a more detailed introduction to the form and there is an analysis of 'Can vei la lauzeta mover' in her chapter 'The Progeny of Bernart de Ventadorn's "Can vei la lauzeta mover"' in *Music and Instruments of the Middle Ages*, ed. Tess Knighton and David Skinner (Boydell Press, 2020): 11–60. The latter is a *Festschrift* for Christopher Page which contains many relevant key texts, not least the comprehensive bibliography of Page's substantial output. For the further history of 'Can vei la lauzeta mover' see David Murray, 'The Clerical Reception of Bernart de Ventadorn's "Can vei la lauzeta mover"', *Medium Ævum* 85/2 (Society for the Study of Medieval Languages and Literature, 2016): 259–77, and Meghan Quinlan, 'Eye, Mouth and Ear: The Female-Voiced Contrafacta of "Can vei la lauzeta mover"', in *Female-Voiced Song in the Middle Ages*, ed. Anna Kathryn Grau and Lisa Colton (Brill Academic Publishers, 2021). The song literature is continually being updated and the reader is referred to the online *Oxford Bibliographies* entries for *Medieval Songs, Troubadours & Trouveres*, and *Cantigas de Santa Maria* for current updates.

There is a transcription (with translation) of 'Can vei la lauzeta mover' in *The Oxford Anthology of Music: Medieval Music*, ed. W. Thomas Marrocco and Nicholas Sandon (Oxford University Press, 1977), which is still a useful introductory anthology of medieval song.

Jerome Weber's online *Troubadour Melodies Discography* (PMMS, last updated August 2020) is a huge resource (it includes my own ECM Dowland Project version of 'Can vei la lauzeta mover' together with those by Catherine Bott, Paul Hillier, Stevie Wishart and more than fifty others).

Katie Chapman's online *Troubadour Melodies Database* is a useful resource containing documentation and transcriptions of 341 troubadour melodies.

The Cambridge Companion to the Literature of the Crusades, ed. Anthony Bale (Cambridge University Press, 2019), is an invaluable guide; see especially Marianne Ailes, 'The Chanson de Geste', and Linda Paterson, 'The Troubadours and Their Lyrics', but the most comprehensive resource to date is Warwick University's AHRC-funded project *Troubadours, Trouvères and the Crusades* and its website. Michael Costen, *The Cathars and the Albigensian Crusade* (Manchester University Press, 1997) is an atmospheric account of Innocent III's tragic adventures in the Languedoc. Oxford University hosts the Centre for the Study of the Cantigas de Santa Maria, which has a comprehensive web presence from which all *Cantigas* manuscipts can be viewed online.

The *trouvère* repertoire has fared less well than its southern counterpart, with the notable exception of Thibaut de Champagne; see Roger Pensom, 'Thibaut de Champagne and the Art of the Trouvère', *Medium Ævum* 57/1 (1988): 1–26. There is a short summary of the significance of the *chansonnier du Roi* in Anne Ibos-Auge, 'The Songs of Thibaut de Champagne (1201–1253)',

The Hudson Review 65/3 (2012): 419–22, and an earlier more substantial account in John Haines, 'The Transformations of the Manuscrit du Roi', *Musica Disciplina* 52 (1998): 5–43. There is a more detailed discussion of the wider repertoire in Mary O'Neill, *Courtly Love Songs of Medieval France: Transmission and Style in the Trouvère Repertoire* (Oxford University Press, 2006). *Chanter m'estuet*, ed. Samuel Rosenberg and Hans Tischler (Faber, 1981), is an early attempt to present music for all the various categories. For a rare analysis of *trouvère* and troubadour song (including a reference to 'Can vei la lauzeta mover') in terms of sound and voice, see Emma Dillon, 'Unwriting Medieval Song', *New Literary History* 46/4 (Autumn 2015): 595–622.

For recordings and scores of the *trouvère* repertoire a good starting point would be *Songs of the Trouvères* (Antico Edition AE36), ed. Christopher Page, recorded by Gothic Voices as *The Spirits of England and France*, Volume 2 (Hyperion, CDA66773).

The *lauda* literature is sparse, but useful sources are Cyrilla Barr, *The Monophonic Lauda and the Lay Religious Communities of Tuscany and Umbria in the Late Middle Ages* (Kalamazoo, MI, 1988), and Blake Wilson, *Music and Merchants: The Laudesi Companies of Republican Florence* (Clarendon Press, 1992). *Il laudario cortonese n91*, ed. Pellegrino Ernetti and Laura Rossi Leidi, is available in print and online. There are many recordings of *laude* ranging from the improbable but fun to the austere and rather more likely: try *Laude di Sancta Maria* by La Reverdie (Arcana A34) or *Laudario di Cortona* by Ensemble Organum (Harmonia Mundi HMC 901582).

Ronald J. Taylor's two-volume *The Art of the Minnesinger* (Cardiff University Press, 1968) pre-dates the early-music revolution and modern unmeasured notation but includes useable versions of almost all surviving songs. Henry Hope's essay, 'Miniatures, Minnesänger, Music: The Codex Manesse', in *Manuscripts and Medieval Song*, ed. Helen Deeming and Elizabeth Eva Leech (Cambridge University Press, 2015), explains that notationless manuscripts may not be entirely music-less.

The *Carmina Burana* has attracted a great deal of critical attention since its rediscovery in 1803. The most recent account is *Revisiting the Codex Buranus: Contents, Contexts, Composition*, ed. Tristan E. Franklinos and Henry Hope (Boydell & Brewer, 2020). Albrecht Classen, 'The Carmina Burana: A Mirror of Latin and Vernacular Literary Traditions from a Cultural-Historical Perspective: Transgression Is the Name of the Game', *Neophilologus* 94 (2010): 477–97, is an overview with a bibliography in German and English. Frederick Goldin, *Walther von der Vogelweide: The Single Stanza Lyrics* (Routledge, 2003) is an excellent introduction to Walther's performing life, with English translations of his shorter poems. *Oswald von Wolkenstein: Frohlich geschray so well wir machen* (Bärenreiter, 1988) is an illustrated edition of twenty-eight of his songs (with commentary in German).

Women in medieval music has become a thriving area of research since Meg Bogin's *The Women Troubadours* (Norton, 1976). Most recent histories and anthologies have a significant female presence; an early-twenty-first-century anthology of insightful articles is *Medieval Woman's Song*, ed. Anne Klinck and Ann Marie Rasmussen (University of Pennsylvania Press, 2002). See also *Songs of the Women Trouvères*, ed. Eglal Doss-Quinby, Joan Tasker Grimbert, Wendy Pfeffer and Elizabeth Aubrey (Yale University Press, 2001), and Brianne Dolce, '"Soit hom u feme": New Evidence for Women Musicians and the Search for the "Women *Trouvères*"', *Revue de musicology* 106/2 (2020). *Women Making Music*, ed. Jane Bowers and Judith Tick (University of Illinois Press, 1986), has become something of a classic, and includes chapters on music in nunneries (Anne Bagnall Yardley) and secular female musicians (Maria Coldwell).

There are now many works on how to perform medieval song. Timothy McGee has been a pioneer in this field and his *The Sound of Medieval Song* (Clarendon Press, 1998) is full of insights. More attention is now given to the role of improvisation in trying to access oral music; see, for example, Angela Mariani, *Improvisation and* Inventio *in the Performance of Medieval Music: A Practical Approach* (Oxford University Press, 2017).

3: Josquin Desprez: 'La Déploration de la mort d'Ockeghem'

The quote from Anna Maria Busse Berger is the title of the first chapter in her *Medieval Music and the Art of Memory* (University of California Press, 2005), the most comprehensive analysis of the topic to date. Her extensive writings include two contributions to *The Cambridge History of Fifteenth-Century Music*, ed. Anna Maria Busse Berger and Jesse Rodin (Cambridge University Press, 2015): 'Oral Composition in Fifteenth-Century Music' and 'How Did Oswald von Wolkenstein Make His Contrafacta?'. If you want to knit your own Leonin you'll need Stephen Immel, 'The Vatican Organum Treatise Re-examined', *Early Music History* 20 (2001): 121–72. There is a comprehensive survey of improvised polyphony in the fifteenth century in Rob C. Wegman, 'From Maker to Composer: Improvisation and Musical Authorship in the Low Countries, 1450–1500', *Journal of the American Musicological Society* 49/3 (Autumn 1996). An excellent account (especially for non-specialists) of how it was done is Ronald Broude, 'To Sing upon the Book: Oral and Written Counterpoint in Early Modern Europe', *Textual Cultures* 13/1 (2020): 75–105. See also *Studies in Historical Improvisation from Cantare super Librum to Partimenti*, ed. Massimiliano Guido (Routledge, 2019).

The facsimile *Le Roman de Fauvel dans l'édition de Mesire Chaillou de Pesstain* (Broude Brothers, 1990), beautiful but unwieldy, has a comprehensive introduction by Edward Roesner, François Avril and Nancy Regalado. *Fauvel Studies: Allegory, Chronicle, Music and Image in Paris Bibliothèque Nationale de France, MS français 146*, ed. Margaret Bent and Andrew Wathey (Clarendon Press, 1998), is a seminal interdisciplinary study of the manuscript with contributions from leading scholars. Emma Dillon's *Medieval Music-Making and the 'Roman de Fauvel'* (Cambridge, 2002) is a very approachable reflection on the manuscript as a book. *The Monophonic Songs in the Roman de Fauvel*, ed. Samuel Rosenberg and Hans Tischler (University of Nebraska Press, 1991), pre-dates the publication of the facsimile, so it appears a little old-fashioned, but as well as editions of all the songs (except the chant pieces and the *ballades* of Jehannot Lescurel) it has a handy 'Summary of the Narrative and Placement of the Songs'. The polyphonic motets are available in *Le Roman de Fauvel* (L'Oiseau-Lyre, 1984), a reprint of Leo Schrade's 1956 edition with a new Introduction by Edward Roesner; Frank Harrison's Introduction to the so-called musicians' motets can be found in *Musicorum Collegio: Fourteenth-Century Musicians' Motets* (L'Oiseau-Lyre, 1986).

There is much more to conductus than I was able to explore in the main text; see Mark Everist, *Discovering Medieval Song: Latin Poetry and Music in the Conductus* (Cambridge University Press, 2018), one of the outcomes of the AHRC-funded *Cantum Pulcriorum Invenire* project, which also generated three CDs from Hyperion by the Conductus Ensemble and a substantial web presence and database.

There is a huge literature (and discography) on Franco-Flemish polyphony. David Fallows's collection of essays, *Songs and Musicians in the Fifteenth Century* (Ashgate, 1996), is a good place to start. His enthusiasm is infectious, and his biography of Dufay (Vintage Books, 1982/1988) is still the standard reference. See also his 'The Most Popular Songs of the Fifteenth Century' in *The Cambridge History of Fifteenth-Century Music*.

The Hilliard Ensemble broadcast a tribute to Ockeghem in February 1997 on the eve of the 500th anniversary of the composer's death. This included all the tribute pieces mentioned in this text apart from *Nymphes des bois*, which the group had recorded in 1983 for the EMI album *Josquin: Motets and Chansons* (which also has 'Scaramella' mentioned in Chapter 4). The BBC recording was later released as a live album, currently available as Coro 16048 together with Andrew Kirkman's article, 'Ockeghem and His Contemporaries', which discusses Compère, Busnois, Lupi and Ockeghem himself. The liner material also has the complete Crétin lament in its original French, excerpts from which are read by Bob Peck in English translation between tracks.

The *New Josquin Edition* (KVM, Utrecht) is one of the most extensive and detailed musicological projects of our time. *Nymphes des bois* can be found in Volume 29 and its companion Critical Commentary, ed. Patrick Macey. *Nymphes des bois* is on my *Secret History* album in a version with Anna Maria Friman (soprano) and vihuelists Ariel Abramovich and Lee Santana (ECM 2119).

There are many recordings of Josquin, Ockeghem and their contemporaries in the one-to-a-part *a cappella* versions favoured by early-music ensembles. To compare the 'manuscript' realisations with what lute players did to their sources, see the two albums of Josquin's tabs by Jacob Heringman: *Josquin des Prez: Sixteenth-Century Lute Settings* (Discipline Global Mobile DGM0006) with explanatory liner notes by David Fallows and Heringman himself, and *Inviolata* (Resonus Classics), which also includes Heringman's own tabs as well as those by Josquin's contemporaries and successors. *Secret*

History has my versions of Josquin and Victoria arranged for voices and lutes. Musicians continue to experiment with Josquin's music: for a recent example see Jean-Christophe Groffe's *Josquin Desprez: Baisiez moy* (Aparte AP259).

4: Cipriano de Rore: 'Ancor che col partire'

James Haar's '*Improvvisatori* and Their Relationship to Sixteenth-Century Music' in his *Essays on Italian Poetry and Music* (University of California Press, 1986) is an introduction to the world of the Italian improvisers. Lewis Lockwood, *Music in Renaissance Ferrara 1400–1505* (Harvard University Press, 1984) contains a chapter on Pietrobono, and Evan MacCarthy's 'The English Voyage of Pietrobono Burzelli', *The Journal of Musicology* 35/4 (2018): 431–59, fills out some details of Pietrobono's probable foreign travels.

The most even-handed account of the *frottola* is to be found in Howard Mayer Brown's *Music in the Renaissance* (Prentice Hall, 1976): 99–106. For more specific information on Isabella's court see William Prizer, 'Isabella d'Este and Lucrezia Borgia as Patrons of Music: The Frottola at Mantua and Ferrara', *Journal of the American Musicological Society* 38/1 (1985): 1–33, and also his 'Una "Virtù Molto Conveniente a Madonne": Isabella D'Este as a Musician', *Journal of Musicology* 17/1 (Winter 1999): 10–49, which chronicles Isabella's musical background and prowess as a singer (and includes a score of Cara's setting of Castiglione's 'Cantai mentre nel cor' which the *marchesa* is known to have sung). The short atmospheric video *Ad Tempo Taci: Songs for Isabella d'Este* (University of North Carolina Press, 2015), filmed in Mantua and featuring songs by Cara and Tromboncino, is available online, as is a digital reconstruction of Isabella's *studiolo*. Stanley Boorman's comprehensive *Ottavio Petrucci: A Catalogue Raisonné* (Oxford University Press, 2006) gives publishing details of all of the *frottola* collections including the two Bossinensis volumes.

Howard Mayer Brown looks at the relationship between three intabulated sources in 'Bossinensis, Willaert and Verdelot: Pitch and the Conventions of Transcribing Music for Lute and Voice in Italy in the Early Sixteenth Century', *Revue de Musicologie* 75/1 (1989): 25–46. Verdelot's *Madrigali* and Willaert's intabulated versions are published by London Pro Musica. Anyone wishing to create a sonnet setting in the style of a fifteenth-century improviser should look at Timothy McGee's 'Cantare all'improvviso' in his edited volume, *Improvisation in the Arts of the Middle Ages and Renaissance* (Western Michigan University, 2003): 61–2.

Bottegari's lute book is reviewed in Carol MacClintock's 'A Court Musician's Songbook: Modena MS C 311', *Journal of the American Musicological Society* 9/3 (Autumn 1956): 177–92. MacClintock is also the editor and translator of *Readings in the History of Music in Performance* (Indiana University Press, 1979/1992), an invaluable sourcebook for performers. Howard Mayer Brown's *Embellishing Sixteenth-Century Music* (Oxford University Press, 1976/1984) is a useful though somewhat jaundiced guide to what he considers the decadent practice of the 'disarrangement' of polyphony for 'slightly suspect artistic purposes'. Richard Wistreich's monograph on the bass Giulio Cesare Brancaccio, *Warrior, Courtier, Singer* (Ashgate, 2007), takes a more positive view of virtuosity in the repertoire of one of the most famous singers of the period and includes a discussion of the tenor-bass version of 'Ancor che col partire'. Much of the 'division repertoire' is published in modern editions by London Pro Musica, including all surviving versions of 'Ancor che col partire'.

There is a considerable literature on the Paston manuscripts. For an introduction to their possible use, see Hector Sequera's 2010 *Performance Practice in the Music Collection of Edward Paston (1550–*

1630), available online, or Philip Brett, 'Edward Paston (1550–1630): A Norfolk Gentleman and His Musical Collection', *Transactions of the Cambridge Bibliographical Society* 4/1 (1964): 51–69. There is no modern edition of Egerton 2971, but Mary Cyr's 'A Seventeenth-Century Source of Ornamentation for Voice and Viol: British Museum Egerton MS 2971', *RMA Research Chronicle* 9 (1971): 53–72, contains basic information, further elaborated on in John Bass 'Would Caccini Approve? A Closer Look at Egerton 2971 and Florid Monody', *Early Music* 36/1 (2008): 81–94. John Bass, 'Improvisation in Sixteenth-Century Italy: Lessons from Rhetoric and Jazz', *Performance Practice Review* 14/1 (2009): 1–32, expands on this with an intriguing and insightful comparison of pedagogical techniques in the division repertoire and jazz, with a particular focus on 'Ancor che col partire'.

Clifford Bartlett published an edition of 'Weepe, weepe, myne eyes' in *Early Music Review* 50 (May 1999), which I used as a basis for my recording with Stephen Stubbs on *Care-Charming Sleep* (ECM 1803). For Wilbye and the English country-house establishments see David Price, *Patrons and Musicians of the English Renaissance* (Cambridge University Press, 1981).

5: John Dowland: 'Flow my tears'

Diana Poulton's *John Dowland* (Faber, 1972, 2nd edn 1982) is still a mine of useful information about the songs and the little we know of Dowland's life; the quote from Sir John Harrington can be found on pages 53–4. Robert Cecil's life is richly documented; see Catherine Loomis, '"Little Man, Little Man": Early Modern Representations of Robert Cecil', *Explorations in Renaissance Culture* 37 (2011–12): 137–56. Philip Heseltine's *The English Ayre* (Oxford, 1926), written under his composer pseudonym Peter Warlock, is the earliest account of the lute-song repertoire and is still worth reading. Both Warlock and Poulton quote Dowland's letter to Cecil in full. Edmund Fellowes's *English Madrigal Composers*, 2nd edn (Oxford, 1972), has a chapter on lutenist composers which includes instructions on how to read tabs. His editions are still available in piano transcriptions and intabulated (the latter revised by Thurston Dart and others). Fellowes's autobiography, *Memoirs of an Amateur Musician* (Methuen, 1946), describes his part in saving the lute song for posterity. For the history of seventeenth-century song beyond Dowland see Ian Spink, *English Song: Dowland to Purcell* (Batsford, 1974).

Dawn Grapes's well-organised and far from dry *John Dowland: A Research and Information Guide* is invaluable for serious students of the composer. Peter Holman's comprehensive guide to the instrumental versions, *Dowland Lachrymae* (Cambridge, 1999), also has an insightful chapter on the rhetoric of the song. All the songbooks are now also available in facsimile.

Almost every early-music soprano, tenor and countertenor since Alfred Deller's 1952 shellac 78 rpm disc has made, or aspires to make, a Dowland recording. Michael and Mollie Hardwick's affectionate memoir, *Alfred Deller: A Singularity of Voice* (Proteus, 1980), chronicles the countertenor's meeting with Desmond Dupré and their subsequent Dowland adventures which included one of the earliest recordings of 'Flow my tears'. My own contribution is ECM's album called simply *Dowland* (ECM 1697), with the ensemble that later became The Dowland Project. There have been many re-releases in various formats of Sting's *Songs from the Labyrinth* (DGG 06025 170 3139). The original also includes readings from Dowland's letter to Cecil. Marenzio's madrigals are performed as lute song by Angela Alesci with Domenico Cerasani and Massimo Lonardi on *Marenzio: Madrigals and Other Works* (Tactus TC531302).

6: Barbara Strozzi: 'Lagrime mie'

Laurie Stras's *Women and Music in Sixteenth-Century Ferrara* (Cambridge University Press, 2018) is a detailed account of women's music-making in the most musically opulent Italian dukedom. She's especially good on the significance of female musicians in the cloister. More general background material can be found in two chapters in Jane Bowers and Judith Tick, eds, *Women Making Music* (University of Illinois Press, 1986): Anthony Newcomb, 'Courtesans, Muses or Musicians? Professional Women Musicians in Sixteenth-Century Italy' (which quotes Ariosto's *Orlando furioso*), and Jane Bowers, 'The Emergence of Women Composers in Italy, 1566–1700'.

The secular monodies from Francesca Caccini's *Il primo libro delle musiche* are published by Indiana University Press in an edition by Ronald James Alexander and Richard Savino, who also provide a biography and commentary with a guide to performance. Suzanne Cusick's *Francesca Caccini at the Medici Court: Music and the Circulation of Power* (University of Chicago Press, 2009) is a groundbreaking and richly documented account of the composer and her world. There are summative chapters on both Caccini and Strozzi in Isabelle Emerson, *Five Centuries of Women Singers* (Praeger, 2005), and Anna Beer, *Sounds and Sweet Airs: The Forgotten Women of Classical Music* (Oneworld, 2016).

At the time of writing there is no biography in English of Barbara Strozzi, but there is a website devoted to her and she also has a Facebook page. *Barbarastrozzi.com* offers a short biography, discography and bibliography together with English translations of song texts. *Cordonatoeditions.com* publishes the complete works; 'Lagrime mie' is available (as hard copy or download) as a single song or in the complete op. 7 volume *Diporti di Euterpe overo cantate e ariette a voce sola*.

For Strozzi's life and career see Beth Glixon's two articles, 'New Light on the Life and Career of Barbara Strozzi', *The Musical Quarterly* 81/2 (1997): 311–35, and 'More on the Life and Death of Barbara Strozzi', *The Musical Quarterly* 83/1 (1999): 134–41. The best introduction to the music of Strozzi is still Ellen Rosand, 'The Voice of Barbara Strozzi', in Jane Bowers and Judith Tick, eds, *Women Making Music* (University of Illinois Press, 1986): 168–90. The case for Bernardo Strozzi's portrait being that of Barbara is made in David Rosand and Ellen Rosand, '"Barbara Di Santa Sofia" and "Il Prete Genovese": On the Identity of a Portrait by Bernardo Strozzi', *The Art Bulletin* 63/2 (1981): 249–58.

In a serendipitous accident of history, Tosti's 'Ideale' was recorded by Alessandro Moreschi, the last castrato, in 1902 (available on *Alessandro Moreschi: The Last Castrato: Complete Vatican Recordings*, Opal CD 9823).

7: Robert Schumann: 'Du Ring an meinem Finger'

There is a rich literature on *Frauenliebe* dating from Ruth Solie's feminist critique, 'Whose Life? The Gendered Self in Schumann's Frauenliebe Songs', in S. Scher, ed., *Music and Text: Critical Inquiries* (Cambridge University Press, 1992): 219–40. Rufus Hallmark's *Frauenliebe und Leben: Chamisso's Poems and Schumann's Songs* (Cambridge University Press, 2014) examines the poems and music in the context of current scholarship. See also Kristina Muxfeldt, '*Frauenliebe und Leben* Now and Then', *19th-Century Music* 25/1 (2001): 27–48. The quote from John Daverio is on page 213 of his comprehensive *Robert Schumann: Herald of a New Poetic Age* (Oxford University Press, 1997).

Sadly, Julia Wirth's 1927 biography of her father Julius Stockhausen, *Julius Stockhausen: Der Sänger des deutschen Liedes*, has never been translated into English. Wilhelmine Schröder-Devrient's colourful career is documented in Chapter 10 of Isabelle Emerson's *Five Centuries of Women Singers* (Praeger, 2005). Walther Dürr, one of the founder editors of the *Neue Schubert Ausgabe* (which includes Vogl's versions as appendices), explains the context, history and importance of the *Singbücher* in 'Schubert and Johann Michael Vogl: A Reappraisal', *19th-Century Music* 3/2 (1979): 126–40. *Gender in Lieder* (Wigmore Hall YouTube channel) is a wide-ranging discussion between leading specialists on the occasion of Roderick Williams's first performance of *Frauenliebe*. For the most positive gloss expounded by some of the finest female Lieder singers see Stephen Eversen's 'Doormat Divas', *The Guardian* (14 May 2004).

Much of the Lieder literature has traditionally focused on song as a written musical or literary entity rather than performance (the 2004 *Cambridge Companion to the Lied*, for example, with the notable exception of Graham Johnson's performance chapter). More recently, there have been in-depth studies of the subtle but supremely important musical and social relationships between singers, composers and their audiences. Jennifer Ronyak's *Intimacy, Performance, and the Lied in the Early Nineteenth Century* (Indiana University Press, 2018) is one of the first to demonstrate the effect of the exigencies of performance in defining the nature of the *Lied*. The most recent publication in this vein is *German Song on Stage: Lieder Performance in the Nineteenth and Early Twentieth Centuries* (Indiana University Press, 2020), ed. Natasha Loges and Laura Tunbridge. All of the separately authored chapters are insightful and revealing, many of them written by scholars who perform (Benjamin Binder's chapter on Robert and Clara Schumann's observations on singers is itself a masterly piece of observation). Natasha Loges' publications include *Brahms in the Home and the Concert Hall: Between Private and Public Performance* (Cambridge University Press, 2014) and *Musical Salon Culture in the Long Nineteenth Century* (Boydell &

Brewer, 2019). The quote from Dean Flower is from 'Bergman's Unseen Masterpiece', *The Hudson Review* 62/1 (Spring 2009): 91–105. For more on Fanny Mendelssohn see Marcia J. Citron, 'The Lieder of Fanny Mendelssohn Hensel', *The Musical Quarterly* 69/4 (Autumn 1983): 570–94.

The Hyperion *Complete Songs* of Schumann (CDS44441-50) comes in a box set, performed by many different artists accompanied by Graham Johnson and including his chronology of Schumann: 'A Life through His Songs'. A more recent project is the eleven-CD Sony box set by Christian Gerhaher and Gerold Huber (*Frauenliebe* is sung by Julia Kleiter). Current editions of the songs are in Volume 6 of Schott's *Neue Ausgabe sämtlicher Werke Robert Schumanns*. Schubert's songs are available in the fourteen volumes of Series 4 of the *Neue Schubert Ausgabe* and on the Hyperion *Complete Songs* of Schubert (CDS44201/40). There are online discographies that list the many recordings of *Frauenliebe*.

The later history of the *Lied* in performance is not so well catered for (compared with the vast amount of scholarly analysis). 'The Dehmel Settings of 1899', Chapter 4 of Walter Frisch, *The Early Works of Arnold Schoenberg 1893–1908* (University of California Press, 1997), includes an analysis of 'Schenk mir deinen goldenen Kamm'. Daniel Jenkins, ed., *Schoenberg's Program Notes and Musical Analyses* (Oxford University Press, 2016) is an invaluable resource with a companion website featuring modern and historical recordings of all of Schoenberg's Lieder. The Moldenhauer Archives in the Library of Congress hold primary material on Webern, Schoenberg, Berg and Hildegard Jone, and much of this is available online (including Lauriejean Reinhardt's note on the Jone settings). Hans Moldenhauer's *Anton von Webern: A Chronicle of His Life and Work* (Gollanz, 1978) is a minutely detailed and engaging narrative of Webern's life and work. Egon Wellesz' *Arnold Schoenberg: The*

Formative Years (new edition Galliard, 1971) is a hagiography but dating from its first publication in 1921 has a colourful immediacy from the hand of one of the master's first students. The Webern complete works were first recorded under the auspices of Robert Craft and have recently been re-released on Sony Classical.

8: Erik Satie: *Ludions*

There has not been space to give *airs de cour* the attention they deserve. Readers interested in these wonderful songs are directed to Jeanice Brooks's sumptuous and encyclopaedic *Courtly Song in Late Sixteenth-Century France* (University of Chicago Press, 2000). Further useful sources are noted in Michael Bane's online *Oxford Bibliographies* entry.

The salon culture and the early history of *romance* and *mélodie* influenced by Schubert is the subject of David Tunley, *Salons, Singers and Songs: A Background to Romantic French Song 1830–1870* (Ashgate, 2002). He also gives brief biographies of Adolphe Nourrit and François Wartel. Nourrit's untimely end is the subject of Henry Pleasants, *The Great Tenor Tragedy: The Last Days of Adolphe Nourrit as Told (Mostly) by Himself* (Amadeus Press, 1995). I have shamelessly plundered Sylvia Kahan's magnificent biography of the Princesse de Polignac, *Music's Modern Muse: A Life of Winnaretta Singer, Princesse de Polignac* (University of Rochester Press, 2003).

The English literature on French song is not as rich or extensive as that for the *Lied*. Frits Noske's *French Song from Berlioz to Duparc*, 2nd edn (Dover Publications, 1970), originally published in French in 1954, is still a fascinating guide to the major figures from the *romances* of Monpou to the *mélodies* of Duparc in the context of their poets and prosody (the Monpou quote is on page 303). For performers the classic reference work is Pierre Bernac, *The Interpretation of French Song* (Kahn & Averill, 1997). Bernac also wrote about Poulenc and is a thoughtful companion if you're learning the songs (he's also very good on how to cope with the French language).

There is a cornucopia of Satie literature ranging from letters and pictures to websites and reference works, and I have drawn heavily on the scholarship of Ornella Volta, Robert Orledge, Steven Moore Whiting and Caroline Potter (no relation). The most recent book on his life and work in a wider Parisian context (and on his legacy) is *Erik Satie: A Parisian Composer and His World* (Boydell & Brewer, 2016) by Caroline Potter, whose first book on the composer was *Erik Satie: Music, Art and Literature* (Ashgate, 2013). Robert Orledge's collection of primary source material, *Satie Remembered* (Faber, 1995), is still essential reading (you'll find the Stravinsky quote on page 105), and his SoundKiosk website is a goldmine of information, with corrected editions of *Ludions* and a comprehensive note on the pieces, among much more. Anything by the late keeper of the Satie flame, Ornella Volta, is similarly valuable; *Satie Seen through His Letters* (Marion Boyars, 1989) is a good starting point. For Satie in a wider cultural context, Roger Shattuck's *The Banquet Years: The Origins of the Avant-Garde in France, 1885 to World War I* (revised edition Vintage, 1968) remains a fascinating study. *Stephen* Moore Whiting's magnificent *Satie the Bohemian: From Cabaret to Concert Hall* (Oxford University Press, 1999) has a comprehensive analysis of *Ludions* in the context of Satie's life in the alternative world of cabaret and theatre. The fullest account of Satie's death is that given by Darius Milhaud in his *Notes without Music* (Calder and Boyars, 1952).

For the wider cultural scene see Roger Nichols, *The Harlequin Years: Music in Paris 1917–1929* (Thames & Hudson, 2002). It's hugely entertaining though you may need a magnifying glass for its tiny font. The only full-length biography of Fargue, Jean-Paul Goujon's *Léon-Paul Fargue: Poète et piéton de Paris* (Gallimard, 1997), exists only in French.

LTM Recordings has released eight CDs of Satie: LTM2459 includes *Socrate* (with three sopranos) and *Ludions*. Hughes Cuénod and Geoffrey Parsons recorded the 1916 *Trois mélodies*, *Ludions* and *Socrate* (Nimbus NI 5027), and there is a live recording of Cuénod singing *Socrate* (with score) on YouTube (complete with a passing police siren which no doubt Satie would have enjoyed). *Ludions* also appears on *An Erik Satie Entertainment* (Heritage TGCD171) performed by Meriel and Peter Dickinson, and there is a rare baritone performance of the complete Satie songs on *Erik Satie: Intégrale des mélodies et des chansons* (Calliope CAL6885). There are recordings of Paulette Darty from 1902, sadly before she met Satie, and these can be found remastered on compilation CDs.

9: George Butterworth: 'The Lads in Their Hundreds'

Stephen Banfield's magisterial *Sensibility and English Song* (Cambridge University Press, 1989) is the bible of twentieth-century English song scholarship; the quote on p. age 195 can be found on p. 139; Trevor Hold's *Parry to Finzi: Twenty English Song Composers* (Boydell & Brewer, 2002) looks at selected songs from a similar period, informed by his own perspective as a composer. Robert Weedon's website and blog, *War Composers: The Music of World War I*, is an invaluable resource for those interested in Farrar, Denis Browne and Frederick Kelly (and the activities of many composers who survived the war). I am much indebted to these three sources. *Race against Time: The Diaries of F.S. Kelly* (National Library of Australia, 2004) has a fascinating and comprehensive biography of Kelly in the Introduction by the editor Thérèse Radic.

Denis Browne's *Six Songs* are published by Thames Publishing, edited with an introduction by Trevor Hold based on Hugh Taylor's unpublished 'The Life and Work of W. Denis Browne' (Barclay

Squire Essay, Cambridge, 1973). Browne's letter to Edward Marsh describing the burial of Rupert Brooke was printed in *The Collected Poems of Rupert Brooke* (Sidgwick & Jackson, 1918, available online). Philip Lancaster's '"Waking Up England": W. Denis Browne and *The Comic Spirit*', *British Music Society* 26 (2004), is reproduced on his website. The source of the Farrar quote by Vaughan Williams is Adrian Officer's 1984 article included in the programme booklet for the recital programme that Stephen Banfield and I toured to commemorate the seventieth anniversary of the First World War. Vaughan Williams's *National Music* (Oxford University Press, 1934) was reprinted many times, most recently in 1972.

Richard Graves, *A.E. Housman the Scholar-Poet* (Oxford University Press, 1981) is a magnificent biography of the poet. Michael Barlow, *Whom the Gods Love: The Life and Music of George Butterworth* (Toccata Press, 1997) has a comprehensive worklist and discography (to 1997). There is footage of Butterworth's elegant dancing on Robert Weedon's War Composers website. The DVD by Stewart Morgan Hajdukiewicz, *All My Life's Buried Here: The Story of George Butterworth* (Hajdukino Productions, 2018), focuses on his interest in folk song (more dancing) with authoritative narration by Anthony Murphy, whose *Banks of Green Willow: The Life and Times of George Butterworth*, 2nd edn (Cappella Archive, 2015), is the most comprehensive biography of the composer to date.

Singers' biographies give a complementary view of song composition and performance. Both Margaret Stewart's *English Singer: The Life of Steuart Wilson* (Duckworth, 1970) and *Gervase Elwes: The Story of His Life* by Winefride and Richard Elwes (Grayson & Grayson, 1935) have the immediacy and intimacy of recollections by family members. Autobiographies of singers are rarer, but many composers kept journals or interpreted their own lives (Spohr and Cyril Scott being notable examples). *The Ordeal of Ivor Gurney*

(Faber, 1978) by Michael Hurd is a beautifully written and moving biography of the composer's life from carefree country childhood to tragic insanity, told through reference to Gurney's often autobiographical poems.

The complete *Shropshire Lad* (including Butterworth's 'The Lads in Their Hundreds') can be heard on *A Shropshire Lad Complete in Verse and Song* with Anthony Rolfe Johnson (tenor), Graham Johnson (piano), and Alan Bates reading the unset poems, together with an extensive note by Andrew Green (Hyperion CDA66471/2). There is a composerly critique of this recording by Wilfrid Mellers: 'Blue Remembered Hills', *The Musical Times* 136/1834 (1995): 654–6 (he loves Butterworth but distrusts Ireland). There is a comparative analysis of settings of 'The Lads in Their Hundreds' by Butterworth, Somervell and Moeran on pages 402–5 of Stephen Banfield's *Sensibility* as part of his critique of Graham Trew's recording (Meridian E77031/2). June Tabor's version with Iain Ballamy (saxophone) and Huw Warren (piano) is on *Quercus* (ECM 2276).

10: George Gershwin: 'Summertime'

The *Oxford Bibliographies* 'People of African Descent in Early Modern Europe' by Annika Bärwald, Josef Köstlbauer and Rebekka von Mallinckrodt is a concise essay for background, followed by suggestions for more focused reading. W.E.B. Du Bois's essay 'Of the Sorrow Songs' is from his 1903 anthology *The Souls of Black Folk: Essays and Sketches* (McClurg, Chicago, 1903; Dover reprint, 2016).

The story of the debate between Vicentino and Lusitano is told in the admirably even-handed Introduction to Maria Rika Maniates *Ancient Music Adapted to Modern Practice: Nicolo Vicentino* (Yale University Press, 1996). The book is a translation of Vicentino's treatise and no mention is made of Lusitano's colour (both theorists are brilliant but quite often didn't seem to understand their own or each other's writing).

The *Letters of the Late Ignatius Sancho, an African*, ed. Vincent Carretta (Penguin, 1998), are a fascinating insight into the urbane world of the friend of Sterne and Garrick (if not very informative about his musical activities). Josephine Wright's *Ignatius Sancho (1729–1780): An Early African Composer in England: The Collected Editions of His Music in Facsimile* (Garland, 1981) contains Sancho's six songs with critical commentary and a biography. Paterson Joseph's *The Secret Diaries of Charles Ignatius Sancho* (Dialogue Books, 2022) is a well-informed and entertaining fictionalised biography.

Josephine Wright's 'George Polgreen Bridgetower: An African Prodigy in England 1789–99', *The Musical Quarterly* 66/1 (1980): 65–82, is a useful source. The British Library holds George Bridgetower manuscripts and there is a brief biography on the BL website. William Hart, 'New Light on George Bridgetower', *The Musical Times* 158/1940 (2017): 95–106, is particularly informative about Bridgetower's background and family. The ballad 'Henry' can be viewed and downloaded from the IMSLP website.

The British Library website has a perceptive essay by Mike Phillips on Samuel Coleridge-Taylor in its Black Europeans Online Gallery, and there is an online exhibition in Google Arts & Culture provided by the Royal College of Music entitled *Samuel Coleridge-Taylor and the Musical Fight for Civil Rights*. The anonymous 'Mr. Coleridge-Taylor', *The Musical Times* 50/793 (1909): 153–8, is a revealing contemporary insight into the composer's work and reputation. The memoir by Jessie Coleridge-Taylor, *Genius and Musician* (Bobby & Co, n.d.), is a touching stream-of-consciousness tribute to her husband. The early biographies are unreliable and speculative; *The Heritage of Samuel Coleridge-Taylor 1875–1912* (Dennis Dobson,

1979) is by Avril Coleridge-Taylor, the composer's daughter. More recently Jeffrey Green's *Samuel Coleridge-Taylor, a Musical Life* (Routledge, 2011) is a detailed and thorough if discursive account of the composer's life in a wider social context. The songs are listed in Stephen Banfield's *Sensibility and English Song*.

Coleridge-Taylor's songs are not well represented in recordings. The first twenty-first-century recording was by The Artsong Collective, *My Heart Is a Singing Bird* (Musaeus MZCD101); the most recent is the 2021 recording by Elizabeth Llewellyn (soprano) and Simon Lepper (piano), *Heart & Hereafter: Songs of Samuel Coleridge-Taylor* (Orchid Classics ORC100164).

Two essential sources for the music of Black America are Eileen Southern's *The Music of Black Americans: A History*, 3rd edn (Norton, 1997) and Tim Brooks's equally monumental *Lost Sounds: Blacks and the Birth of the Recording Industry 1890–1919* (University of Illinois Press, 2004), which includes a section on Harry Burleigh (pages 473–85). The songs by the first Black African composers working in Europe are listed in Dominique-René de Lerma, 'Black Composers in Europe: A Works List', *Black Music Research Journal* 10/2 (1990): 275–334. The African American Art Song Alliance is the first port of call for the performance or research of art song by Black American musicians.

Derek Healey's thoughtful 2003 publication for the Philadelphia branch of the Delius Society, *The Influence of African-American Music on the Works of Frederick Delius*, looks at the subtle influences of Black music on the composer's work. Daniel Grimley's illustrated article 'Delius and America' on the British Library website discusses the composer's American visits and their effect on his music.

The often unread history of the stuttering relationship between Black and white classical music is the subject of Joseph Horowitz's *Dvořák's Prophecy and the Vexed Fate of Black Classical Music* (Norton,

2022). He is particularly scathing about music historians' tendency to overlook or oversimplify an extraordinarily complex and delicate cultural divide. The peculiarly low profile of Harry Burleigh is discussed in Samuel Floyd, 'The Invisibility and Fame of Harry T. Burleigh: Retrospect and Prospect', *Black Music Research Journal* 24/2 (2004): 179–94.

The Library of Congress site has a biography of Will Marion Cook, and Cook's tribute to Burleigh is taken from Marva Carter, *Swing Along: The Musical Life of Will Marion Cook* (Oxford University Press, 2008): 31 (also quoted in Jean Snyder's excellent biography *Harry T. Burleigh: From the Spiritual to the Harlem Renaissance* (University of Illinois Press, 2016): 352).

The literature on *Porgy and Bess* and on 'Summertime' is vast and continues to grow. Among the more recent contributions is Howard Pollack's *George Gershwin: His Life and Work* (University of California Press, 2007; California Scholarship Online, May 2012). Pollack's chapter on the subsequent life of both *Porgy* and 'Summertime' on disc, stage and screen is comprehensive and includes a brief analysis of the song. John Szwed, *Billie Holiday: The Musician and the Myth* (William Heinemann, 2015) is one of the few sources that mention the circumstances of the first non-operatic recording.

Naomi André, 'Complexities in Gershwin's *Porgy and Bess*: Historical and Performing Contexts', in A. Celenza, ed., *The Cambridge Companion to Gershwin* (Cambridge University Press, 2019): 182–96, is a thoughtful discussion of performance contexts, both now and in the 1930s. James Maycock's 2011 film *Gershwin's Summertime: The Song that Conquered the World* is a history of the song from 1935 to the early twenty-first century and includes some very evocative contextual archive footage.

Rouben Mamoulian's description of his first encounter with the *Porgy and Bess* score can be found in Merle Armitage's 1938 tribute anthology *George Gershwin* (Da Capo, 1995, with an introduction by Edward Jablonski): 47–57. Todd Duncan's account is in *The George Gershwin Reader*, ed. Robert Wyatt and John Andrew Johnson (Oxford University Press, 2004): 221–8. Both these anthologies are essential collections of elegantly written source material.

I have focused on the one element of diversity in song that currently impinges on the life of musicians today, but the question of non-European influences is a much wider one. Slightly tangential to my main narrative, for example, is the early-twentieth-century fascination with Orientalism. Nalini Ghuman's British Library essay 'Holst and India' discusses the influence of Indian culture on Gustav Holst's music. Those interested in English song may be familiar with the Chinese poetry set by Constant Lambert, Granville Bantock, Peter Warlock, Bernard van Dieren and Arthur Oldham, among many others. Porgy is also the first homeless and disabled operatic hero, a fact that (for the moment) hovers in the background of a story coloured by race.

11: Benjamin Britten: 'O might those sighes and teares returne againe'

As mentioned above, the definitive work on English song post-First World War is Stephen Banfield's *Sensibility and English Song*. Erudite, opinionated and beautifully written, it also contains a catalogue of over five hundred songs. There are significant composers' biographies, notably Valerie Langfield's *Roger Quilter: His Life and Music* (Boydell & Brewer, 2002) and Stephen Lloyd's *H. Balfour Gardiner* (Cambridge University Press, 1984), both of which I have drawn on here; also Ian Maxwell's comprehensive *Ernest John Moeran: His Life and Music* (Boydell & Brewer, 2021). *Gervase Elwes: The Story of His Life*, mentioned above, is an affectionate tribute and paints a vivid picture of the Elwes circle. Thomas Armstrong's musings on the Frankfurt Group are insightful and of their time: 'The Frankfurt Group', *Proceedings of the Royal Musical Association* 85 (1958). There is a Norman O'Neill website created by researchers at the Royal College of Music which holds many of his manuscripts.

There have been many attempts to get to grips with the life of Philip Heseltine and much information was made available thanks to the indefatigable efforts of the Peter Warlock Society and its long-time chairman the late Fred Tomlinson. Banfield and Hold are illuminating on the music (especially *The Curlew*). Of the many colourful biographies, Barry Smith's *Peter Warlock: The Life of Philip Heseltine* (Clarendon, 1994) is probably the most authoritative. Wilfrid Mellers's comparison of 'The Fox' with 'Der Leiermann' is from 'Rebel without Applause: Wilfrid Mellers Reflects on the Chaotic Life and Enduring Achievements of Peter Warlock . . .', *The Musical Times* 135 (1994): 500–3. There is no biography of Peter Pope, and thanks are due to Jacob Heringman for a sight of his manuscripts and to Tessa Reid, the composer's daughter, and Lucy Reid, his granddaughter, for biographical details.

Boris Ford's *Benjamin Britten's Poets* (Carcanet, 1994/2013) is a key resource, the poems presented in chronological order of setting and with insightful essays by the editor Peter Porter (who references the Donne sonnets). Britten specialists have tended to give less attention to 'O might those sighes and teares returne againe' than to the other songs in the set. The quote from Christopher Headington is from his *Peter Pears: A Biography* (Faber, 1992): 147. For a musical-literary analysis of the cycle see David Fuller, 'Sin, Death and Love: Britten's *The Holy Sonnets of John Donne*', in *Literary Britten: Words and Music in Britten's Vocal Works*, ed. Kate Kennedy (Boydell & Brewer, 2018): 243–55. Rebekah Scott's chapter in the same book, 'Britten's Drops: The Lyric into Song': 124–43, discusses Britten's handling of the drop image in 'O might those sighes and teares'. Graham Johnson discusses the performance of the sonnets in *Britten, Voice & Piano: Lectures on the Vocal Music of Benjamin Britten* (Ashgate, 2003): 127–37.

A lot of creative effort has gone into keeping the song recital a living entity. See Jane Manning's publications (and their earlier incarnations) *Vocal Repertoire for the Twenty-First Century, Volume 1: Works Written before 2000* and *Volume 2: Works Written from 2000 Onwards* (Oxford University Press, 2020), and *Songs for the Twenty-First Century* compiled and introduced by David Blake and John Potter, ed. Michael Hooper (University of York Music Press, 2010).

The pessimistic prognostications for the future of song are taken from Arthur Jacobs, 'The British Isles', in *A History of Song*, ed. Denis Stevens (Hutchinson, 1960/2013): 180; Peter Pears, 'Text and Voice in English Song', in *Yehudi Menuhin Music Guides: The Voice*, ed. Sir Keith Falkner (Macdonald, 1983; Kahn & Averill, 1998): 116; and Stephen Varcoe, 'European Art Song', in *The Cambridge Companion to Singing*, ed. John Potter (Cambridge University Press, 2000/2011): 122.

12: Luciano Berio: *Sequenza III*

The letter from Yeats to Dolmetsch is quoted in Margaret Campbell, *Dolmetsch: The Man and His Work* (Hamish Hamilton, 1975): 142. For his attempts to reinvigorate poetic declamation see Yeats's 'Speaking to the Psaltery', in *Ideas of Good and Evil* (A.H. Bullen, 1903, available online), which also includes some sample notation. The context for all this is provided by Ronald Schuchard, '*The Countess Cathleen* and the Revival of the Bardic Arts', *The South Carolina Review* 32/1 (Fall 1999): 24–37. Appendix 1 of Stephen Banfield's *Sensibility and English Song* contains C.W. Orr's poem 'The Story of *The Joyce Book*' (from one who was there).

Ezra Pound's musical reputation has been rescued by two Pound scholars who write with the insights of performers. Robert Hughes's *Cavalcanti: A Perspective on the Music of Ezra Pound* (Second Evening Art Publishing, 2003) and Margaret Fisher's *Ezra Pound's Radio Operas: The BBC Experiments, 1931–1933* (MIT Press, 2002) are fascinating accounts of Pound's creative endeavours, as is Margaret Fisher's article 'The Music of Ezra Pound', *The Yale University Library Gazette* (2006): 139–60.

Pierrot Lunaire continues to perplex performers, audiences and scholars more than a century after its first performance. The indispensable guide to the problems of the piece (to which I am much indebted) is *Inside Pierrot Lunaire: Performing the Sprechstimme in Schoenberg's Masterpiece* by soprano Phyllis Bryn-Julson and musicologist Paul Mathews (Scarecrow Press, 2009). This is one of the few accounts to document the part played by Albertine Zehme in the genesis of the work, and it is as complete a guide to the history, structure and performance of the work as any performer could wish to have. Martha Elliott, also a performer herself, gives much useful information on Schoenberg performance in her *Singing in Style: A Guide to Performance Practices* (Yale University Press, 2006). Albertine Zehme's book, *Die Grundlagen künstlerischen Sprechens und Singens* (Verlag Karl Merseburger, 1920), is as yet not translated into English.

The quotes from Constant Lambert's wonderfully entertaining *Music Ho! A Study of Music in Decline* (2nd edn, Faber, 1937; The Hogarth Press Ltd, 1985) can be found on pages 64 (the Sitwell poem) and 294 (the 'wrong turning'). The 1929 recording of Edith Sitwell and Constant Lambert reciting Walton's *Façade*, played on an HMV Model 1A Record Changer of the period, is available online. *Joseph Holbrooke: Composer, Critic, and Musical Patriot*, ed. Paul Watt and Anne-Marie Forbes (Rowman & Littlefield, 2014), is a serious resource for Holbrooke enthusiasts.

Five of the Otto Vrieslander songs which inspired Albertine Zehme are sung by Ursula Behrens and Lothar Odinius on *Ein Clown hinter den Masken der Musik* (Musicaphon 56817), which also features the Schoenberg and other *Pierrot* settings by Max Kowalski and Eduard Künneke. *Schoenberg Conducts Schoenberg: Pierrot Lunaire* is a recording with Erika Stiedry-Wagner dating from 1940, released on CD in 1989 (CBS MPK 45695). Many other singers have recorded *Pierrot* including Jane Manning and jazz singer Cleo Laine. Phyllis Bryn-Julson's persuasive arguments are reflected in her two recordings of *Pierrot* and Schoenberg's other vocal works. Björk performed *Pierrot* at the Verbier Festival in 1996 (there's a brief very lo-fi excerpt on the web) but did not go on to make a studio recording.

The story of Mallarmé's *Un coup de dés* and its impact are the subject of R. Howard Bloch's *One Toss of the Dice* (Norton, 2017). It includes a translation of the poem by J.D. McClatchy, printed to reflect something of the original typography. Hausmann's *Poèmes phonétiques* are available remastered on vinyl read by the poet himself (Erratum 024). There are many performances of *Ursonata* online, including one of the scherzo by Schwitters himself (the complete recording by Schwitters's son Ernst is rather tame in comparison). Eberhard Blum's 2000 Berlinische Galerie recording of *fmsbw* includes three other Hausmann works and the four movements of the final version of *Ursonata*.

There are very few biographies of the significant singers of the early avant-garde. The Marya Freund papers relating to Arnold Schoenberg are held by the New York Public Library and there is a substantial biographical note on the library's website. Cathy Berberian is well represented in the literature. A comprehensive starting point is Pamela Karantonis, Francesca Placanica and Pieter Verstraete, eds, *Cathy Berberian: Pioneer of Contemporary Vocality* (Routledge, 2014), which also includes David Osmond-Smith's 'The Tenth Oscillator:

The Work of Cathy Berberian 1958–1966' originally published in *Tempo* 58 (2004). See also Arman Schwartz, 'The Absent Diva: Notes toward a Life of Cathy Berberian', *The Opera Quarterly* 30/1 (2014): 93–104, and Jennifer Paull's illustrated *Cathy Berberian and Music's Muses* (Lulu, 2007), marking the twenty-fifth anniversary of Cathy's death. *A-Ronne* was recorded by Swingle II on Decca 425 620-2.

Cathy Berberian can be seen online performing *Sequenza III* live and her first recording of the work is available on *Luciano Berio* (Wergo WER 6021-2). Her discography is extensive; *Recital 1 for Cathy* is on RCA Victor (09026 62540 2) together with *Folksongs* and Berio's Kurt Weill arrangements. There are many recordings of *Sequenza III* on disc and online by other singers, notably Linda Hirst's 1986/7 live recording, *Songs Cathy Sang: Music Composed for the Voice of Cathy Berberian* (Virgin Classics), which also includes John Cage's *Aria*. The official Berio website, *Centro Studi Luciano Berio*, has a complete discography. There is a Cathy Berberian website hosted by her daughter Cristina.

The scholarly literature on contemporary music is often as creative as the compositions critiqued. For a kind of reverse-musicology where you get the interpretation straight from the source you won't do better than *Luciano Berio: Two Interviews with Rossanta Dalmonte & Bálint András Varga*, ed. David Osmond-Smith (Marion Boyars, 1985). The quote in the first paragraph is the last line of Berio's interview with Bálint András Varga on page 167. Berio's own programme notes are available online in English and Italian from the *Centro Studi Luciano Berio*. Markus Kutter's text is reproduced here courtesy of UE (Luciano Berio, *Sequenza III*, text by Markus Kutter © Copyright 1968 by Universal Edition (London) Ltd., London, © Copyright assigned to Universal Edition A. G., Wien).

Roy Hart's occasional writings on the voice can be viewed in the online *Roy Hart Theatre Archives*, which also contain links to the work of Alfred Wolfsohn. There is a comprehensive 'official' Georges Aperghis website, with a discography and an annotated list of works. The definitive recording is by the dedicatee Martine Viard (Montaigne 782118).

History and Future Song

Laura Mvula's first album was the 2013 *Sing to the Moon*, recorded the following year with orchestra. There is an *a cappella* arrangement of the title song on *All Things Are Quite Silent* by the chapel choir of Pembroke College Cambridge (Signum SIGCD642). Errollyn Wallen's website has a discography that features the many sides to her songwriting. Pwyll ap Siôn's article in the December 2020 issue of *Gramophone* covers her career in some detail.

Jacob Collier's vocal music is presented online and in live performance, and includes compositions for his audiences.

Sting's explorations of classical singing can be found on *Songs from the Labyrinth* (DGG 06025 170 3139), *If on a Winter's Night* (DGG 0605 170 1743) and *Welcome to the Voice* (DGG 4776524). 'Bury Me Deep' together with songs by Tony Banks and John Paul Jones are on my *Amores Pasados* (ECM 2441).

Jeff Buckley completed only one studio album (*Grace*, which has Britten's 'Corpus Christi'), but the web is awash with bootlegs, including his 1995 Meltdown Festival performance of 'When I am laid in earth'. Iain Ballamy's arrangement of 'The Lads in Their Hundreds' is sung by June Tabor on Quercus (ECM2276). Maria Pia de Vito's 'Ancor che col partire' is on *Phoné* (EGEA – SCA 063).

Björk and the Brodsky Quartet perform Tavener's 'Prayer of the Heart' on *John Tavener: A Portrait* (Naxos 8.558152-53). Meredith Monk's original version of 'Gotham Lullaby' is on *Dolmen Music* (ECM 1197); Björk performs it with the Brodsky Quartet on *Monk*

Mix (The House Foundation for the Arts MONKMIX01). Gavin Bryars's website has a comprehensive list of the singers he has worked with. The songs of singing cellists Nathaniel Pierce, Mara, Laura Moody, Ashia Grzesik, Abel Selaocoe and Ayanna Witter-Johnson are best explored via their respective websites. Michael Blackwood's 1993 film *The Sensual Nature of Sound: 4 Composers, Laurie Anderson, Tania Leon, Meredith Monk, Pauline Oliveros* is a documentary about the working lives of four New York songwriters.

Benjamin Bagby's performance of *Beowulf* is available on DVD. The European Music Archaeology Project (EMAP) is the inspiration for many experiments in recovering and repurposing music of the distant past. For examples of 'Very Early Music' see *In Praise of Saint Columba: The Sound-World of the Celtic Church* by Barnaby Brown (pipes and lyre) and the choir of Gonville and Caius College, Cambridge, directed by Geoffrey Webber (Delphian DCD34137-CD), and Stef Conner's *Riddle Songs* based on the twentieth-century *Exeter Book*.

The John Donne quote is from the *Hymn to God the Father* set by Pelham Humfrey (and many more recent composers, including Elizabeth Maconchy). The Errollyn Wallen albums taken to the International Space Station are *ERROLLYN*, *Meet Me at Harold Moores* and *The Girl in My Alphabet*.

INDEX

Greenwood, Jonny 297
Gregory, Lady Augusta 265
Greig 230
Gropius, Walter 162
Gross, Valentine 187
Grzesik, Ashia 302
Guarini, Anna 133
Guildhall School of Music 290
Guilhem de Tudela 50
Guilhem IX of Aquitaine (also VII,
    count of Poitou) 41–2
Guillaume de Villehardouin 52
Gurney, Ivor 196, 201, 214–15, 216, 251,
    291
Gutheil-Schoder, Marie 168–9

Hadewijch of Brabant 31
Hales, Robert 113, 121
Hall, Adelaide 300
Halle, Adam de la 63, 66, 68, 69
Hamilton, Cicely 202
Hamilton, Jane 216
Hancock, Herbie 240
Handel 143, 196, 197, 198
Harding, Archie 268
Hardy, Thomas 217
Harmonice Musices Odhecaton 90
harmony 10, 47, 121, 127, 134, 136, 149,
    150, 216, 231, 232, 240, 248, 256
Harrington, Sir John 117
Harrison, Frank 78
Hart, Roy 282–3, 301, 340
Hartleben, Otto 270
Hausmann, Raoul 275, 339
    fmsbw 275, 339
Haydn 150, 197, 208
Hayes, Roland 235, 248
Headington, Christopher 257
Heath, Edward 240
Heim, Emmy 169
Heine 196, 211
Henry VIII, King of England 110
Henze, Hans Werner 283
Herbert, Muriel 216
Heringman, Jacob 84, 302, 318, 336
Herrick, Robert 196
Heseltine, Philip (Peter Warlock) 123,
    248, 252, 321–2, 336
Hess, Myra 206
Heyward, DuBose 237
Hildegard von Bingen 21*ff*, 44, 50, 276,
    288, 308, 310–11

anchoress 22–3
Causae et curae 24
and chant 26
childhood 22–3
'Columba aspexit' 27–9, 308
medical and botanical writings 24
medical conditions 24
migraine 24
modern revival of her works 22, 29–30
Ordo virtutum 22
Scivias 24, 30
*Symphonia armonie celestium
    revelationum* 22, 24–5, 30
visions 24
Hilliard Ensemble 30, 83, 100, 222, 302,
    311, 318
Hindemith, Paul 123, 232
Holbrooke, Joseph 201, 245, 269, 273
Hold, Trevor 260, 336
Holiday, Billie 239–40
Holst, Gustav 201, 245, 335
Hopkins, Arthur 216
Hopkins, Gerald Manley 216
Horace 18
Housman, Alfred 195–6, 210–12, 214,
    216, 217
    A Shropshire Lad 211
    'The Lads in their hundreds' 212
Howells, Herbert 214
Hrotswitha of Gandersheim 31
Huang, Hsin-Chien 305
Hugh-Jones, Elaine 260
Hugo, Victor 175, 179, 180
Humfrey, Pelham 197, 342
Humperdinck, Engelbert 270
Humplik, Josef 166
Hyspa, Vincent 186

improvisation 65–6, 88, 89, 113, 118,
    119, 127, 136, 316, 319, 320, 321
improvvisatori 88, 90, 304, 319
Innocent III (pope) 51
intabulation *see* tab
intermedii 115
Ireland, John 201, 212, 216, 254, 259,
    291
    'Goal and Wicket' 212
    Land of Lost Content 216
    'The Lent Lily' 216
Isaac, Heinrich 75
Isabella d'Este 92–3, 135, 319
isorhythm 73